Rick Steves'® POCKET PARIS

Rick Steves, Steve Smith & Gene Openshaw

Contents

Introduction

Paris—the City of Light—has been a beacon of culture for centuries. As a world capital of art, fashion, food, literature, and ideas, it stands as a symbol of all the fine things human civilization can offer. Come prepared to celebrate this, rather than judge our cultural differences, and you'll capture the romance and *joie de vivre* that Paris exudes.

Paris offers sweeping boulevards, chatty crêpe stands, chic boutiques, and world-class art galleries. Sip decaf with deconstructionists at a sidewalk café, then step into an Impressionist painting in a tree-lined park. Climb Notre-Dame and rub shoulders with the gargoyles. Cruise the Seine, zip up the Eiffel Tower, and saunter down avenue des Champs-Elysées. Master the Louvre and Orsay museums. Save some after-dark energy for one of the world's most romantic cities.

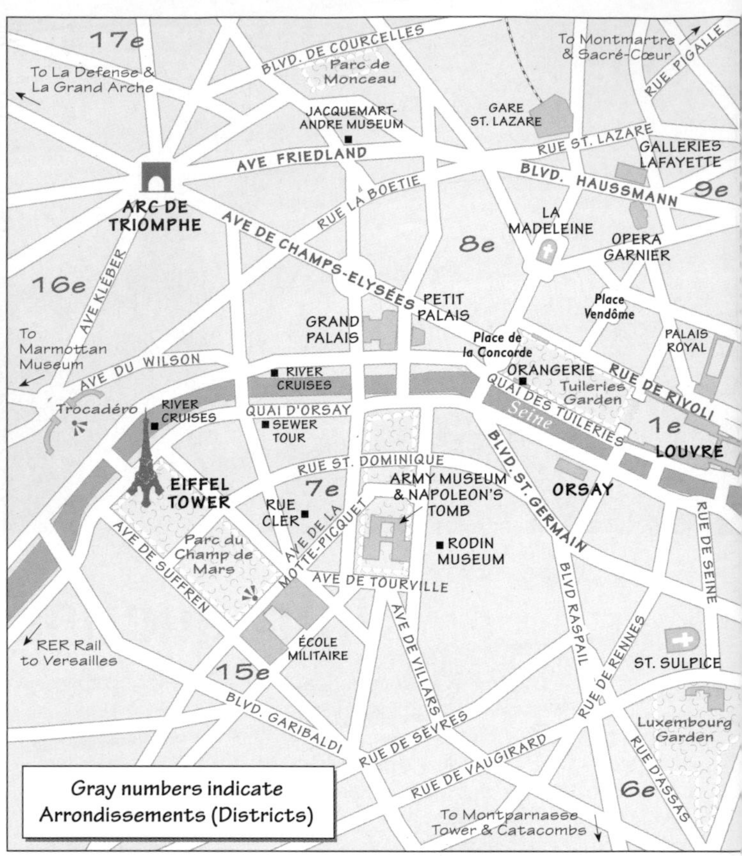

Map Legend

View Point
Entry Arrow
Restroom
Taxi Stand
Batobus Boat Stop
Cité Metro Stop
Bus Stop
Tourist Info
Point of Interest
Church
Parking
Park

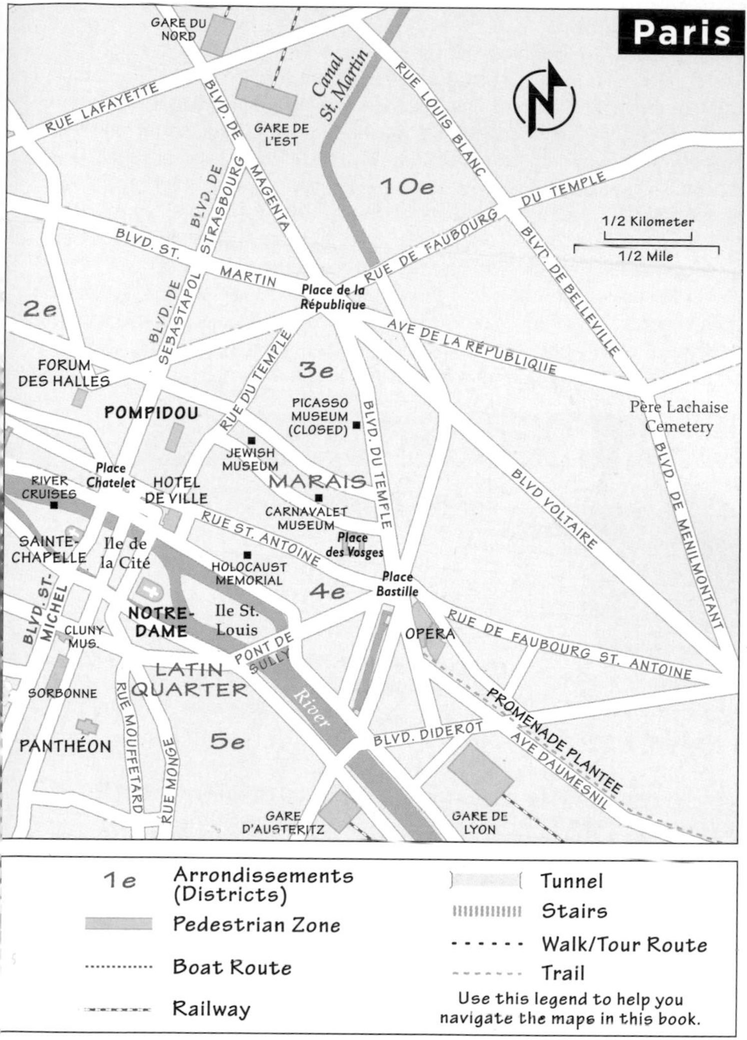

Paris

GARE DU NORD
RUE LAFAYETTE
BLVD. DE MAGENTA
GARE DE L'EST
Canal St. Martin
RUE LOUIS BLANC
10e
BLVD. DE STRASBOURG
RUE DE FAUBOURG DU TEMPLE
BLVD. ST. MARTIN
1/2 Kilometer
1/2 Mile
BLVD. DE BELLEVILLE
Place de la République
2e
BLVD. DE SEBASTAPOL
AVE DE LA RÉPUBLIQUE
RUE DU TEMPLE
FORUM DES HALLES
3e
POMPIDOU
PICASSO MUSEUM (CLOSED)
BLVD. DU TEMPLE
Père Lachaise Cemetery
JEWISH MUSEUM
Place Chatelet
RIVER CRUISES
HOTEL DE VILLE
MARAIS
BLVD. DE MENILMONTANT
BLVD VOLTAIRE
CARNAVALET MUSEUM
RUE ST. ANTOINE
SAINTE-CHAPELLE
Ile de la Cité
Place des Vosges
HOLOCAUST MEMORIAL
4e
Place Bastille
BLVD. ST-MICHEL
NOTRE-DAME
Ile St. Louis
OPERA
CLUNY MUS.
PONT DE SULLY
RUE DE FAUBOURG ST. ANTOINE
LATIN QUARTER
SORBONNE
RUE MOUFFETARD
River
PROMENADE PLANTEE
PANTHÉON
RUE MONGE
5e
BLVD. DIDEROT
AVE DAUMESNIL
GARE D'AUSTERITZ
GARE DE LYON

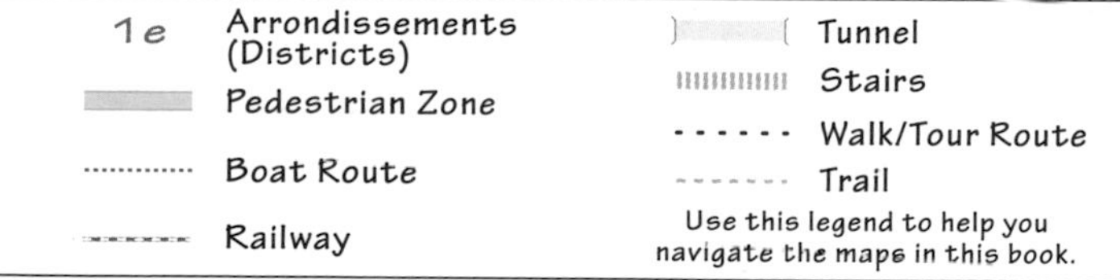

About This Book

With this book, I've selected only the best of Paris—admittedly, a tough call. The core of the book is six self-guided tours that zero in on Paris's greatest sights and neighborhoods. The Historic Paris Walk takes you through the heart of the city—soaring Notre-Dame, the bustling Latin Quarter, and the stained-glass wonder of Sainte-Chapelle. You'll see all the essentials of the vast Louvre and Orsay museums, while still leaving time for browsing. Ascend the 1000-foot Eiffel Tower at sunset and watch the City of Light light up. Stroll Rue Cler's friendly (and odiferous) shops, and take a side trip to Versailles for chandeliered palaces and manicured gardens.

The rest of the book is a traveler's tool kit. You'll find plenty more about Paris's attractions, from shopping to nightlife to less touristy sights. And there are helpful hints on saving money, avoiding crowds, getting around on the Métro, finding a great meal, and much more.

Key to Symbols

Sights are rated:

▲▲▲	Don't miss
▲▲	Try hard to see
▲	Worthwhile if you can make it
No rating	Worth knowing about

For opening times, if a sight is listed as "May–Oct daily 9:00–16:00," it's open from 9 a.m. until 4 p.m. from the first day of May until the last day of October.

Tourist information offices are abbreviated as TI, bathrooms are WCs, and Métro stops are Mo.

If you'd like more information than this Pocket Guide offers, I've sprinkled the book liberally with web references, including my own website. For updates to this book, feedback from fellow travelers, in-depth travel tips, and much more, visit **www.ricksteves.com**.

Paris by Neighborhood

Central Paris (population 2,170,000) is circled by a ring-road, and split in half by the Seine River, which runs east–west. If you were on a boat floating downstream, the Right Bank would be on you right, and the Left Bank on your left. The bull's-eye on your map is Notre-Dame, on an island in the middle of the Seine.

Twenty arrondissements (administrative districts) spiral out from the center, like an escargot shell. If your hotel's zip code is 75007, you know (from the last two digits) that it's in the 7th arrondissement. The city is speckled with Métro stops, and most Parisians locate addresses by the closest stop nearby. So in Parisian jargon, the Eiffel Tower is on *la Rive Gauche* (the Left Bank) in the *7ème* (7th arrondissement), zip code 75007, Mo: Trocadéro (the closest Métro stop).

Think of Paris as a series of neighborhoods, cradling major landmarks.

The Historic Core: Paris got its start around Notre-Dame, on the Ile

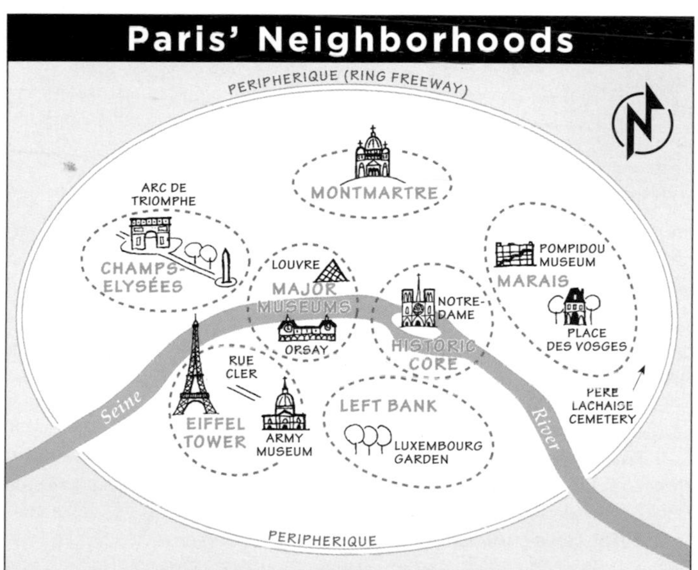

Daily Reminder

Sunday: Many sights are free on the first Sunday of the month, including the Louvre, Orsay, Rodin, and Cluny museums, the Arc de Triomphe (Oct–March only), and Pompidou Center. These free days at popular sights attract hordes of visitors.

Versailles is more crowded than usual on Sunday—but on the upside, the garden's fountains are running (April–Oct).

Look for organ concerts at St. Sulpice and possibly other churches. The American Church often hosts a free concert (often classical piano and vocals, generally Sept–June at 17:00—but not every week). Summer brings puppet shows to Luxembourg Garden and the Champ de Mars park.

Most of Paris' stores are closed on Sunday, but shoppers will find relief along the Champs-Elysées and in the Marais neighborhood's lively Jewish Quarter, where many stores are open. Many recommended restaurants in the rue Cler neighborhood are closed for dinner.

Monday: These sights are closed today: Orsay, Rodin, Marmottan, Carnavalet, Catacombs, Petit Palais, Victor Hugo's House, Montmartre Museum, Deportation Memorial, and Paris Archaeological Crypt. Versailles, outside of Paris, is also closed. The Louvre and Eiffel Tower are more crowded because of these closings. From fall through spring, the Army Museum (and Napoleon's Tomb) is closed the first Monday of every month. Some small stores don't open until 14:00. Market streets such as rue Cler

de la Cité ("Island of the City"). There you'll find Paris' oldest sights, from Roman ruins to the medieval Sainte-Chapelle church.

The Major Museums: To the west, the Louvre, Orsay, and Orangerie museums cluster around the fringes of the Tuileries Garden.

The Champs-Elysées: The greatest 19th-century boulevard—stretching two miles from the Tuileries to the Arc de Triomphe—anchors a neighborhood of grand Right Bank sights, including the Opéra Garnier.

Eiffel Tower neighborhood: In the Tower's shadow lies colorful rue Cler, with its village-like market and recommended hotels and restaurants.

and rue Mouffetard are dead today. Some banks are closed. It's discount night at many cinemas.

Tuesday: Many sights are closed today, including the Louvre, Orangerie, Cluny, and Pompidou museums, as well as the Grand Palais. The Eiffel Tower, Orsay, and Versailles are particularly busy today.

Wednesday: All sights are open (Louvre until 21:45). The weekly *Pariscope* magazine comes out today. Most schools are closed, so many kids' sights are busy, and in summer the puppet shows play in Luxembourg Garden and the Champ de Mars park. Some cinemas offer discounts.

Thursday: All sights are open except the Sewer Tour. The Orsay is open until 21:45 (last entry 21:00). Some department stores are open late.

Friday: All sights are open (Louvre until 21:45; last entry 21:00) except the Sewer Tour. Afternoon trains and roads leaving Paris are crowded; TGV train reservation fees are higher. Restaurants are busy—it's smart to book ahead at popular places.

Saturday: All sights are open except the Jewish Art and History Museum. The fountains run at Versailles (April–Oct). Department stores are jammed. The Jewish Quarter is quiet. In summer, puppet shows are held at Luxembourg Garden and the Champ de Mars park. Restaurants get packed; reserve in advance if you have a particular place in mind.

Sights include the Rodin Museum and the Army Museum and Napoleon's Tomb.

The Left Bank: Between the river and the Luxembourg Garden, the Left Bank is known for Paris' intellectual, artistic, and café life. It's also one of Paris' best boutique shopping areas.

The Marais: Stretching between the Pompidou Center and place Bastille, this neighborhood is the upwardly mobile Paris of today—with trendy restaurants, shops, nightlife, and artistic sights such as the Pompidou Center and Picasso Museum (currently closed for renovation).

Paris at a Glance

▲▲▲**Notre-Dame Cathedral** Paris' most beloved church, with towers and gargoyles. **Hours:** Cathedral daily 8:00–18:45, Sat–Sun until 19:15; tower daily April–Sept 10:00–18:30, June–Aug Sat–Sun until 23:00, Oct–March 10:00–17:30; Treasury Mon–Fri 9:30–18:00, Sat–Sun 9:30–18:30. See page 18.

▲▲▲**Sainte-Chapelle** Gothic cathedral with peerless stained glass. **Hours:** Daily March–Oct 9:30–18:00, Nov–Feb 9:00–17:00. See page 33.

▲▲▲**Louvre** Europe's oldest and greatest museum, starring *Mona Lisa* and *Venus de Milo*. **Hours:** Wed–Mon 9:00–18:00, Wed and Fri until 21:45 (except on holidays), closed Tue. See page 45.

▲▲▲**Orsay Museum** Nineteenth-century art, including Europe's greatest Impressionist collection. **Hours:** Tue–Sun 9:30–18:00, Thu until 21:45, closed Mon. See page 71.

▲▲▲**Eiffel Tower** Paris' soaring exclamation point. **Hours:** Daily mid-June–Aug 9:00–24:00 in the morning, Sept–mid-June 9:30–24:00. See page 101.

▲▲▲**Arc de Triomphe** Triumphal arch with viewpoint, marking start of Champs-Elysées. **Hours:** Always viewable; inside open daily April–Sept 10:00–23:00, Oct–March 10:00–22:30. See page 168.

▲▲▲**Versailles** The ultimate royal palace (Château), with a Hall of Mirrors, vast gardens, a grand canal, plus a queen's playground (Trianon Palaces and Domaine de Marie-Antoinette). **Hours:** Château April–Oct Tue–Sun 9:00–18:30, Nov–March Tue–Sun 9:00–17:30, closed Mon year-round. Trianon/Domaine April–Oct Tue–Sun 12:00–18:30, Nov–March Tue–Sun 12:00–17:30, closed Mon year-round; in winter only the two Trianon Palaces are open. Gardens generally open April–Oct daily 9:00–20:30, Nov-March Tue–Sun 8:00–18:00, closed Mon. See page 127.

▲▲**Orangerie Museum** Monet's water lilies, plus works by Utrillo, Cézanne, Renoir, Matisse, and Picasso, in a lovely setting. **Hours:** Wed–Mon 9:00–18:00, closed Tue. See page 157.

▲▲**Army Museum and Napoleon's Tomb** The emperor's imposing tomb, flanked by museums of France's wars. **Hours:** Daily April–Sept 10:00–18:00, Sun until 18:30 and Tue until 21:00, July–Aug tomb open until 19:00; daily Oct–March 10:00–17:00, Sun until 17:30; Oct–June closed first Mon of each month. See page 160.

▲▲**Rodin Museum** Works by the greatest sculptor since Michelangelo, with many statues in a peaceful garden. **Hours:** Tue–Sun 10:00–17:45, closed Mon. See page 159.

▲▲**Marmottan Museum** Untouristy art museum focusing on Monet. **Hours:** Tue–Sun 10:00–18:00, Thu until 21:00, closed Mon. See page 161.

▲▲**Cluny Museum** Medieval art with unicorn tapestries. **Hours:** Wed–Mon 9:15–17:45, closed Tue. See page 163.

▲▲**Champs-Elysées** Paris' grand boulevard. **Hours:** Always open. See page 167.

▲▲**Jacquemart-André Museum** Art-strewn mansion. **Hours:** Daily 10:00–18:00. See page 170.

▲▲**Pompidou Center** Modern art in colorful building with city views. **Hours:** Wed–Mon 11:00–21:00, closed Tue. See page 173.

▲▲**Carnavalet Museum** Paris' history wrapped up in a 16th-century mansion. **Hours:** Tue–Sun 10:00–18:00, closed Mon. See page 174.

▲**Sacré-Cœur** White basilica atop Montmartre with spectacular views. **Hours:** Daily 6:00–22:30. See page 176.

▲**Panthéon** Neoclassical monument celebrating the struggles of the French. **Hours:** Daily 10:00–18:30 in summer, until 18:00 in winter. See page 165.

▲**Opéra Garnier** Grand belle époque theater with a ceiling by Chagall. **Hours:** Generally daily 10:00–17:00, mid-July–Aug until 18:00. See page 169.

▲**Père Lachaise Cemetery** Final home of Paris' illustrious dead. **Hours:** Mon–Fri 8:00–18:00, Sat 8:30–18:00, Sun 9:00–18:00, until 17:30 in winter. See page 175.

▲**Jewish Art and History Museum** Displays history of Judaism in Europe. **Hours:** Mon–Fri 11:00–18:00, Sun 10:00–18:00, closed Sat. See page 174.

Montmartre: This hill, topped by the bulbous white domes of Sacré-Cœur, hovers on the northern fringes of your Paris map. The neighborhood still retains some of the untamed rural charm that once drew Impressionist painters and turn-of-the-century bohemians.

Planning Your Time

The following day-plans give an idea of how much an organized, motivated, and caffeinated person can see. Trying to do too much would drive you in-Seine, so leave a few things for your next visit to Paris. Paris is a great one-week getaway. If you have less than a week, start with the Day 1 plan—the most important sights—and add on from there.

Day 1: Follow this book's Historic Paris Walk. In the afternoon, tour the Louvre. Then enjoy the Trocadéro scene and a twilight ride up the Eiffel Tower.

Day 2: Stroll the Champs-Elysées from the Arc de Triomphe to the Tuileries Garden. Tour the Orsay Museum. In the evening, take a nighttime tour by cruise boat, taxi, bus, or retro-chic Deux Chevaux car.

Day 3: Catch the RER suburban train by 8:00 to arrive early at Versailles. Tour the palace's interior, then the gardens and Trianon/Domaine. Have dinner in Versailles town or return to Paris.

Day 4: Visit Montmartre and the Sacré-Cœur Basilica. Have lunch on Montmartre. Continue your Impressionist theme by touring the Orangerie. Enjoy dinner on Ile St. Louis, then a floodlit walk by Notre-Dame.

Day 5: Concentrate on the morning market in the rue Cler neighborhood, then afternoon sightseeing at the Rodin Museum and the Army Museum and Napoleon's Tomb.

Day 6: Ride scenic bus #69 to the Marais and tour this neighborhood, including the Pompidou Center. In the afternoon, visit the Opéra

Garnier, and end your day with rooftop views from the Galeries Lafayette or Printemps department stores.

Day 7: See more in Paris (rue Montorgueil market, Left Bank shopping stroll, Père Lachaise Cemetery, Marmottan or Jacquemart-André museum), or take a day-trip to Chartres or Giverny.

These are busy day-plans, so be sure to schedule in slack time for picnics, laundry, people-watching, leisurely dinners, shopping, and recharging your touristic batteries. Slow down and be open to unexpected experiences and the courtesy of Parisians.

Here are a few quick sightseeing tips to get you started: Consider the handy Paris Museum Pass (✪ see page 218), which covers admission to many sights and lets you skip ticket-buying lines. Reservations are recommended for the Eiffel Tower. Since opening hours are variable, get the latest information from museum websites, at www.parisinfo.com, or from local publications when you arrive. For more sightseeing tips, ✪ see page 217.

And finally, remember that—although Paris' sights can be crowded and stressful—the city itself is all about gentility and grace, so...be flexible.

I hope you have a great trip! Traveling like a temporary local, you'll get the absolute most out of every mile, minute, and euro. As you visit places I know and love, I'm happy you'll be meeting my favorite Parisians.

Bon voyage!

Historic Paris Walk

Ile de la Cité and the Latin Quarter

Paris has been the cultural capital of Europe for centuries. We'll start where it did, on Ile de la Cité, with a foray onto the Left Bank, on a walk that laces together 80 generations of history—from Celtic fishing village to Roman city, bustling medieval capital, birthplace of the Revolution, bohemian haunt of the 1920s, and the working world of modern Paris. Along the way, we'll step into two of Paris' greatest sights: Notre-Dame and Sainte-Chapelle.

ORIENTATION

Length of This Walk: Allow four hours for this three-mile walk.

Paris Museum Pass: Since many sights on this walk are covered by the pass, consider picking it up before your walk (or, on the Ile de la Cité, at the *tabac* by Sainte-Chapelle at 5 boulevard du Palais). ✪ For more information, see page 218.

Notre-Dame Cathedral: Free, open Mon–Fri 8:00–18:45, Sat–Sun 8:00–19:15. Modest dress expected. The cathedral hosts several masses every morning, plus Vespers at 17:45. For a schedule of services, organ concerts, and summer night spectacles, call or check the website. Tel. 01 42 34 56 10, www.notredamedeparis.com.

Tower Climb: The entrance for Notre-Dame's towers is outside the cathedral, on the left side. It's 387 steps up, but it's worth it for the gargoyle's-eye view of the cathedral, Seine, and city. It costs €8, and is covered by the Museum Pass, but there's no bypass line for passholders. Open daily April–Sept 10:00–18:30, also June–Aug Sat–Sun until 23:00, Oct–March 10:00–17:30, last entry 45 minutes before closing. To avoid crowds in peak season, arrive before 10:00 or after 17:00.

Paris Archaeological Crypt: €4, covered by Museum Pass, Tue–Sun 10:00–18:00, last entry 30 minutes before closing, closed Mon.

Deportation Memorial: Free, Tue–Sun April–Sept 10:00–19:00, Oct–March 10:00–18:00, closed Mon year-round.

Shakespeare and Company Bookstore: Mon–Fri 10:00–23:00, Sat–Sun 11:00–23:00; tel. 01 43 25 40 93.

Sainte-Chapelle: €8, €11 combo-ticket with Conciergerie, covered by Museum Pass. Open March–Oct daily 9:30–18:00, Wed until 21:30 mid-May–mid-Sept; Nov–Feb daily 9:00–17:00, last entry 30 minutes before closing. Avoid the ticket line with a Museum Pass or a combo-ticket bought at the less crowded Conciergerie. Security is strict at the entrance.

Conciergerie: €7, €11 combo-ticket with Sainte-Chapelle, covered by Museum Pass. Open daily March–Oct 9:30–18:00, Nov–Feb 9:00–17:00, last entry 30 minutes before closing. Tel. 01 53 40 60 80.

Free Audio Tour: A free Rick Steves audio tour is available on iTunes or at www.ricksteves.com.

Services: There's a free public WC in front of Notre-Dame. Find others at Sainte-Chapelle, the Conciergerie, and cafés.

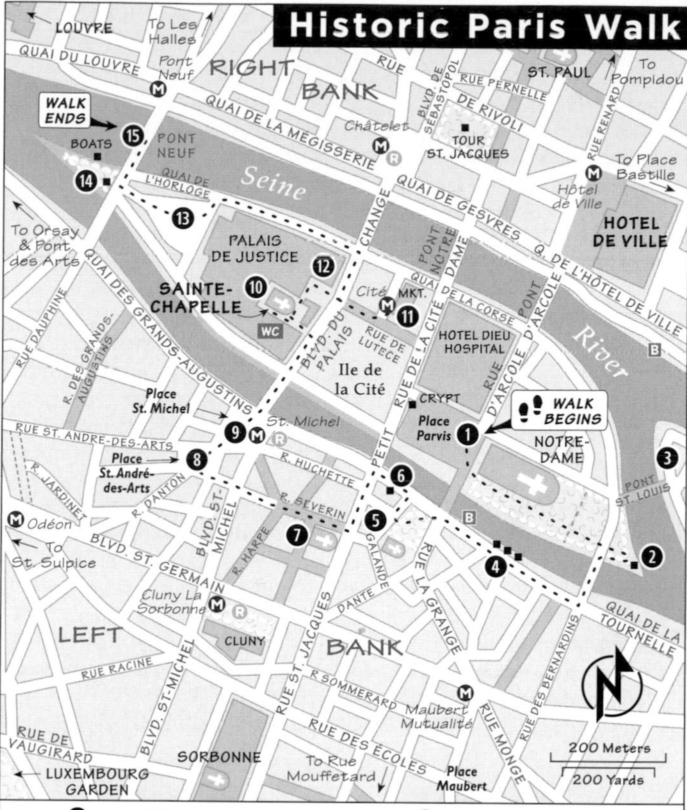

1. Point Zero
2. Deportation Memorial
3. Ile St. Louis
4. Left Bank Booksellers
5. Medieval Paris
6. Shakespeare & Co. Bookstore
7. St. Séverin
8. Place St. André-des-Arts
9. Place St. Michel
10. Sainte-Chapelle
11. Cité Métro Stop
12. Conciergerie
13. Place Dauphine
14. Statue of Henry IV
15. Pont Neuf

THE WALK BEGINS

Start at Notre-Dame Cathedral on the island in the Seine River, the physical and historic bull's-eye of your Paris map. The closest Métro stops are Cité, Hôtel de Ville, and St. Michel, each a short walk away.

► *On the square in front of the cathedral, stand far enough back to take in the whole facade. Find the circular window in the center.*

Notre-Dame Cathedral

For centuries, the main figure in the Christian pantheon has been Mary, the mother of Jesus. This church is dedicated to "Our Lady" *(Notre Dame),* and there she is, cradling God, right in the heart of the facade, surrounded by the halo of the rose window.

Imagine the faith of the people who built this cathedral. They broke ground in 1163 with the hope that someday their great-great-great-great-great-great grandchildren might attend the dedication Mass, which finally took place two centuries later, in 1345. Look up the 200-foot-tall bell towers and imagine a tiny medieval community mustering the money and energy for construction. Master masons supervised, but the people did much of the grunt work themselves for free—hauling the huge stones from distant quarries, digging a 30-foot-deep trench to lay the foundation, and treading like rats on a wheel designed to lift the stones up, one by one. This kind of backbreaking, arduous manual labor created the real hunchbacks of Notre-Dame.

► *"Walk this way" toward the cathedral, and view it from the bronze plaque on the ground (30 yards from the central doorway) marked...*

Notre-Dame's impressive facade

Rose window framing "Our Lady"

❶ Point Zero

You're standing at the center of France, the point from which all distances are measured. It was also the center of Paris 2,300 years ago, when the Parisii tribe fished where the east–west river crossed a north–south road. The Romans conquered this Celtic tribe and built their Temple of Jupiter where Notre-Dame stands today (52 B.C.). When Rome fell, the Germanic Franks sealed their victory by replacing the temple with the Christian church of St. Etienne in the sixth century.

The grand equestrian statue (to your right, as you face the church) is of Charlemagne ("Charles the Great," 742–814), King of the Franks, whose reign marked the birth of modern France.

When Notre-Dame was first built, this square was filled with higgledy-piggledy buildings. The church's huge bell towers rose above this tangle of smaller buildings, inspiring Victor Hugo's story of a deformed bell-ringer who could look down on all of Paris. Looking two-thirds of the way up Notre-Dame's left tower, find Paris' most photographed gargoyle. Propped on his elbows on the balcony rail, he watches all the tourists in line.

► *Much of Paris' history is right under your feet. Some may consider visiting it in the Archeological Crypt, a small museum located 100 yards in front of Notre-Dame. Otherwise, turn your attention to the...*

Notre-Dame Facade

► *Start with the left doorway and, to the left of the door, find the statue of St. Denis, with his head in his hands.*

Left Door—St. Denis: When Christianity began making converts in Roman Paris, the bishop of Paris, Denis, was beheaded by the Romans. But those early Christians were hard to keep down. Denis simply got up,

Point Zero: Step on the center of France.

Charlemagne, whose "Franks" became "France"

Paris Through History

250 B.C. Small fishing village of the Parisii, a Celtic tribe.

52 B.C. Julius Caesar conquers the Parisii, and the Romans soon establish a capital on the Left Bank.

A.D. 497 Roman Paris falls to the Germanic Franks. King Clovis (482–511) converts to Christianity and makes Paris his capital.

885–886 Paris gets wasted in a siege by Viking Norsemen = Normans.

1163 Notre-Dame cornerstone laid.

c. 1250 Paris is a bustling commercial city with a newly built university, Notre-Dame, and Sainte-Chapelle.

c. 1600 King Henry IV beautifies Paris with structures such as the Pont Neuf.

c. 1700 Louis XIV makes Versailles his capital. Parisians grumble.

1789 Paris is the heart of France's Revolution, which condemns thousands to the guillotine.

1804 Napoleon Bonaparte crowns himself emperor in a ceremony at Notre-Dame.

c. 1860 Napoleon's nephew, Napoleon III, builds Paris' wide boulevards.

1889 The centennial of the Revolution is celebrated with the Eiffel Tower. Paris enjoys the prosperity of the belle époque (beautiful age).

1920s After the draining Great War, Paris is a cheap place to live, attracting expatriates such as Ernest Hemingway.

1940–1944 Occupied Paris spends the war years under gray skies and gray Nazi uniforms.

1968 In May student protests and a general strike bring Paris to a halt.

1981–1995 Paris modernizes: the TGV, the new Louvre Pyramid, Musée d'Orsay, La Grande Arche de la Défense, and Opéra Bastille.

1998 Playing at its home stadium, France wins the World Cup.

2005 Lance Armstrong wins his seventh Tour de France.

2010 France wins its bid to host the Europe 2016 soccer championship.

tucked his head under his arm, "headed" north, paused at a fountain to wash it off, and continued until he found just the right place to meet his maker. Christianity gained ground, and a church soon replaced the pagan temple.

Central Door—Last Judgment Relief: Above the doorway (just under the arches), witness the end of the world. Christ sits on the throne of judgment holding both hands up. Beneath him an angel and a demon weigh souls in the balance; the demon cheats by pressing down. The good

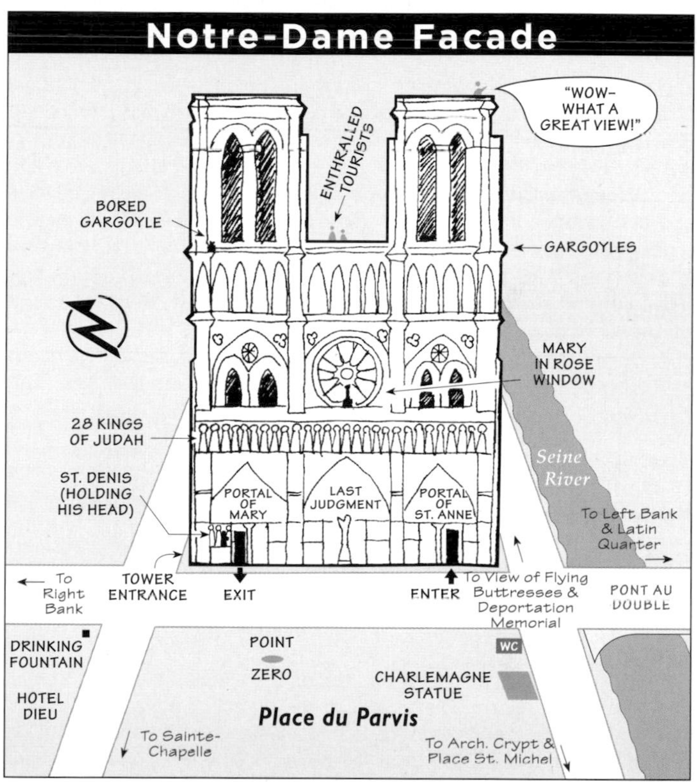

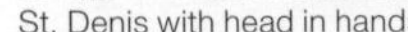
St. Denis with head in hands

Last Judgment (over the central door)

souls stand to the left, gazing up to heaven. The bad souls to the right are chained up and led off to a six-hour tour of the Louvre on a hot summer day. (The ugly souls must be the crazy demons farther to the right, at the base of the arch. Find the flaming cauldron with the sinner diving headfirst into it.)

Above the Doors—The Kings of Judah: Take a dozen paces back and look up to find the row of 28 kings. In the days of the French Revolution (1789–1799), these Biblical kings were mistaken for the hated French kings. The citizens stormed the church, crying, "Off with their heads!" Plop—they lopped off the crowned heads of these statues with glee, creating a row of St. Denises that wasn't repaired for decades.

But the story doesn't end there. A schoolteacher collected the heads and buried them in his backyard for safekeeping. There they slept until 1977, when they were accidentally unearthed. Today, they're on display in the Cluny Museum, a few blocks away (✪ see page 163).

► *Now let's head into the...*

Notre-Dame Interior

► *Enter the church at the right doorway and find a spot where you can view the long, high central aisle. (Be careful: Pickpockets attend church here religiously.)*

Nave

Remove your metaphorical hat and become a simple bareheaded peasant, entering the dim medieval light of the church. Take a minute to let your pupils dilate, then take in the subtle, mysterious light show that God beams through the stained-glass windows. Follow the slender columns up 10 stories to the praying-hands arches of the ceiling, and contemplate the heavens.

This is Gothic. Taller and filled with light, Notre-Dame was a major improvement over the earlier Romanesque style. Gothic architects needed only a few structural columns, topped by crisscrossing pointed arches, to support the weight of the roof. This let them build higher than ever, freeing up the walls for windows.

Notre-Dame has the typical basilica floor plan: a long central nave lined with columns and flanked by side aisles. It's designed in the shape of a cross, with the altar placed where the crossbeam intersects. The church can hold up to 10,000 faithful. It's probably buzzing with visitors now, just as it was 600 years ago, when churches were the busy center of every community.

▸ *Walk up to the main altar.*

Altar

This marks the place where Mass is said and the bread and wine of Communion are blessed and distributed. In olden days, there were no chairs. This was the holy spot for Romans, Christians...and even atheists during the Revolution. France today, though nominally Catholic, remains aloof from Vatican dogmatism. Instead of traditional wooden confessional booths, there's an inviting **glass-walled room** (right aisle), where modern sinners seek counseling as much as forgiveness.

Just past the altar is the so-called "choir," the area enclosed with carved-wood walls, where more intimate services can be held in this spacious building. At the far end of the choir (under the cross) is a fine

Notre-Dame's soaring Gothic arches

Pietà behind the altar

Notre-Dame Interior

1. St. Denis & Exit
2. Last Judgment
3. Entrance
4. Glass-Walled Confessional Room
5. Pietà Flanked by Louis XIII & Louis XIV
6. Joan of Arc Statue
7. Rose-Shaped Window
8. Thomas Aquinas Painting
9. Scenes of the Resurrected Jesus

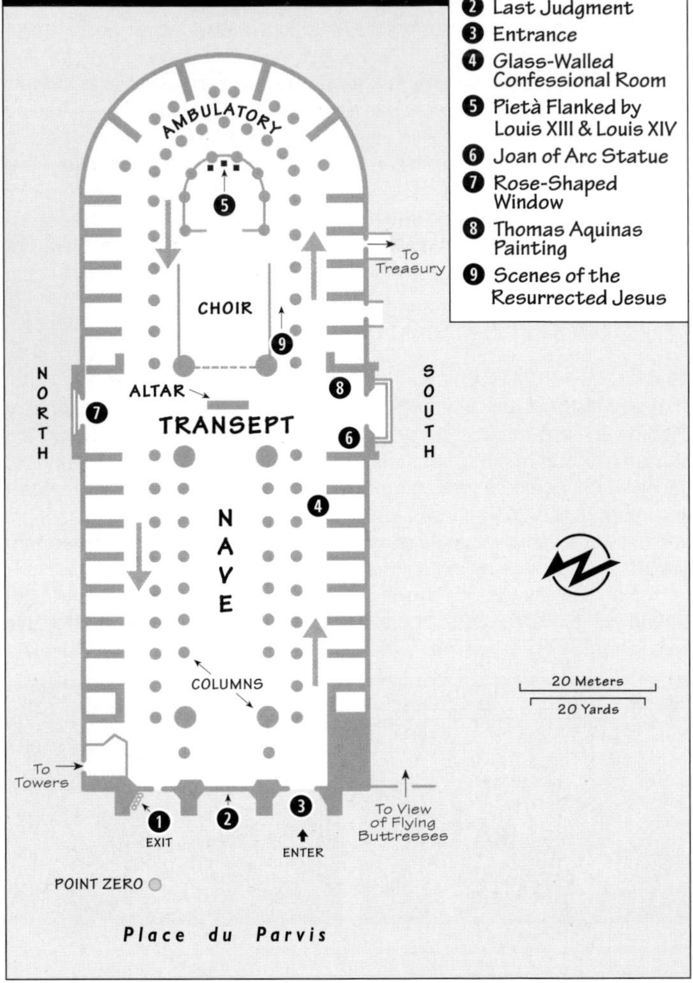

17th-century *pietà* flanked by a kneeling King Louis XIV (1638–1715) and his less-famous father.

Right Transept

A statue of **Joan of Arc** (Jeanne d'Arc, 1412–1431), dressed in armor and praying, honors the French teenager who rallied her country's soldiers to try to drive English invaders from Paris. The English and their allies burned her at the stake for claiming to hear heavenly voices. Almost immediately, Parisians rallied to condemn Joan's execution, and finally, in 1909, here in Notre-Dame, the former "witch" was beatified.

Join the statue in gazing up to the blue-and-purple, **rose-shaped window** in the opposite transept, still with its original medieval glass.

A large painting back down to your right shows portly **Thomas Aquinas** (1225–1274) teaching, while his students drink from the fountain of knowledge. This Italian monk taught at the multicultural University of Paris, using Aristotle's logic to examine the Christian universe, aiming to fuse faith and reason.

▸ *Continue toward the far end of the church, pausing at the top of the three stair steps.*

Circling the Choir

The back side of the choir walls feature **scenes of the resurrected Jesus** (c. 1350) appearing to his followers, starting with Mary Magdalene. The nearby **Treasury** contains lavish robes, golden reliquaries, and the humble tunic of King (and St.) Louis IX, but it probably isn't worth the €3 entry fee.

Surrounding the choir are chapels, each dedicated to a particular

Joan of Arc—former heretic, now saint

Original rose window in north transept

saint. One chapel displays a model showing how the medieval church was built—with pulleys, wagons, hamster-wheel cranes, and lots of elbow grease. At other chapels, the faithful can pause to light a candle as an offering, and meditate in the cool light of the stained glass.

▸ *Amble around the ambulatory, spill back outside, and make a slow U-turn left. Enter the park (recently renamed "Square Jean XXIII") through the iron gates along the riverside.*

Notre-Dame Side View

Alongside the church you'll notice the flying buttresses. These 50-foot stone beams that stick out of the church were the key to the complex Gothic architecture. The pointed arches we saw inside cause the weight of the roof to push outward rather than downward. The "flying" buttresses support the roof by pushing back inward. This opens up the walls for stained-glass windows.

The gargoyles at the base of the roof stick out from pillars and buttresses, representing souls caught between heaven and earth. They also function as rainspouts—from the same French root word as "gargle."

The Neo-Gothic 300-foot spire is a product of the 1860 reconstruction of the dilapidated old church. Find the restoration's chief architect, Eugène-Emmanuel Viollet-le-Duc, among the statues at the base of the spire, looking up, admiring his fine work.

▸ *Behind Notre-Dame, cross the street and enter through the iron gate into the park at the tip of the island. Look for the stairs and head down to reach the...*

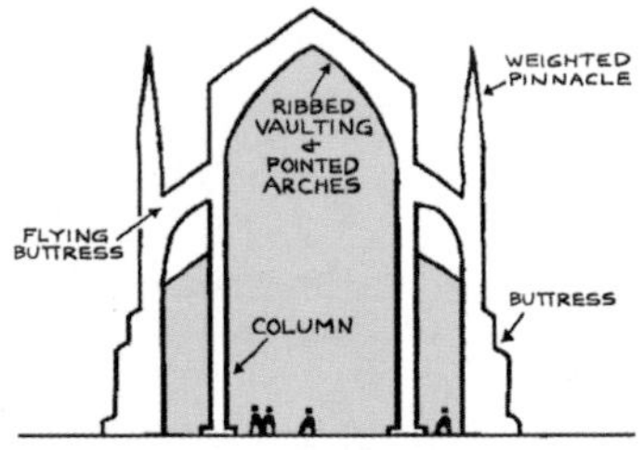

It takes 13 tourists to build a Gothic church: one steeple, six columns, and six buttresses.

Gargoyle—hideous yet functional

❷ Deportation Memorial (Mémorial de la Déportation)

This memorial to the 200,000 French victims of the Nazi concentration camps (1940–1945) draws you into their experience. France was quickly overrun by Nazi Germany, and Paris spent the war years under Nazi occupation. Jews and dissidents were rounded up and deported—many never returned.

As you descend the steps, the city around you disappears. Surrounded by walls, you have become a prisoner. Inside, the hallway is lined with 200,000 lighted crystals, one for each French citizen who died. Flickering at the far end is the eternal flame of hope. Above the exit as you leave is the message you'll find at other Holocaust sites: "Forgive, but never forget."

► *Back on street level, look across the river (north) to the island called...*

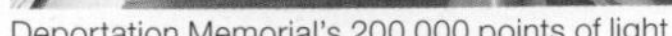

Deportation Memorial's 200,000 points of light

Booksellers line the Seine River.

❸ Ile St. Louis

If the Ile de la Cité is a tugboat laden with the history of Paris, it's towing this classy little residential dinghy, laden only with high-rent apartments, boutiques, and characteristic restaurants. The Ile is most famous for its ice-cream shops. Berthillon has outlets at 31 rue St. Louis-en-l'Ile, another across the street, and a third around the corner on rue Bellay. Gelato-lovers head instead to Amorino Gelati at 47 rue St. Louis-en-l'Ile.

► *From the Deportation Memorial, cross the bridge onto the Left Bank and turn right (west). Walk along the river, toward the front end of Notre-Dame. This side view of the church from across the river is one of Europe's great sights and is best from river level.*

LEFT BANK

❹ Left Bank Booksellers

The Rive Gauche, or the Left Bank of the Seine—"left" if you were floating downstream—still has many of the twisting lanes and narrow buildings of medieval times. The Right Bank is more modern and business-oriented, with wide boulevards and stressed Parisians in suits. Here along the riverbank, the "big business" is secondhand books, displayed in the green metal stalls on the parapet. With flexible hours and (literally) no overhead, these literary entrepreneurs run their businesses as they have since medieval times.

► *When you reach the bridge (pont au Double) that crosses over in front of Notre-Dame, veer to the left across the street to a small park called Square Viviani (fill your water bottle from the fountain on the left).*

Angle across the square and pass by Paris' oldest inhabitant—an acacia tree nicknamed Robinier, after the guy who planted it in 1602. Imagine that this same tree might once have shaded the Sun King, Louis XIV. Just beyond the tree you'll find the small rough-stone church of St. Julien-le-Pauvre.

❺ Medieval Paris (1000–1400)

Picture Paris in 1250, when the church of St. Julien-le-Pauvre was still new. Notre-Dame was nearly done (so they thought), Sainte-Chapelle had just opened, the university was expanding human knowledge, and Paris was fast becoming a prosperous industrial and commercial center. The area around the church (and along nearby rue Galande) gives you some of the medieval feel of ramshackle architecture and old houses leaning every which way. In medieval days, people were piled on top of each other, here along the main commercial artery of the day—the Seine. The smell of fish competed with the smell of neighbors in this knot of humanity.

▸ *Return to the river and turn left on rue de la Bûcherie. At #37, drop into the...*

❻ Shakespeare and Company Bookstore

In addition to hosting butchers and fishmongers, the Left Bank has been home to scholars, philosophers, and poets since medieval times. This funky bookstore—a reincarnation of the original shop from the 1920s on rue de l'Odéon—has picked up the literary torch.

Sylvia Beach, an American with a passion for free thinking, opened Shakespeare and Company for the post-WWI Lost Generation, who came to Paris to find themselves. American expatriates flocked here for

St. Julien-le-Pauvre and 400-year-old tree

This bookstore carries on expatriate bohemian life.

the cheap rent and free-flowing booze, fleeing the uptight, Prohibition-era United States. Beach's bookstore was a meeting place for the likes of Ernest Hemingway, Gertrude Stein, and Ezra Pound. James Joyce struggled to find a publisher for his now-classic novel *Ulysses*—until Sylvia Beach published it.

▸ *Continue to rue du Petit-Pont (which becomes rue St. Jacques), and turn left. This bustling north–south boulevard was the Romans' busiest street 2,000 years ago, with chariots racing in and out of the city.*

A block south of the Seine, turn right at the Gothic church of St. Séverin and walk into the Latin Quarter.

❼ St. Séverin

Don't ask me why, but it took a century longer to build this church than Notre-Dame. This is Flamboyant, or "flame-like," Gothic, and you can see how the short, prickly spires are meant to make this building flicker in the eyes of the faithful. The church gives us a close-up look at gargoyles, the decorative drain spouts that also functioned to keep evil spirits away.

Inside, see stained-glass windows in the greens and reds popular in Flamboyant Gothic. In the apse, admire the lone twisted Flamboyant Gothic column, the fan vaulting, and the colorful modern stained-glass windows that echo the fan-vaulting. The church has an impressive organ (on the entrance wall) and hosts evening concerts.

▸ *At #22 rue St. Séverin, you'll find the skinniest house in Paris, two windows wide. Rue St. Séverin leads right through...*

St Séverin flickers with flamboyant flames.

The Latin Quarter looks "Greek" today.

The Latin Quarter

Although it may look more like the Greek Quarter today (cheap gyros abound), this area is the Latin Quarter, named for the language you'd have heard on these streets in medieval times. Latin-speaking scholars from across Europe gathered at the University of Paris (founded 1215), one of Europe's first universities, which was (and still is) nearby.

As you walk along rue St. Séverin, notice how the street slopes into a central channel of bricks. In the days before plumbing and toilets, flushing meant throwing it out the window. *"Garde de l'eau!"* they'd holler, "Watch out for the water!", and heave it into the streets, where it would eventually wash down into the Seine.

Until the 19th century, all of Paris was like this—a medieval tangle of small streets. The ethnic feel of this area is nothing new, as it's been a melting pot and university district for almost 800 years.

► *Keep wandering straight, and you'll come to...*

Boulevard St. Michel

Busy boulevard St. Michel (or "boul' Miche") is the main artery for the Latin Quarter, culminating a block away (to the left) at the intersection with boulevard St. Germain. There's still a bohemian vibe at cafés and boutiques nearby, although nowadays you're more likely to find pantyhose at 30 percent off.

The Sorbonne—the University of Paris' humanities department—is two blocks south, if you want to make a detour. (You can gaze at the dome from the place de la Sorbonne courtyard, but visitors are not allowed to enter.) Originally founded as a theological school in medieval times, the Sorbonne expanded to include secular subjects and gained a world-wide reputation for bold new ideas. Nonconformity is still a tradition here, and Paris remains a world center for new intellectual trends.

► *Cross boulevard St. Michel. Just ahead is...*

❽ Place St. André-des-Arts

This tree-filled square is lined with Paris' social watering holes—cafés. Every great French writer—from Voltaire and Jean-Jacques Rousseau to Jean-Paul Sartre and Jacques Derrida—had his favorite café, offering a warm place to sit and stimulating conversation for the price of a cup of coffee.

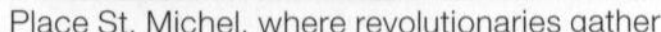
Place St. Michel, where revolutionaries gather

Sainte-Chapelle—built for the Crown of Thorns

► *Adjoining this square toward the river is the triangular place St. Michel, with a Métro stop and a statue of St. Michael killing a devil.*

9 Place St. Michel

You're standing at the traditional core of the Left Bank's artsy, bohemian district of poets, philosophers, and winos. Nearby (especially west of the square along rue St. André-des-Arts), you'll find international eateries, far-out bookshops, street singers, pale girls in black berets, jazz clubs, avant-garde cinemas, and—these days—tourists. The Left Bank's best action is after dark.

In less commercial times, place St. Michel was a gathering point for the city's malcontents and misfits. In 1830, 1848, and again in 1871, the citizens took the streets from the government troops, set up barricades *Les Miz*–style, and fought against royalist oppression. During World War II, the locals rose up against their Nazi oppressors—read the plaques under the dragons at the foot of the St. Michel fountain.

In the spring of 1968, a time of social upheaval all over the world, young students battled riot batons and tear gas by digging up the cobblestones on the street and hurling them at police. They took over the square and declared it an independent state. Factory workers followed their call to arms and went on strike, challenging the de Gaulle government and forcing change. Even today, whenever there's a student demonstration, it starts here. But the Latin Quarter's cobblestones have been replaced with pavement, so scholars can never again use the streets as weapons.

► *From place St. Michel, look across the river and find the prickly steeple*

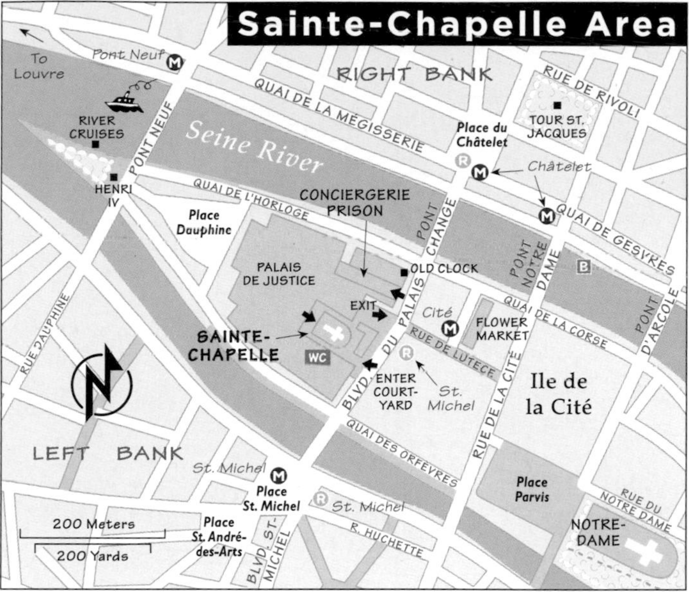

of the Sainte-Chapelle church. Head toward it. Cross the river on pont St. Michel and continue north along the boulevard du Palais. On your left, you'll see the doorway to Sainte-Chapelle.

⑩ Sainte-Chapelle

► *You'll need to pass through a strict security checkpoint to get into the Sainte-Chapelle complex. (This is more than a tourist attraction—France's Supreme Court meets to the right of Sainte-Chapelle.) Past security, you'll enter the courtyard outside Sainte-Chapelle, where you'll find WCs and information about upcoming church concerts. The ticket-buying line into the church may be long.*

If you have a Museum Pass or a Conciergerie combo-ticket, you may be able to skip some of the security line (look for signs), and can certainly bypass the ticket-buying line.

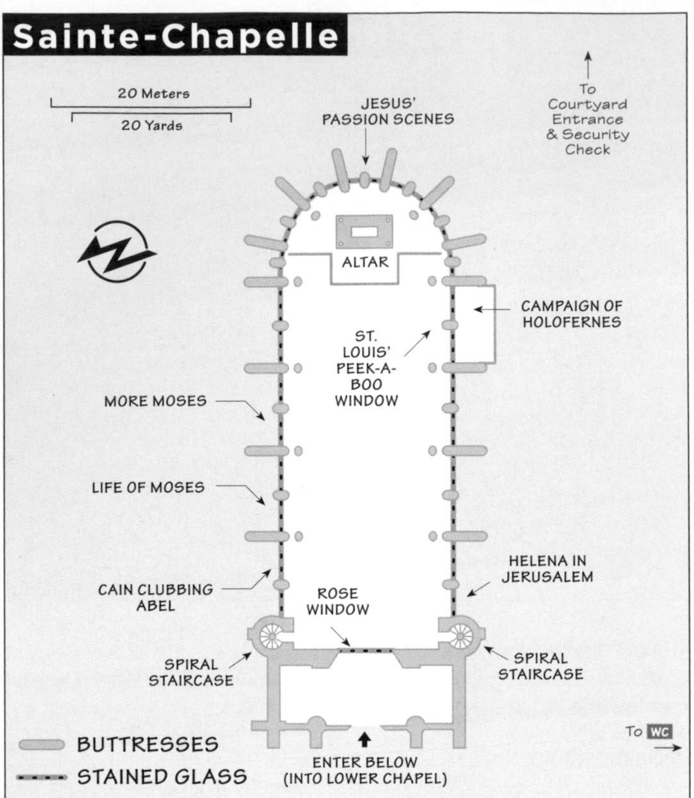

Exterior

This triumph of Gothic church architecture is a cathedral of glass like no other. It was speedily built between 1242 and 1248 for King Louis IX—the only French king who is now a saint—to house the supposed Crown of Thorns. Its architectural harmony is due to the fact that it was completed under the direction of one architect and in only six years—unheard of in Gothic times. Recall that Notre-Dame took over 200 years.

Though the inside is beautiful, the exterior is basically functional. The

1,100 scenes of stained glass; 6,500 square feet

muscular buttresses hold up the stone roof, so the walls are essentially there to display stained glass. The lacy spire is Neo-Gothic—added in the 19th century.

► *Enter. First you see the relatively humble ground floor. Then climb the spiral staircase to the Chapelle Haute. Leave the rough stone of the earth and step into the light.*

Interior: The Stained Glass

Fiat lux. "Let there be light." From the first page of the Bible, it's clear: Light is divine. Light shines through stained glass like God's grace shining down to earth. Gothic architects used their new technology to turn dark stone buildings into lanterns of light. The glory of Gothic shines brighter here than in any other church.

Fifteen separate panels of stained glass cover 6,500 square feet—two thirds of it 13th-century original. There are more than 1,100 different scenes, mostly from the Bible. These tell the entire Christian history of the world, from the Creation in Genesis (first window on the left, as you face the altar), to the coming of Christ (over the altar), to the end of the world (the round "rose"-shaped window at the rear of the church). Each individual scene is interesting, and the whole effect is overwhelming. Allow yourself a few minutes to bask in the glow of the colored light, then zero in on some of the individual panels.

► *Working clockwise from the entrance, look for these worthwhile scenes. (Note: The sun lights up different windows at various times of day. Overcast days give the most even light. On bright, sunny days, some sections are glorious, while others look like sheets of lead.)*

Genesis—Cain Clubbing Abel (first window on the left, always dark because of a building butted up against it): On the bottom level in the third circle from the left, we see God create the round earth and hold it up. On the next level up, we catch glimpses of naked Adam and Eve. On the third level (far right circle), Cain, in red, clubs his brother Abel, committing the first murder.

Life of Moses (second window, the bottom row of diamond panels): The first panel shows baby Moses in a basket, placed by his sister in the squiggly brown river. Next he's found by the pharaoh's daughter. Then he grows up. And finally, he's a man, a prince of Egypt on his royal throne.

More Moses (third window, in middle and upper sections): You'll see various scenes of Moses, the guy with the bright yellow horns—the result of a medieval mistranslation of the Hebrew word for "rays of light," or halo.

Jesus' Passion Scenes (over the altar and likely hidden by scaffolding until 2013): These scenes from Jesus' arrest and crucifixion were the backdrop for the Crown of Thorns (originally displayed on the altar), which was placed on Jesus' head when the Romans were torturing and humiliating him before his execution. Stand a few steps back from the altar to look through the canopy and find Jesus in yellow shorts, carrying his cross (fifth frame up from right bottom). A little below that, see Jesus in purple, being fitted with the painful Crown of Thorns.

Campaign of Holofernes (window to the right of the altar wall): On the bottom row are four scenes of colorful knights (refer to map to get oriented). The second circle from the left is a battle scene, the campaign of Holofernes. Three soldiers with swords are slaughtering three other men. The background is blue. The men have different-colored clothes—red,

Stained Glass Supreme

Craftsmen made glass—which is, essentially, melted sand—using this recipe:

- Melt one part sand with two parts wood ash.
- Mix in rusty metals to get different colors—iron makes red; cobalt makes blue; copper, green; manganese, purple; cadmium, yellow.
- Blow glass into a cylinder shape, cut lengthwise, and lay flat.
- Cut into pieces with an iron tool, or by heating and cooling a select spot to make it crack.
- Fit pieces together to form a figure, using strips of lead to hold them in place.
- Place masterpiece so high on a wall that no one can read it.

blue, green, mauve, and white. You can see the folds in the robes, the hair, and facial features. The victim in the center has his head splotched with blood. Such details were created by scratching on the glass or baking on paint. It was a painstaking process of finding just the right colors, fitting them together to make a scene...and then multiplying by 1,100.

Rose Window (above entrance): It's Judgment Day, with a tiny Christ in the center of the chaos and miracles that accompany the Apocalyptic last days.

Altar

The altar was raised up high to better display the Crown of Thorns, the

Campaign of Holofernes, one detail of many

Altar for the Crown of Thorns

Criss-cross arches on Saint-Chapelle's ceiling

relic around which this chapel was built. Notice the staircase: Access was limited to the priest and the king, who wore the keys to the shrine around his neck.

The Crown is supposedly the one placed on Jesus' head as he was being tortured before his crucifixion. Legend has it that the Crown was discovered in Jerusalem by Emperor Constantine's mother (circa 300 A.D.) and brought to the city of Constantinople (today's Istanbul). There it sat until French Crusaders arrived in the 13th century. King Louis IX, convinced he'd found the real McCoy, paid £135,000 for the Crown...and a mere £40,000 to build Sainte-Chapelle to house it. Today, the supposed Crown of Thorns is kept by the Notre-Dame Treasury and shown only on Good Friday and on the first Friday of the month at 15:00.

Before leaving, lay your camera on the ground and shoot the ceiling. Those pure and simple ribs growing out of the slender columns are the essence of Gothic structure.

► *Exit Sainte-Chapelle. Back outside, walk counter-clockwise around the church to reach the street.*

You'll pass the giant Palais de Justice, now the home of the French Supreme Court. During the Revolution, here is where they enforced the motto "Liberté, Egalité, Fraternité," *sentencing many to prison in the Conciergerie or to death at the guillotine.*

Now pass through the big iron gate to the noisy boulevard du Palais. Cross the street to the wide, pedestrian-only rue de Lutèce and walk about halfway down.

⓫ Cité "Metropolitain" Métro Stop

Of the 141 original early-20th-century subway entrances, this is one of only a few survivors—now preserved as a national art treasure. (New York's Museum of Modern Art even exhibits one.) It marks Paris at its peak in 1900—on the cutting edge of Modernism, but with an eye for beauty. The curvy, plantlike ironwork is a textbook example of Art Nouveau, the style that rebelled against the erector-set squareness of the Industrial Age.

Nearby is the flower and plant market on place Louis Lépine. On Sundays the square flutters with a busy bird market.

► *Double back to the Palais de Justice, turn right onto boulevard du Palais, and enter the...*

⓬ Conciergerie

The Conciergerie was the gloomy prison famous as the last stop for 2,780 victims of the guillotine, including France's last *ancien régime* queen, Marie-Antoinette. Inside, pick up a free map and breeze through.

Original Art Nouveau Métro entrance

Marie-Antoinette's cell in the Conciergerie

Conciergerie—photogenic torture chamber

See the spacious, low-ceilinged Hall of Men-at-Arms (Room 1), used as the guards' dining room, with four large fireplaces (look up the chimneys). Pass through the bookstore (Room 4 on the map) to find the Office of the Keeper, or "Concierge" of the place (who monitored torture...and recommended nearby restaurants). Next door is the *Toilette,* where condemned prisoners combed their hair or touched up their lipstick before their final public appearance—waiting for the open-air cart (tumbrel) to carry them to the guillotine on place de la Concorde.

Upstairs is a memorial room with the names of the 2,780 citizens condemned to death by the guillotine. Find Anne Elisabeth Capet, whose crime was being "sister of the tyrant." Charlotte Corday *("dite d'Armais")* was a noblewoman who snuck into the bathroom of the revolutionary writer Jean-Paul Marat and stabbed him while he bathed. Georges Danton was a prominent revolutionary who was later condemned for being insufficiently liberal—a nasty crime. Louis XVI (called "Capet: last king of France") deserves only a modest mention, as does his wife, Marie-Antoinette (*veuve* means she's widowed). And finally—oh, the irony—there's Maximilien de Robespierre, the head of the Revolution, the man who sent so many to the guillotine before he was eventually toppled, humiliated, imprisoned here, and beheaded.

Back downstairs, you eventually arrive at a re-creation of Marie-Antoinette's cell. Mannequins, period furniture, and a video set the scene. Imagine the queen spending her last days—separated from her 10-year-old son, and now widowed because the king had already been executed. The guard stands modestly behind a screen, while the queen psyches herself up with a crucifix. On October 16, 1793, the queen walked the corridor, stepped onto the cart, and was slowly carried to place de la Concorde, where she had a date with "Monsieur de Paris"—the guillotine.

▸ *Back outside, turn left on boulevard du Palais and head north. On the corner is the city's oldest public clock. The mechanism of the present clock is from 1334, and even though the case is Baroque, it keeps on ticking.*

Turn left onto quai de l'Horloge and walk west along the river. The bridge up ahead is the pont Neuf, where we'll end this walk. At the first corner, veer left into a sleepy triangular square called...

⓭ Place Dauphine

It's amazing to find such coziness in the heart of Paris. This city of two million is still a city of neighborhoods, a collection of villages. The French Supreme Court building looms behind like a giant marble gavel. The Caveau du Palais restaurant is a nice spot for a drink or light meal. You may see lawyers on their lunch break lobbing metal balls at a target, playing *boules.*

▸ *Continue through place Dauphine. As you pop out the other end, you're face to face with a...*

⑭ Statue of Henry IV

Henry IV (1553–1610) is not as famous as his grandson, Louis XIV, but Henry helped make Paris what it is today—a European capital of elegant buildings and quiet squares. He built the place Dauphine (behind you), the pont Neuf (to the right), residences (to the left, down rue Dauphine), the Louvre's long Grand Gallery (downriver on the right), and the tree-filled square Vert-Galant (directly behind the statue, on the tip of the island). The square is one of Paris' make-out spots; its name comes from Henry's nickname, the Green Knight, as Henry was a notorious ladies' man. The park is a great place to relax: dangle your legs over the concrete prow of this boat-shaped island.

▸ *From the statue, turn right onto the old bridge. Pause at the little nook halfway across.*

⑮ Pont Neuf

This "new bridge" is now Paris' oldest. Built during Henry IV's reign (about 1600), its arches span the widest part of the river. Unlike other bridges, this one never had houses or buildings growing on it. The turrets were originally for vendors and street entertainers. From the bridge, look downstream

Place Dauphine—oasis of peace

Pont Neuf—400-year old "new bridge"

View of the Seine from Pont Neuf

(west) to see the next bridge, the pedestrian-only pont des Arts. Ahead on the Right Bank is the long Louvre Museum. Beyond that, on the Left Bank, is the Orsay. And what's that tall black tower in the distance?

The Seine

Our walk ends where Paris began—on the Seine River. From Dijon to the English Channel, the Seine meanders 500 miles, cutting through the center of Paris. The river is shallow and slow within the city, but still dangerous enough to require steep stone embankments (built in 1910) to prevent occasional floods.

In summer, the roads that run along the river are replaced with acres of sand, as well as beach chairs and tanned locals, creating Paris Plage. Any time of year, you'll see tourist boats and the commercial barges that carry 20 percent of Paris' transported goods. And on the banks, sportsmen today cast into the waters once fished by Paris' original Celtic inhabitants.

► *We're done. From here, you could take a boat tour (Vedettes du Pont Neuf) leaving from the base of pont Neuf on the island side. The Pont Neuf Métro stop is across the bridge on the Right Bank. Bus #69 heads east along quai du Louvre (at the north end of the bridge) and west along rue de Rivoli (a block farther north). In fact, you can go anywhere—you're standing in the heart of Paris.*

Louvre Tour

Musée du Louvre

Paris' world-class museums walk you through world history, and the best place to start your "art-yssey" is at the Louvre. With more than 30,000 works of art, the Louvre is a full inventory of Western civilization. To cover it all in one visit is impossible. Let's focus on the Louvre's specialties—Greek sculpture, Italian painting, and French painting.

We'll see "Venuses" through history, from the curvy *Venus de Milo* to the wind-blown *Winged Victory of Samothrace,* from placid medieval Madonnas to the *Mona Lisa* to the symbol of modern democracy. Each generation defined beauty differently, and we'll gain insight into long-ago civilizations by admiring what they found beautiful.

ORIENTATION

Cost: €9.50, free on first Sun of month, covered by Museum Pass. Tickets good all day; reentry allowed. Optional additional charges apply for temporary exhibits.

Hours: Wed–Mon 9:00–18:00, Wed and Fri until 22:00, closed Tue, last entry 45 minutes before closing. Galleries begin closing 30 minutes before official closing time.

When to Go: Crowds are worst on Sun, Mon, Wed, and mornings. Evenings are peaceful.

Getting There: Métro stop Palais Royal–Musée du Louvre is the closest. Handy bus #69 heading east (from rue Cler) stops along the Seine River at quai François Mitterand. The westbound bus stops along rue de Rivoli at the Palais Royal–Musée du Louvre Métro stop. You'll also find a taxi stand on rue de Rivoli, next to the Palais Royal–Musée du Louvre Métro station.

Getting In:

Main Pyramid Entrance: There is no grander entry than through the glass pyramid in the central courtyard, but metal detectors (not ticket-buyers) can create a long line.

Museum Pass/Group Entrance: Museum Passholders can use the group entrance in the pedestrian passageway (labeled *Pavilion Richelieu*) between the pyramid and rue de Rivoli. It's under the arches, a few steps north of the pyramid; find the uniformed guard at the security checkpoint entrance, at the down escalator.

Underground Mall Entrance: There's a less crowded underground entrance located within the Carrousel du Louvre shopping mall at

Main Pyramid Entrance

The underground mall entrance is less crowded.

99 rue de Rivoli (the door with the red awning). You can also reach the mall directly from the Métro stop Palais Royal–Musée du Louvre: stepping off the train, exit at the end of the platform and follow signs to *Musée du Louvre–Le Carrousel du Louvre*. At the Louvre entrance, Museum Pass–holders can skip to the head of the security line.

Information: Tel. 01 40 20 53 17, recorded info tel. 01 40 20 51 51, www.louvre.fr.

Buying Tickets: Located under the pyramid, the self-serve ticket machines are faster to use than the ticket windows (machines accept euro notes, coins, and Visa cards). The *tabac* in the underground mall at the Louvre also sells tickets and Museum Passes (cash only).

Tours: Ninety-minute guided tours leave daily (except the first Sun of the month) at 11:00 and 14:00 from the *Accueil des Groupes* area under the pyramid (€5 plus your entry ticket, tel. 01 40 20 52 63). Audioguides are €6. A free Rick Steves audio tour of the Louvre is available on iTunes (search for "Rick Steves Audio Tours") or at www.ricksteves.com.

Length of This Tour: Allow at least two hours.

Baggage Check: Large bags must be checked (it's free), and you can also check small bags to lighten your load. You can't check cameras, money, passports, or other valuables.

Services: WCs are located under the pyramid. Once you're in the galleries, WCs are scarce.

Photography: Photography without a flash is allowed.

Cuisine Art: The Louvre has several cafés, including Café Mollien, located near the end of our tour (€12 for sandwich and drink on terrace overlooking pyramid). Under the pyramid, a self-service lunch cafeteria (€9 *plats du jour*) is just up the escalator in the Richelieu wing. But your best bet is in the Carrousel du Louvre underground shopping mall (west of the pyramid), which has an assortment of decent-value, multiethnic fast-food eateries. Outside the Louvre, try the venerable Café le Nemours or the classy Le Fumoir.

Starring: *Venus de Milo, Winged Victory, Mona Lisa,* Leonardo da Vinci, Raphael, Michelangelo, the French painters, and many of the most iconic images of Western civilization.

SURVIVING THE LOUVRE

► *Start under the glass pyramid—pick up a free map at the information desk and get oriented.*

The Louvre, the largest museum in the Western world, fills three wings of this immense, U-shaped palace. The Richelieu wing (north side)

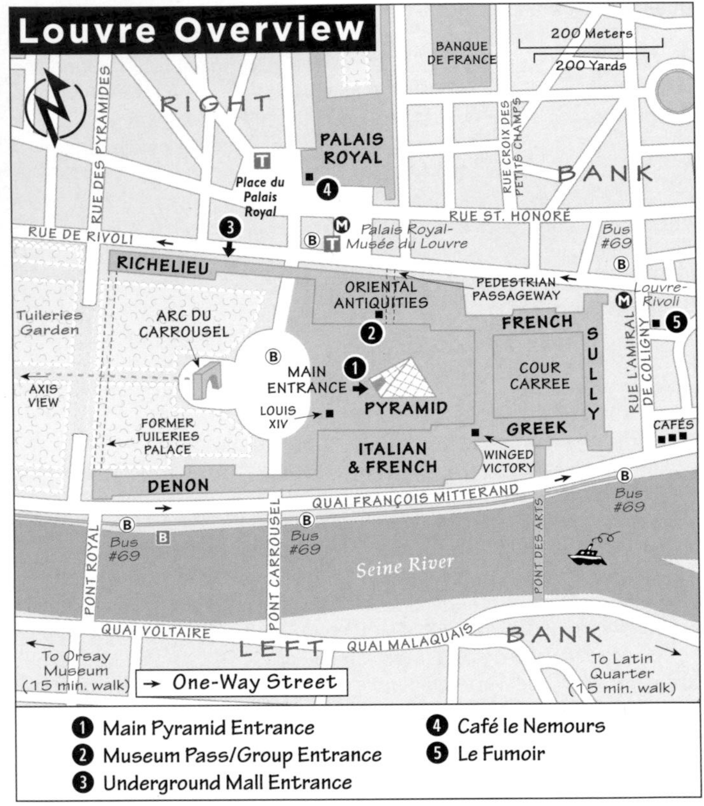

Glass pyramid and Pavilion Richelieu

houses Oriental Antiquities, plus French, Dutch, and Northern art. The Sully wing (east side) has extensive French painting and ancient Egypt collections.

We'll concentrate on the Louvre's south side: the Denon and Sully wings, which hold many of the superstars, including ancient Greek sculpture, Italian Renaissance painting, and French Neoclassical and Romantic painting.

Expect changes—the sprawling Louvre is constantly in flux. Rooms are periodically closed for renovation, and pieces are often being restored or on loan.

The bottom line: You could spend a lifetime here. Concentrate on seeing the biggies quickly, and try to finish the tour with enough energy left to browse.

THE TOUR BEGINS

▶ *Start at the famous Venus de Milo statue. You'll find her not far from another famous statue, the Winged Victory of Samothrace.*

To reach the Venus de Milo from inside the big glass pyramid, head for the Denon wing.

Escalate up one floor. After showing your ticket, continue up the stairs until you reach the top. Glance at the pyramid out the window, then turn right, heading down a long sculpture hall. When you reach the base of a grand staircase, look up at the Winged Victory of Samothrace. We'll return to her later.

To find the Venus de Milo, walk to the left around the big staircase. After about 50 yards, you'll reach Salle 16 (Room 16), where you'll see Venus floating above a sea of worshipping tourists. It's been said that, among the warlike Greeks, this was the first statue to unilaterally disarm.

Greece (500 B.C.–A.D. 1)

The great Greek cultural explosion that changed the course of history unfolded over 50 years (starting around 450 B.C.) in Athens, a Greek town smaller than Muncie, Indiana. The art shows their love of rationality, order, and balance. The balance between timeless stability and fleeting movement made beauty. Most of the art that we'll see in the Louvre either came from Greece or was inspired by it.

Venus de Milo (*Aphrodite*, c. 100 B.C.)

The *Venus de Milo* (or goddess of love, from the Greek island of Melos) created a sensation when it was discovered in 1820. Europe was already

Venus de Milo—balance of opposites

Athena in the Gallery of Statues

in the grip of a classical fad, and this statue seemed to sum up all that ancient Greece stood for. The optimistic Greeks pictured their gods in human form (meaning humans are godlike), and Venus' well-proportioned body captures the perfection of the Greek universe.

Split *Venus* down the middle from nose to toes and see how the two halves balance each other. Venus rests on her right foot (called *contrapposto,* or "counterpoise"), then lifts her left leg, setting her whole body in

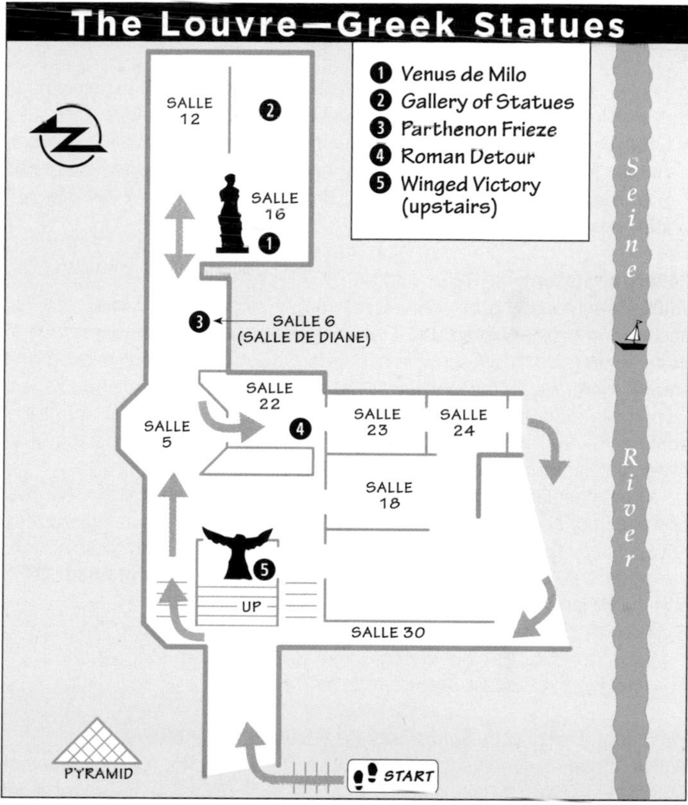

motion. As the left leg rises, her right shoulder droops down. And as her knee points one way, her head turns the other, giving a pleasing S-curve to her body (especially noticeable from the back). *Venus* is a harmonious balance of opposites, orbiting slowly around a vertical axis.

Other opposites balance as well, like the smooth skin of her upper half that sets off the rough-cut texture of her dress (size 14). She's actually made from two different pieces of stone plugged together at the hips (the seam is visible). The face is anatomically accurate, but it's also idealized, a perfect goddess. This isn't any particular woman, but Everywoman—all the idealized features that appealed to the Greeks.

What were her missing arms doing? Some say her right arm held her dress, while her left arm was raised. Others say she was hugging a male statue or leaning on a column. I say she was picking her navel.

► *Orbit* Venus. *This statue is interesting and different from every angle. Remember the view from the back—we'll see it again later. Now make your reentry to earth. From* Venus, *browse around Salle 7 and the adjoining rooms.*

Gallery of Statues

You'll see statues of gods, satyrs, soldiers, athletes, and everyday people engaged in ordinary activities. Greek statues feature the human body in all its splendor. The anatomy is accurate, and the poses are relaxed and natural. Greek sculptors learned to capture people in motion, and to show them from different angles, not just face-forward. The classic *contrapposto* pose—with the weight resting on one leg—captures a balance between timeless stability and fleeting motion.

For Athenians, the most popular goddess was their patron, Athena. She's usually shown as a warrior, wearing a helmet and carrying a spear, ready to fight for her city. Whatever the statue, Golden Age artists sought the perfect balance between down-to-earth humans (with human flaws and quirks) and the idealized perfection of a Greek god.

► *Head for Salle 6 (also known as Salle de Diane), located behind the* Venus de Milo. *(Facing* Venus, *make a loop to the right, of about 20 paces.) You'll find two carved panels on the wall.*

Parthenon Frieze (*Les Sculptures du Parthenon,* c. 440 B.C.)

These stone fragments once decorated the exterior of the greatest Athenian temple, the Parthenon, built at the peak of the Greek Golden Age.

A model of the Parthenon shows where the panels might have hung. The centaur panel would have gone above the entrance. The panel of girls was placed under the covered colonnade, but above the doorway (you'll have to crouch way down and look up to see the frieze of panels).

One panel shows a centaur sexually harassing a woman, telling the story of how these rude creatures crashed a party of humans. But the Greeks fought back and threw the brutes out, just as Athens (metaphorically) conquered its barbarian neighbors and became civilized.

The other relief shows the sacred procession of young girls who marched up the hill every four years with an embroidered veil for the 40-foot-high statue of Athena, the goddess of wisdom. Though headless, the maidens speak volumes about Greek craftsmanship. Carved in only a couple of inches of stone, they're amazingly realistic. They glide along horizontally (their belts and shoulders all in a line), while the folds of their dresses drape down vertically. The man in the center is relaxed, realistic, and *contrapposto*. Notice the veins in his arm. The maidens' pleated dresses make them look as stable as fluted columns, but their arms and legs step out naturally—their human forms emerging gracefully from the stone.

► *Make another 20-step loop into the nearby Salle 5 and turn left into Salle 22, the Roman Antiquities room (Antiquités Romaines), for a...*

Roman Detour (Salles 22–30)

Stroll among the Caesars and try to see the person behind the public persona. Besides the many faces of the ubiquitous Emperor *Inconnu* ("unknown"), you might spot Augustus (Auguste), the first emperor, and his wily wife, Livia (Livie). Their son Tiberius (Tibère) was the Caesar that Jesus

Parthenon frieze—natural movement

Roman busts—warts-and-all realism

Christ "rendered unto." Caligula was notoriously depraved, curly-haired Domitia murdered her husband, Hadrian popularized the beard, Trajan ruled the Empire at its peak, and Marcus Aurelius (Marc Aurèle) presided stoically over Rome's slow fall.

The pragmatic Romans (500 B.C.–A.D. 500) were great conquerors but bad artists. One area in which they excelled was realistic portrait busts, especially of their emperors, who were worshipped as gods on earth. The Romans also loved Greek statues and made countless copies, adding a veneer of sophistication to their homes, temples, and offices.

▶ *Continue clockwise through the Roman collection of sarcophagi and mosaics, eventually spilling out at the base of the stairs leading up to the first floor and the dramatic...*

Winged Victory of Samothrace (*Victoire de Samothrace*, c. 190 B.C.)

This woman with wings, poised on the prow of a ship, once stood on a hilltop to commemorate a naval victory. Her clothes are windblown and sea-sprayed, clinging close enough to her body to win a wet T-shirt contest. Originally, her right arm was stretched high, celebrating the victory like a Super Bowl champion, waving a "we're number one" finger.

This is the *Venus de Milo* gone Hellenistic, from the time after the culture of Athens was spread around the Mediterranean by Alexander the Great (c. 325 B.C.). As *Victory* strides forward, the wind blows her and her wings back. Her feet are firmly on the ground, but her wings (and missing arms) stretch upward. She is a pillar of vertical strength, while the clothes curve and whip around her. These opposing forces create a feeling of great energy, making her the lightest two-ton piece of rock in captivity.

Winged Victory—wind-blown exuberance

Crown jewels in the Apollo Gallery

In the glass case nearby is *Victory*'s open right hand with an outstretched finger, found in 1950, a century after the statue itself was unearthed. When the French discovered this was in Turkey, they negotiated with the Turkish government for the rights to it. Considering all the other ancient treasures that France had looted from Turkey in the past, the Turks thought it only appropriate to give the French the finger.

▶ *Enter the octagonal room to the left as you face the* Winged Victory, *with Icarus bungee-jumping from the ceiling. Find a friendly window and look out toward the pyramid.*

View from the Octagonal Room: The Louvre as a Palace

The former royal palace, the Louvre was built in stages over eight centuries. On your right (the eastern Sully wing) was the original medieval fortress. About 500 yards to the west, in the now-open area past the pyramid and the triumphal arch, is where the Tuileries Palace used to stand. Succeeding kings tried to connect these two palaces, each one adding another section onto the long, skinny north and south wings. Finally, in 1852, after three centuries of building, the two palaces were connected, creating a rectangular Louvre. Nineteen years later, the Tuileries Palace burned down during a riot, leaving the U-shaped Louvre we see today.

The glass pyramid was designed by the American architect I. M. Pei (1989). Many Parisians hated the pyramid, just as they hated another new and controversial structure 100 years ago—the Eiffel Tower.

In the octagonal room, a plaque at the base of the dome explains that France's Revolutionary National Assembly (the same people who brought you the guillotine) founded this museum in 1793. What could be more logical? You behead the king, inherit his palace and art collection, open the doors to the masses, and *voilà!* You have Europe's first public museum.

▶ *From the octagonal room, enter the Apollo Gallery (Galerie d'Apollon).*

Apollo Gallery

This gallery gives us a feel for the Louvre as the glorious home of French kings (before Versailles). Imagine a chandelier-lit party in this room, drenched in stucco and gold leaf, with tapestries of leading Frenchmen and paintings featuring mythological and symbolic themes. The inlaid tables made from marble and semiprecious stones, and many other art objects, show the wealth of France, Europe's number-one power for two centuries.

Stroll past glass cases of royal dinnerware to the far end of the room. In a glass case are France's crown jewels. The display varies, but you may see the jewel-studded crown of Louis XV and the 140-carat Regent Diamond, which once graced crowns worn by Louis XV, Louis XVI, and Napoleon.

▸ *A rare WC is not far away, near Salle 38 in the Sully wing. The Italian collection (Peintures Italiennes) is on the other side of Winged Victory. Cross back in front of Winged Victory to Salle 1, where you'll find two Botticelli frescoes that give us a preview of how ancient Greece would be "reborn" in the Renaissance. Now continue into the large Salle 3.*

THE MEDIEVAL WORLD (1200–1500)

Cimabue—*The Madonna of the Angels* (1280)

During the Age of Faith (1200s), almost every church in Europe had a painting like this one. Mary was a cult figure—even bigger than the 20th-century Madonna—adored and prayed to by the faithful for bringing baby Jesus into the world. After the collapse of the Roman Empire (c. A.D. 500), medieval Europe was a poor and violent place, with the Christian Church as the only constant in troubled times.

Altarpieces tended to follow the same formula: somber iconic faces, stiff poses, elegant folds in the robes, and generic angels. Cimabue's holy figures are laid flat on a gold background like cardboard cutouts, existing

Giotto—hints of 3-D and humanism

Giotto detail—St. Francis

Cimabue—2-D cardboard cutouts

in a golden never-never land, as though the faithful couldn't imagine them as flesh-and-blood humans inhabiting our dark and sinful earth.

Giotto—*St. Francis of Assisi Receiving the Stigmata* (c. 1290–1295)

Francis of Assisi (c. 1181–1226), a wandering Italian monk of renowned goodness, kneels on a rocky Italian hillside, pondering the pain of Christ's torture and execution. Suddenly, he looks up, startled, to see Christ himself, with six wings, hovering above. Christ shoots lasers from his wounds to the hands, feet, and side of the empathetic monk, marking him with the stigmata. Francis went on to breathe the spirit of the Renaissance into medieval Europe. His humble love of man and nature inspired artists like Giotto to portray real human beings with real emotions, living in a physical world of beauty.

Like a good filmmaker, Giotto (c. 1266–1337, JOT-toh) doesn't just *tell* us what happened, he *shows* us in the present tense, freezing the scene at its most dramatic moment. Though the perspective is crude—Francis' hut is smaller than he is, and Christ is somehow shooting at Francis while facing us—Giotto creates the illusion of 3-D, with a foreground (Francis), middle ground (his hut), and background (the hillside). Painting a 3-D world on a 2-D surface is tough, and after a millennium of Dark Ages, artists were rusty.

In the predella (the panel of paintings below the altarpiece), Francis gives a sermon in the open-air, while birds gather at his feet to catch a few words from the beloved hippie of Assisi.

▸ *The long Grand Gallery displays Italian Renaissance painting—some masterpieces, some not.*

ITALIAN RENAISSANCE

The Grand Gallery

Built in the late 1500s to connect the old palace with the Tuileries Palace, the Grand Gallery displays much of the Louvre's Italian Renaissance art. From the doorway, look to the far end and consider this challenge: I hold the world's record for the Grand Gallery Heel-Toe-Fun-Walk-Tourist-Slalom, going end to end in 1 minute, 58 seconds (only two injured). Time yourself. Along the way, notice some of the...

Features of Italian Renaissance Painting

• **Religious:** Lots of Madonnas, children, martyrs, and saints.

• **Symmetrical:** The Madonnas are flanked by saints—two to the left, two to the right, and so on.

• **Realistic:** Real-life human features are especially obvious in the occasional portrait.

• **Three-Dimensional:** Every scene gets a spacious setting with a distant horizon.

• **Classical:** You'll see some Greek gods and classical nudes, but even Christian saints pose like Greek statues, and Mary is a *Venus* whose face and gestures embody all that was good in the Christian world.

Andrea Mantegna—*St. Sebastian* (c. 1480)

This isn't the patron saint of acupuncture. St. Sebastian was a Christian martyr, although here he looks more like a classical Greek statue. Notice the *contrapposto* stance (all of his weight resting on one leg) and the

The Louvre—Grand Gallery

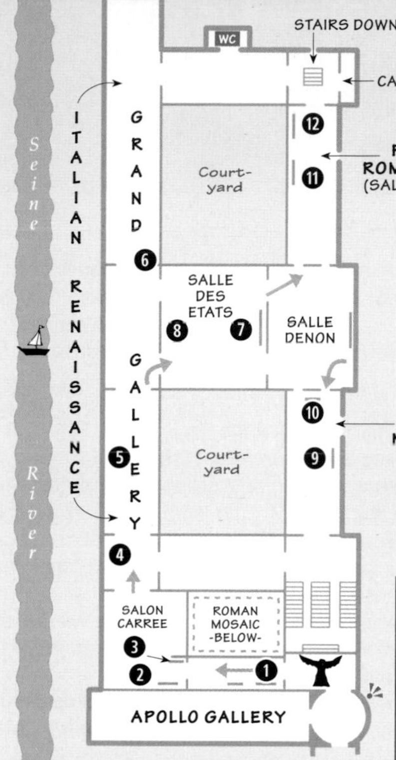

1. BOTTICELLI - Frescoes
2. CIMABUE - The Madonna of the Angels
3. GIOTTO - St. Francis of Assisi
4. MANTEGNA - St. Sebastian
5. LEONARDO - Virgin, Child & St. Anne
6. RAPHAEL - La Belle Jardinière
7. LEONARDO - Mona Lisa
8. VERONESE - The Marriage at Cana
9. DAVID - The Coronation of Napoleon
10. INGRES - La Grande Odalisque
11. GERICAULT - The Raft of the Medusa
12. DELACROIX - Liberty Leading the People
13. MICHELANGELO - Slaves

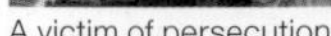

A victim of persecution

A victim of the Louvre

Greek ruins scattered around him. His executioners look like ignorant medieval brutes bewildered by this enlightened Renaissance man. Let the Renaissance begin.

▸ *Look for the following masterpieces by Leonardo 50 yards down the Grand Gallery, on the left.*

Leonardo da Vinci—*Virgin, Child, and St. Anne* (*La Vierge à l'Enfant Jésus avec Sainte-Anne*, c. 1510)

Three generations—grandmother, mother, and child—are arranged in a pyramid, with Anne's face as the peak and the lamb as the lower right corner. Within this balanced structure, Leonardo sets the figures in motion. Anne's legs are pointed to our left. (Is Anne *Mona?* Hmm.) Her daughter Mary, sitting on her lap, reaches to the right. Jesus looks at her playfully while turning away. The lamb pulls away from him. But even with all the twisting and turning, this is still a placid scene. It's as orderly as the geometrically perfect universe created by the Renaissance god.

There's a psychological kidney punch in this happy painting. Jesus, the picture of childish joy, is innocently playing with a lamb—the symbol of his inevitable sacrificial death.

The Louvre has the greatest collection of Leonardos in the world—five of them. Look for the neighboring *Virgin of the Rocks* and *John the Baptist.* Leonardo was the consummate Renaissance man: a musician, sculptor, engineer, scientist, and sometime painter, he combined knowledge from all of these areas to create beauty. If he were alive today, he'd create a Unified Field Theory in physics—and set it to music.

▸ *You'll likely find Raphael's art on the right side of the Grand Gallery, just past the statue of* Diana the Huntress.

Leonardo's Virgin—three generations of love

Raphael—*La Belle Jardinière* (1507)

Raphael (roff-eye-ELL) perfected the style Leonardo pioneered. The Madonna, Child, and John the Baptist form a Leonard-esque pyramid, and the scene is softened with a hazy grace. Mary is a mountain of maternal tenderness (the title translates as "The Beautiful Gardener"), as she eyes her son with a knowing look and holds his hand in a gesture of union. Jesus looks up innocently, standing *contrapposto* like a chubby Greek statue. Baby John the Baptist kneels lovingly at Jesus' feet, holding a cross that hints at his playmate's sacrificial death. The interplay of gestures and gazes gives the masterpiece both intimacy and cohesiveness, while Raphael's blended brushstrokes varnish the work with an iridescent smoothness.

With Raphael, the Greek ideal of beauty—reborn in the Renaissance—reached its peak. His work spawned so many imitators who cranked out

Raphael's *La Belle Jardinière*

Italian Renaissance (1400–1600)

A thousand years after Rome fell, plunging Europe into the Dark Ages, the Greek ideal of beauty was reborn in 15th-century Italy. The Renaissance—or "rebirth" of the culture of ancient Greece and Rome—was a cultural boom that changed people's thinking about every aspect of life. In politics, it meant democracy. In religion, it meant a move away from Church dominance and toward the assertion of man (humanism) and a more personal faith. Science and secular learning were revived after centuries of superstition and ignorance. In architecture, it was a return to the balanced columns and domes of Greece and Rome.

In painting, the Renaissance meant realism, and for the Italians, realism was spelled "3-D." Artists rediscovered the beauty of nature and the human body. With pictures of beautiful people in harmonious 3-D surroundings, they expressed the optimism and confidence of this new age.

sickly sweet, generic Madonnas that we often take him for granted. Don't. This is the real thing.

▶ *The* Mona Lisa (La Joconde) *is near the statue of* Diana, *in Salle 6—the Salle des Etats—midway down the Grand Gallery on the right. After several years and a €5 million renovation,* Mona *is alone behind glass on her own false wall. Six million heavy-breathing people crowd in each year to glimpse the most ogled painting in the world. (You can't miss her. Just follow the signs and the people...it's the only painting you can hear. With all the groveling crowds, you can even smell it.)*

Leonardo da Vinci—*Mona Lisa* (1503–1506)

Leonardo was already an old man when François I invited him to France. Determined to pack light, he took only a few paintings with him. One was a portrait of Lisa del Giocondo, the wife of a wealthy Florentine merchant. When Leonardo arrived, François immediately fell in love with the painting, making it the centerpiece of the small collection of Italian masterpieces that would, in three centuries, become the Louvre museum. He called it *La Gioconda* (*La Joconde* in French)—both her last name and a play on the

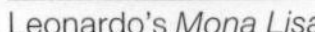

Leonardo's *Mona Lisa*

Veronese's Venetian party scene

Italian word for "happy woman." We know it as a contraction of the Italian for "my lady Lisa"—*Mona Lisa.*

Mona may disappoint you. She's smaller than you'd expect, darker, engulfed in a huge room, and hidden behind a glaring pane of glass. So why all the hubbub? Let's take a closer look. As you would with any lover, you've got to accept her for what she is, not what you'd like her to be.

The famous smile attracts you first. Leonardo used a hazy technique called *sfumato,* blurring the edges of her mysterious smile. Try as you might, you can never quite see the corners of her mouth. Is she happy? Sad? Tender? Or is it a cynical supermodel's smirk? All visitors read it differently, projecting their own moods onto her enigmatic face. *Mona* is a Rorschach inkblot...so, how are you feeling?

Now look past the smile and the eyes that really do follow you (most eyes in portraits do) to some of the subtle Renaissance elements that make this painting work. The body is surprisingly massive and statue-like, a perfectly balanced pyramid turned at an angle, so we can see its mass. Her arm is resting lightly on the chair's armrest, almost on the level of the frame itself, as if she's sitting in a window looking out at us. The folds of her sleeves and her gently folded hands are remarkably realistic and relaxed. The typical Leonardo landscape shows distance by getting hazier and hazier.

Though the portrait is most likely of Lisa del Giocondo, the 20-something wife of a Florentine businessman, there are many other hypotheses about her identity, including the idea that it's Leonardo himself. Or she might be the Mama Lisa. A recent infrared scan revealed that she has a barely visible veil over her dress, which may mean (in the custom of the day) that she had just had a baby.

The overall mood is one of balance and serenity, but there's also an element of mystery. *Mona*'s smile and long-distance beauty are subtle and elusive, tempting but always just out of reach, like strands of a street singer's melody drifting through the Métro tunnel. *Mona* doesn't knock your socks off, but she winks at the patient viewer.

► *Before leaving* Mona, *step back and just observe the paparazzi scene. The huge canvas opposite* Mona *is...*

Paolo Veronese—*The Marriage at Cana* (1562–1563)

Stand 10 steps away from this enormous canvas to where it just fills your field of vision, and suddenly...you're in a party! Help yourself to a glass of wine. This is the Renaissance love of beautiful things gone hog-wild.

In a spacious setting of Renaissance architecture, colorful lords and ladies, decked out in their fanciest duds, feast on a great spread of food and drink, while the musicians fuel the fires of good fun. Servants prepare and serve the food, jesters play, and animals roam. In the upper left, a dog and his master look on. A sturdy linebacker in yellow pours wine out of a jug (right foreground). The man in white samples some wine and thinks, "Hmm, not bad," while nearby a ferocious cat battles a lion. The wedding couple at the far left is almost forgotten.

Believe it or not, this is a religious work showing the wedding celebration in which Jesus turned water into wine. And there's Jesus in the dead center of 130 frolicking figures, wondering if maybe beer might not have been a better choice. With true Renaissance optimism, Venetians pictured Christ as a party animal, someone who loved the created world as much as they did.

Now, let's hear it for the band! On bass—the bad cat with the funny hat—Titian the Venetian! And joining him on viola—Crazy Veronese!

► *Exit behind* Mona *into the Salle Denon. The dramatic Romantic room is to your left, and the grand Neoclassical room is to your right. Entering the Neoclassical room (Salle Daru), kneel before the largest canvas in the Louvre.*

FRENCH NEOCLASSICISM (1780–1850)

Jacques-Louis David—*The Coronation of Napoleon* (1806–1807)

Napoleon holds aloft an imperial crown. This common-born son of immigrants is about to be crowned emperor of a "New Rome." He has just made his wife, Josephine, the empress, and she kneels at his feet. Seated behind Napoleon is the pope, who journeyed from Rome to place the imperial crown on his head. But Napoleon feels that no one is worthy of the task. At the last moment, he shrugs the pope aside, grabs the crown, holds it up for all to see...and crowns himself. The pope looks p.o.'d.

After the French people decapitated their king during the Revolution (1793), their fledgling democracy floundered in chaos. France was united by a charismatic, brilliant, temperamental, upstart general who kept his feet on the ground, his eyes on the horizon, and his hand in his coat—Napoleon Bonaparte. Napoleon quickly conquered most of Europe and

Napoleon crowns his wife and himself.

insisted on being made emperor.

The painter David (dah-VEED) recorded the coronation for posterity. (Find his self-portrait using the key on the picture frame telling who's who. He's way up in the second balcony, peeking around the tassel directly above Napoleon's crown.) David was the new emperor's official painter and propagandist, in charge of color-coordinating the costumes and flags for public ceremonies and spectacles. The coronation ceremony took place in Notre-Dame cathedral, where interior decorators fitted the church with fake columns and arches to reflect the glories of Greece and the grandeur of Rome. As a painter, David's simple style and Greek themes championed the "Neoclassical" style that influenced generations of artists.

The radiant woman in the gallery in the background center was added later. Since she couldn't make it to Paris to watch her boy become the most powerful man in Europe, Napoleon had David paint his mom in anyway.

▶ *As you double back toward the Romantic room, stop at...*

Jean-Auguste-Dominique Ingres—*La Grande Odalisque* (1819)

Take *Venus de Milo,* turn her around, lay her down, and stick a hash pipe next to her, and you have the *Grande Odalisque.* OK, maybe you'd have to add a vertebra or two. Ingres (ang-gruh, with a soft "gruh") exaggerates the S-curve of a standing Greek nude. Using cool colors, sculptural lines, and idealized features, Ingres preserves *Venus'* backside for posterior—I mean, posterity.

▶ *Cross back through the Salle Denon (where you might spot a painting high up titled* The Death of Walter Mondale*) and into a room gushing with...*

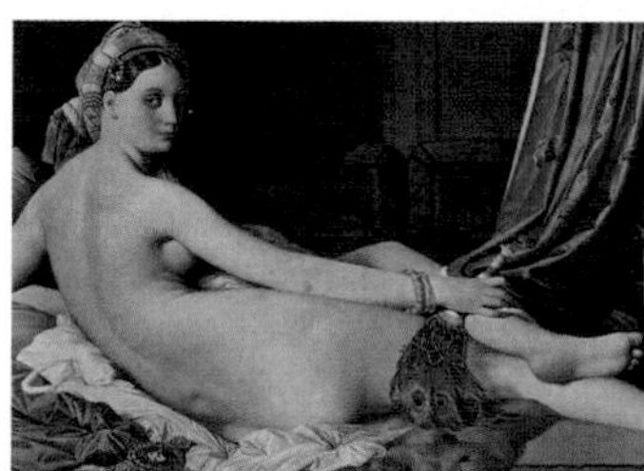

Ingres' *Odalisque*—cool Neoclassicism

Géricault's *Raft*—fevered Romanticism

FRENCH ROMANTICISM (1800–1850)

Théodore Géricault—*The Raft of the Medusa* (*Le Radeau de la Méduse,* 1819)

In the artistic war between hearts and minds, the heart style was known as Romanticism. Stressing motion and emotion, it was the flip side of cool, balanced Neoclassicism, though they both flourished in the early 1800s.

What better setting for an emotional work than a shipwreck? Clinging to a raft is a tangle of bodies and lunatics sprawled over each other. The scene writhes with agitated, ominous motion—the ripple of muscles, churning clouds, and choppy seas. On the right, a deathly green corpse dangles overboard. The face of the man at left, cradling a dead body, says it all—the despair of spending weeks stranded in the middle of nowhere.

This painting was based on an actual event—150 shipwrecked people were set adrift on the open seas for 12 days, suffering hardship and hunger, even resorting to cannibalism. The story was made to order for a painter determined to shock the public—young Géricault (ZHAIR-ee-ko). To reproduce the raw emotion, he interviewed survivors. He sketched dead bodies in the morgue and the twisted faces of lunatics in asylums, capturing the moment when all hope is lost.

But wait. There's a stir in the crowd. They've spotted something. The bodies rise up in a pyramid of hope, culminating in a waving flag. They signal frantically, trying to catch the attention of the tiny ship on the horizon, their last desperate hope...which did finally save them. If art controls your heartbeat, this is a masterpiece.

Eugène Delacroix—*Liberty Leading the People* (*La Liberté Guidant le Peuple,* 1830)

The year is 1830. King Charles has been restored to the throne after Napoleon's exile, and his subjects are angry. The Parisians take to the streets once again, *Les Miz*–style, to fight royalist oppressors. Leading them on through the smoke and over the dead and dying is the figure of Liberty, a strong woman waving the French flag. Does this symbol of victory look familiar? It's the *Winged Victory*, wingless and topless. Delacroix shows the full range of France's social classes—the hard-bitten proletarian with a sword (far left), an intellectual with a top hat and a sawed-off shotgun, and even a little boy brandishing pistols. Eventually, the people would

Delacroix—Lady Liberty leads the French

triumph, replacing the king with Louis-Philippe, who was happy to rule within the constraints of a modern constitution.

To stir our emotions, Delacroix (del-ah-kwah) uses only three major colors—the red, white, and blue of the French flag. France is the symbol of Revolution and modern democracy, and this painting has long stirred its citizens' passion for liberty.

This symbol of freedom is a fitting tribute to the Louvre, the first museum ever opened to the common rabble of humanity. The good things in life don't belong only to a small, wealthy part of society, but to everyone. The motto of France is *Liberté, Egalité, Fraternité*—liberty, equality, and brotherhood for all.

► *Exit the room at the far end (past the Café Mollien) and go downstairs, where you'll bump into the bum of a large, twisting male nude looking like he's just waking up after a thousand-year nap.*

EPILOGUE

Michelangelo—*Slaves* (1513–1515)

These two statues by earth's greatest sculptor are an appropriate end to this museum—works that bridge the ancient and modern worlds. Michelangelo, like his fellow Renaissance artists, learned from the Greeks. The perfect anatomy, twisting poses, and idealized faces appear as if they could have been created 2,000 years earlier.

The so-called *Dying Slave* (also called the *Sleeping Slave,* looking like he should be stretched out on a sofa) twists listlessly against his T-shirt-like bonds, revealing his smooth skin. Compare the polished detail of the rippling, bulging left arm with the sketchy details of the face and neck. With Michelangelo, the body does the talking. This is probably the most sensual nude Michelangelo, the master of the male body, ever created.

The *Rebellious Slave* fights against his bondage. His shoulders rotate one way, his head and leg turn the other. He looks upward, straining to get free. He even seems to be trying to free himself from the rock he's made of. Michelangelo said that his purpose was to carve away the marble to reveal the figures God put inside. This slave shows the agony of that process and the ecstasy of the result.

▸ *Tour over! These two may be slaves of the museum, but you are free to go or browse at your leisure. To leave the museum, head for the end of the hall, turn right, and follow signs down the escalators to the* Sortie.

Michelangelo's *Slaves* bridge ancient and modern.

Orsay Museum Tour

Musée d'Orsay

The Musée d'Orsay (mew-zay dor-say), housing French art from 1848–1914, picks up where the Louvre's art collection leaves off. That means Impressionism, the art of sun-dappled fields, bright colors, and crowded Parisian cafés. The Orsay houses the best general collection anywhere of Manet, Monet, Renoir, Degas, Van Gogh, Cézanne, and Gauguin. If you like Impressionism, visit this museum. If you don't like Impressionism, visit this museum. I personally find it a more enjoyable and rewarding place than the Louvre. Sure, ya gotta see the *Mona Lisa* and *Venus de Milo,* but after you get your gottas out of the way, enjoy the Orsay.

ORIENTATION

Renovation: The Orsay's top-floor Impressionist and Post-Impressionist rooms have been recently renovated. Some works of art have been moved; for the current layout see www.musee-orsay.fr.

Cost: €8, €5.50 Fri–Wed after 16:15 and Thu after 18:00, free first Sun of month, covered by Museum Pass. Tickets are good all day.

Hours: Tue–Sun 9:30–18:00, Thu until 21:45, closed Mon, last entry one hour before closing (45 minutes before on Thu). The top-floor Impressionist galleries begin closing 45 minutes early.

Free Entry near Closing Time: Right when the ticket booth stops selling tickets, you're welcome to scoot in free of charge (Tue–Wed and Fri–Sun at 17:00, Thu at 21:00; they won't let you in much after that, however). See the Impressionist galleries first; they close earliest.

Getting There: The museum is alongside the Seine River at 1 rue de la Légion d'Honneur. It's well-connected by Métro (to Solférino), RER-C (Musée d'Orsay), bus #69, Batobus, and taxi. From the Louvre, it's a 15-minute walk through the Tuileries Garden and across the pedestrian bridge.

Avoiding Lines: The ticket-buying line can be long (especially on Tue and Sun), but if you have a Museum Pass or advance ticket, you can waltz right in through Entrance C (to the right). Buy advance tickets at TIs or FNAC department stores, or online for pick-up in Paris (see www.musee-orsay.fr).

Information: Tel. 01 40 49 48 14, www.musee-orsay.fr.

Tours: Audioguides cost €6. English guided tours usually run daily (except Sun) at 11:30 (€7.50/90 minutes). A free Rick Steves audio tour is available on iTunes or at www.ricksteves.com.

Length of This Tour: Allow two hours.

Cloakroom *(Vestiaire)*: Checking bags or coats is free. Day bags (but nothing bigger) are allowed in the museum. No valuables (cameras, passports, money) can be stored in checked bags.

Photography: It's forbidden.

Cuisine Art: A pricey but *très* elegant restaurant is on the second floor, with affordable tea and coffee served 14:45–17:30 (daily except Thu). A fifth-floor café is sandwiched between the Impressionists.

Starring: Manet, Monet, Renoir, Degas, Van Gogh, Cézanne, Gauguin, and Rodin.

Orsay Ground Floor—Overview

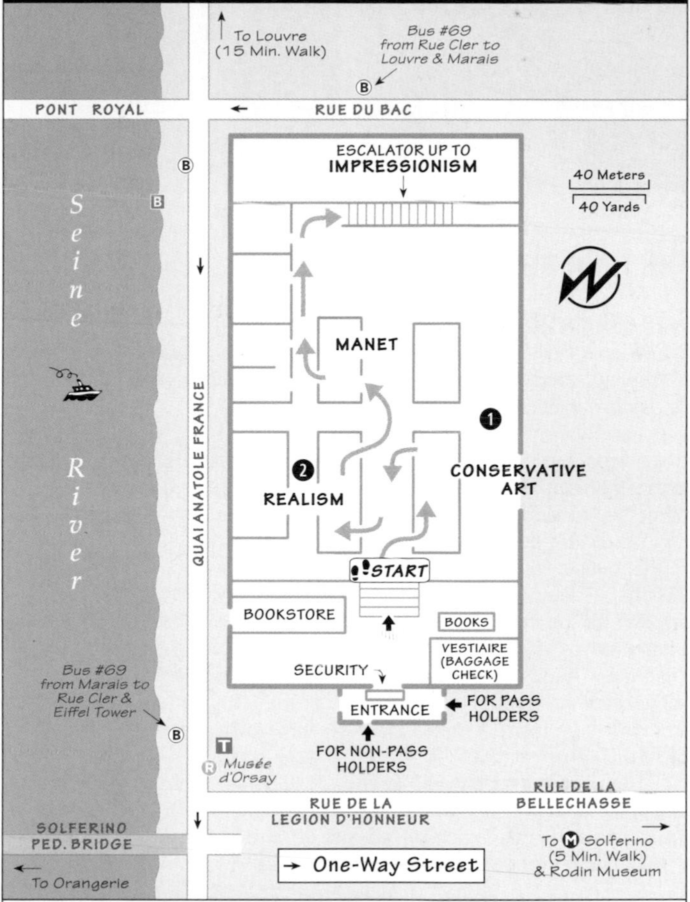

To Louvre (15 Min. Walk)

Bus #69 from Rue Cler to Louvre & Marais

PONT ROYAL

RUE DU BAC

ESCALATOR UP TO IMPRESSIONISM

40 Meters

40 Yards

Seine River

MANET

CONSERVATIVE ART

REALISM

QUAI ANATOLE FRANCE

START

BOOKSTORE

BOOKS

VESTIAIRE (BAGGAGE CHECK)

SECURITY

ENTRANCE

FOR PASS HOLDERS

FOR NON-PASS HOLDERS

Bus #69 from Marais to Rue Cler & Eiffel Tower

Musée d'Orsay

RUE DE LA LEGION D'HONNEUR

RUE DE LA BELLECHASSE

SOLFERINO PED. BRIDGE

To Orangerie

One-Way Street

To Solferino (5 Min. Walk) & Rodin Museum

1. Temporary Impressionist & Post-Impressionist Rooms
2. Temporary Van Gogh & Gauguin Rooms

The Orsay's main hall—former train station

Ingres' *Source*—clean, sculptural lines

THE TOUR BEGINS

Gare d'Orsay: The Old Train Station

► *Pick up a free English map upon entering, get updates on the renovation, and check your bag. Belly up to the stone balustrade overlooking the main floor, and orient yourself.*

Trains used to run right under our feet down the center of the gallery. This former train station, or *gare,* barely escaped the wrecking ball in the 1970s, when the French realized it'd be a great place to house the enormous collections of 19th-century art scattered throughout the city.

The main floor has early 19th-century art—as usual, Conservative on the right, Realism on the left. On the top floor (not visible from here) is the core of the collection—the Impressionist rooms. We'll start with the Conservatives and early rebels on the ground floor, then head upstairs to see how a few visionary young artists bucked the system and revolutionized the art world, paving the way for the 20th century. We'll end the tour with the "other" Orsay on the mezzanine level. Clear as Seine water? *Bien.*

Remember, because of the renovation, some paintings will be moved elsewhere or simply not on display. Use your current Orsay map to learn the latest arrangement, and be ready to go with the flow.

► *Walk down the steps to the main floor, a gallery filled with statues.*

CONSERVATIVE ART

Main Gallery Statues

No, this isn't ancient Greece. These statues are from the same era as the Theory of Relativity. It's the Conservative art of the French schools, and it was very popular for its beauty—balanced poses, perfect anatomy, sweet faces, curving lines, and gleaming white stone. (I'll bad-mouth it later, but for now appreciate the exquisite craftsmanship of this "perfect" art.)

► *Take your first right into the small Room 1, marked* Ingres et l'Ingrisme. *Look for a nude woman with a pitcher of water.*

Jean-Auguste-Dominique Ingres—*The Source* (*La Source*, 1856)

Let's start where the Louvre left off. Ingres (ang-gruh, with a soft "gruh"), who helped cap the Louvre collection, championed a Neoclassical style. *The Source* is virtually a Greek statue on canvas. Like *Venus de Milo,* she's a balance of opposite motions—her hips tilt one way, her breasts the other; one arm goes up, the other down; the water falling from the pitcher

The Orsay's "19th Century" (1848–1914)

Einstein and Geronimo. Abraham Lincoln and Karl Marx. The train, the bicycle, the horse and buggy, the automobile, and the balloon. Freud and Dickens. Darwin's *Origin of Species* and the Church's Immaculate Conception. Louis Pasteur and Billy the Kid. Ty Cobb and V. I. Lenin.

The 19th century was a mix of old and new, side by side. Europe was entering the modern Industrial Age, with cities, factories, rapid transit, instant communication, and global networks. At the same time, it clung to the past with traditional, rural—almost medieval—attitudes and morals.

According to the Orsay, the "19th century" began in 1848 with the socialist and democratic revolutions (Marx's *Communist Manifesto*). It ended in 1914 with the pull of an assassin's trigger, which ignited World War I and ushered in the modern world. The museum shows art that is also both old and new, conservative and revolutionary.

matches the fluid curve of her body. Her skin is porcelain-smooth, painted with seamless brushstrokes.

Ingres worked on this painting over the course of 35 years and considered it his "image of perfection." Famous in its day, *The Source* influenced many artists whose classical statues and paintings are in this museum.

► *Walk uphill (quickly, as this is background stuff) to the last room (Room 3), and find a pastel blue-green painting.*

Alexandre Cabanel—*The Birth of Venus* (La Naissance de Vénus, 1863)

Cabanel lays Ingres' *The Source* on her back. This goddess is a perfect fantasy, an orgasm of beauty. The Love Goddess stretches back seductively, recently birthed from the ephemeral foam of the wave. This is art of a pre-Freudian society, when sex was dirty and mysterious and had to be exalted into a more pure and divine form. French folk would literally swoon in ecstasy before these works of art.

The art world of Cabanel's day was dominated by two conservative institutions: the Academy (the state-funded art school) and the Salon, where works were exhibited to the buying public. The public loved Cabanel's *Venus* (and Napoleon III purchased it).

Get a feel for the ideal beauty and refined emotion of these Greek-style works. (Out in the gallery, you'll find a statue of another swooning Venus.) Go ahead, swoon. If it feels good, enjoy it. Now, take a mental cold shower, and let's cross over to the "wrong side of the tracks," to the art of the early rebels.

► *Exit Room 3 into the main gallery, turn left, and head back toward the entrance, turning right into Room 4, marked* Daumier *(opposite the Ingres room).*

Cabanel's *Venus*—soft-porn fantasy

Millet's *Gleaners*—hard-core Realism

REALISM—EARLY REBELS

Honoré Daumier—*Celebrities of the Happy Medium* (*Célébrités du juste milieu,* 1832–1835)

This is a liberal's look at the stuffy bourgeois establishment that controlled the Academy and the Salon. In these 36 bustlets, Daumier, trained as a political cartoonist, exaggerates each subject's most distinct characteristic to capture with vicious precision the pomposity and self-righteousness of these self-appointed arbiters of taste. The labels next to the busts give the name of the person being caricatured, his title or job (most were members of the French parliament), and an insulting nickname (like "gross, fat, and satisfied" or Monsieur "Platehead"). Give a few nicknames yourself. Can you find Reagan, Clinton, Kerry, Sarkozy, Al Sharpton, and Gingrich?

These people hated the art you're about to see. Their prudish faces tightened as their fantasy world was shattered by the Realists.

► *Go uphill four steps and through one room to the final room, #6.*

Jean-François Millet—*The Gleaners* (*Les Glaneuses,* 1867)

Millet (mee-yay) shows us three gleaners, the poor women who pick up the meager leftovers after a field has already been harvested by the wealthy. Millet grew up on a humble farm. He didn't attend the Academy and despised the uppity Paris art scene. Instead of idealized gods, goddesses, nymphs, and winged babies, he painted simple rural scenes. He was strongly affected by the socialist revolution of 1848, with its affirmation of the working class. Here he captures the innate dignity of these stocky, tanned women who bend their backs quietly in a large field for their small reward.

This is "Realism" in two senses. It's painted "realistically," unlike the prettified pastels of Cabanel's *Birth of Venus.* And it's the "real" world—not the fantasy world of Greek myth, but the harsh life of the working poor.

► *Exit Room 6 into the main gallery and make a U turn to the left, climbing the steps to a large alcove with huge canvases. On the left is...*

Gustave Courbet—*The Painter's Studio* (*L'Atelier du Peintre,* 1855)

The Salon of 1855 rejected this dark-colored, sprawling, monumental painting of..."What's it about?" In an age when "Realist painter" was equated with "bomb-throwing Socialist," it took courage to buck the system. Dismissed by the so-called experts, Courbet (coor-bay) held his own one-man exhibit. He built a shed in the middle of Paris, defiantly hung his art out, and basically mooned the shocked public.

Courbet's painting takes us backstage, showing us the gritty reality behind the creation of pretty pictures. We see Courbet himself in his studio, working diligently on a Realistic landscape, oblivious to the confusion around him. Milling around are ordinary citizens, not Greek heroes. The woman who looks on is not a nude Venus but a naked artist's model. And the little boy with an adoring look on his face? Perhaps it's Courbet's inner child, admiring the artist who sticks to his guns, whether it's popular or not.

Courbet—behind the scenes at his studio

Couture's decadence before the revolution

► *Return to the main gallery. Back across "the tracks," the huge canvas you see is...*

Thomas Couture—*The Romans of the Decadence* (*Les Romains de la Décadence,* 1847)

We see a *fin de siècle* (end-of-century) society that looks like it's packed in a big hot tub. It's stuffed with too much luxury, wasted, burned out, and in decay. The old, backward-looking order was about to be slapped in the face.

► *Continue up the gallery, then left into Room 14 (Manet). Find the reclining nude.*

Edouard Manet—*Olympia* (1863)

"This brunette is thoroughly ugly. Her face is stupid, her skin cadaverous. All this clash of colors is stupefying." So wrote a critic when Edouard Manet's nude hung in the Salon. The public hated it, attacking Manet (man-ay) in print and literally attacking the canvas.

Think back on Cabanel's painting, *The Birth of Venus:* an idealized, pastel, Vaseline-on-the-lens beauty. It's basically soft-core pornography, the kind you see today selling lingerie and perfume.

Manet's nude doesn't gloss over anything. The pose is classic, used by Titian, Goya, and countless others. But this is a Realist's take on the classics. The sharp outlines and harsh, contrasting colors are new and shocking. Her hand is a clamp, and her stare is shockingly defiant, with not a hint of the seductive, hey-sailor look of most nudes. This prostitute, ignoring the flowers sent by her last customer, looks out as if to say, "Next." Manet replaced soft-core porn with hard-core art.

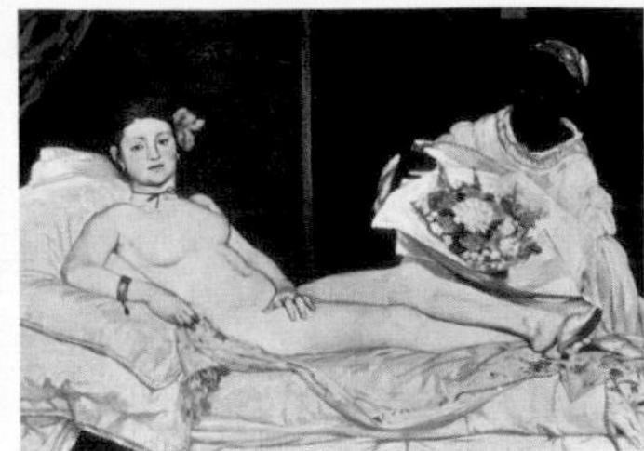

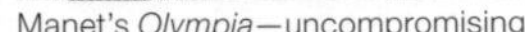
Manet's *Olympia*—uncompromising

Manet—Impressionist hors d'oeuvre

Edouard Manet (1832–1883) had an upper-class upbringing and some formal art training, and he had been accepted by the Salon. He could have cranked out pretty nudes and been a successful painter. Instead, he surrounded himself with a group of young artists experimenting with new techniques. Because of his reputation and strong personality, he was their master, though he learned equally from them.

▸ *Climb the small set of stairs in Room 14. Across the hall (and slightly to the right), you'll find...*

Edouard Manet—*Luncheon on the Grass* (Le Déjeuner sur l'Herbe, 1863)

A shocked public looked at this and wondered: What are these scantily clad women doing with these men? Or rather, what will they be doing after the last baguette is eaten? It isn't the nudity, but the presence of the men in ordinary clothes, that suddenly makes the nudes look naked. Once again, the public judged the painting on moral rather than artistic terms.

A new revolutionary movement was starting to bud—Impressionism. Notice the background: the messy brushwork of trees and leaves, the play of light on the pond, and the light that filters through the trees onto the woman who stoops in the haze. Also note the strong contrast of colors (white skin, black clothes, green grass). This is a true out-of-doors painting, not a studio production. Let the Impressionist revolution begin.

▸ *Get a sneak peek of that revolution in nearby rooms, with a fine collection of works by Monet. Otherwise, continue to the far end of the gallery, where you'll walk on a glass floor over a model of Paris.*

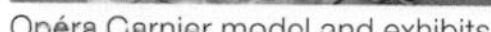

Opéra Garnier model and exhibits

It's Impressionist time.

Opéra Exhibit

Expand to 100 times your size and hover over this scale-model section of the city. In the center sits the 19th-century Opéra Garnier, with its green domed roof. Nearby, you'll also see a cross-section model of the Opéra house, and models of set designs from some famous productions. These days, Parisians enjoy their Verdi and Gounod at the modern opera house at place de la Bastille.

► *Next up—the Orsay's Impressionist and Post-Impressionist collection. Take the escalator up to the top floor Impressionist rooms. The top floor offers a commanding view of the Orsay. Continue on past a bookshop and a giant "backward" clock (with great city views) to the art, starting in Room 29.*

The Impressionist collection is scattered somewhat randomly through the next few rooms. Shadows dance and the displays mingle. Where they're hung is a lot like their brushwork...delightfully sloppy. If you don't see a described painting, ask a guard or just move on. It's either hanging farther down or it's on vacation.

IMPRESSIONISM

Rooms 29–36: Manet, Degas, Monet, Renoir, and More

Light! Color! Vibrations! You don't hang an Impressionist canvas—you tether it. Impressionism features bright colors, easygoing open-air scenes, spontaneity, broad brushstrokes, and the play of light.

The Impressionists made their canvases shimmer by using a simple but revolutionary technique. Let's say you mix red, yellow, and green together—you'll get brown, right? But Impressionists didn't bother to mix them. They'd slap a thick brushstroke of yellow down, then a stroke of green next to it, then red next to that. Up close, all you see are the three messy strokes, but as you back up...*voilà!* Brown! The colors blend in the eye, at a distance. But while your eye is saying "bland old brown," your subconscious is shouting, "Red! Yellow! Green! Yes!"

There are no lines in nature, yet someone in the classical tradition (Ingres, for example) would draw an outline of his subject, then fill it in with color. Instead the Impressionists built a figure with dabs of paint...a snowman of color.

▸ *Start with the non-Impressionist but equally famous...*

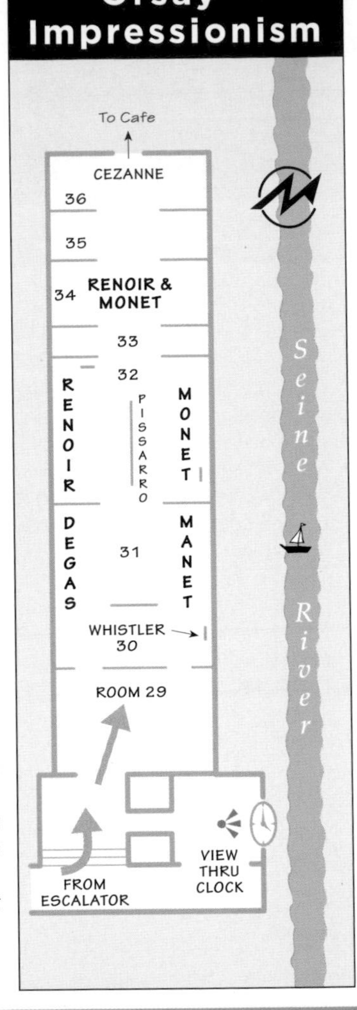

James Abbott McNeill Whistler—*Portrait of the Artist's Mother* (*Portrait de la Mère de l'Auteur,* 1871)

Why's it so famous? I don't know either. Perhaps because it's by an American, and we see in his mother some of the monumental solidity of our own ancestral moms, who were made tough by pioneering the American wilderness.

Or perhaps because it was so starkly different for its day. In a roomful of golden goddesses, it'd stand out like a fish in a tree. The alternate title is *Arrangement in Gray and Black, No. 1,* and the whole point is the subtle variations of dark shades softened by the rosy tint of her cheeks. Nevertheless, the critics kept waiting for it to come out in Colorization.

► *In the next couple of rooms, find works by Edgar Degas.*

Edgar Degas—*The Dance Class* (*La Classe de Danse,* c. 1873–1875)

Clearly, Degas loved dance and the theater. (Catch his statue, *Tiny Dancer, 14 Years Old,* in the glass case.) The play of stage lights off his dancers, especially the halos of ballet skirts, is made to order for an Impressionist. In *The Dance Class,* bored, tired dancers scratch their backs restlessly at the end of a long rehearsal. And look at the bright green bow on the girl with her back to us. In the Impressionist style, Degas slopped green paint onto her dress and didn't even say, *"Excusez-moi."*

Edgar Degas (1834–1917, day-gah) was a rich kid from a family of bankers, and he got the best classical-style art training. He painted in the Academic style, exhibited in the Salon, gained a good reputation, and then...he met the Impressionists.

Degas combined Ingres' classical lines with Impressionist color, spontaneity, and everyday subjects from urban Paris. Degas loved the unposed

Whistler's *Mother*—exploring gray areas

Degas—Impressionist snapshot of dancers

Impressionism

The camera threatened to make artists obsolete. Now a machine could capture a better likeness faster than you could say "Etch-a-Sketch."

But true art is more than just painting reality. It gives us reality from the artist's point of view, with the artist's personal impressions of the scene. Impressions are often fleeting, so working quickly is essential.

The Impressionist painters rejected camera-like detail for a quick style more suited to capturing the passing moment. Feeling stifled by the rigid rules and stuffy atmosphere of the Academy, the Impressionists grabbed their berets and scarves and went on excursions to the country. They set up their easels (and newly invented tubes of premixed paint) on riverbanks and hillsides, or they sketched in cafés and dance halls. Gods, goddesses, nymphs, and fantasy scenes were out; common people and rural landscapes were in.

The quick style and everyday subjects were ridiculed and called childish by the "experts." They brashly took their name from an insult thrown at them by a critic who laughed at one of Monet's "impressions" of a sunrise. Rejected by the Salon, the Impressionists staged their own exhibition in 1874. The public, opposed at first, was slowly won over by the simplicity, color, and vibrancy of Impressionist art.

"snapshot" effect, catching his models off guard. Dance students, women at work, and café scenes are approached from odd angles that aren't always ideal, but make the scenes seem more real.

Edgar Degas—*In a Café,* or *The Glass of Absinthe* (*Au Café, dit L'Absinthe,* 1876)

Degas hung out with low-life Impressionists, discussing art, love, and life in the cheap cafés and bars in Montmartre. Here, a weary lady of the evening meets morning with a last, lonely, nail-in-the-coffin drink in the glaring light of a four-in-the-morning café. The pale green drink at the center of the composition is the toxic substance absinthe, which fueled many artists and burned out many more.

► *The next few rooms (32–36) feature works by two Impressionist masters*

Degas—unvarnished reality

at their peak, Monet and Renoir. You're looking at the quintessence of Impressionism. The two were good friends, often working side by side, and their canvases now hang side by side in these rooms.

Pierre-Auguste Renoir—*Dance at the Moulin de la Galette* (*Bal du Moulin de la Galette,* 1876)

On Sunday afternoons, working-class folk would dress up and head for the fields on butte Montmartre (near Sacré-Cœur basilica) to dance, drink, and eat little crêpes *(galettes)* till dark. Pierre-Auguste Renoir (1841–1919, ren-wah) liked to go there to paint the common Parisians living and loving in the afternoon sun. The sunlight filtering through the trees creates a kaleidoscope of colors, like the 19th-century equivalent of a mirror ball throwing darts of light onto the dancers.

He captures the dappled light with quick blobs of yellow staining the ground, the men's jackets, and the sun-dappled straw hat (right of center).

Renoir—belle époque joie de vivre

Smell the powder on the ladies' faces. The painting glows with bright colors. Even the shadows on the ground, which should be gray or black, are colored a warm blue. The scene is lighthearted, with light colors, almost pastels. Like a photographer who uses a slow shutter speed to show motion, Renoir paints a waltzing blur.

Claude Monet—*The Cathedral of Rouen* (*La Cathédrale de Rouen,* 1893)
Claude Monet (1840–1926, mo-nay) is the father of Impressionism. He fully explored the possibilities of open-air painting and tried to faithfully reproduce nature's colors with bright blobs of paint.

Monet went to Rouen, rented a room across from the cathedral, set up his easel...and waited. He wanted to catch "a series of differing impressions" of the cathedral facade at various times of day and year. He often had several canvases going at once. In all, he did 30 paintings of the cathedral, and each is unique. The time-lapse series shows the sun passing

Monet prefigures abstract art.

slowly across the sky, creating different-colored light and shadows. The labels next to the art describe the conditions: in gray weather, in the morning, morning sun, full sunlight, and so on.

As Monet zeroes in on the play of colors and light, the physical subject—the cathedral—is dissolving. It's only a rack upon which to hang the light and color. Later artists would boldly throw away the rack, leaving purely abstract modern art in its place.

Claude Monet—Paintings from Monet's Garden at Giverny

One of Monet's favorite places to paint was the garden he landscaped at his home in Giverny, west of Paris (and worth a visit, provided you like Monet more than you hate crowds). The Japanese bridge and the water lilies floating in the pond were his two favorite subjects. As Monet aged and his eyesight failed, he made bigger canvases of smaller subjects. The final water lilies (at the Orangerie and Marmottan museums) are monumental smudges of thick paint surrounded by paint-splotched clouds reflected on the surface of the pond.

► *Before moving on, check out some of the "lesser" pioneers of the Impressionist style—Pissarro, Sisley, and others. There's a café up ahead.*

The tour continues with Post-Impressionism. After the renovation, Post-Impressionism will likely be spread over the upper level and in Rooms 70–72 of Level 2 (niveau 2). The enigmatic Toulouse-Lautrec was last seen on the ground floor, Room 10.

POST-IMPRESSIONISM

Paul Cézanne

Paul Cézanne (1839–1906, say-zahn) brought Impressionism into the 20th century. Compared with the colors of Monet, the warmth of Renoir, and Van Gogh's passion, Cézanne's rather impersonal canvases can be difficult to appreciate. Bowls of fruit, landscapes, and a few portraits were Cézanne's passion. Because of his style (not his content), he is often called the first modern painter.

Paul Cézanne—*Self-Portrait* (*Portrait de l'Artiste*, c. 1873–1876)

Cézanne was virtually unknown and unappreciated in his lifetime. He worked alone, lived alone, and died alone, ignored by all but a few

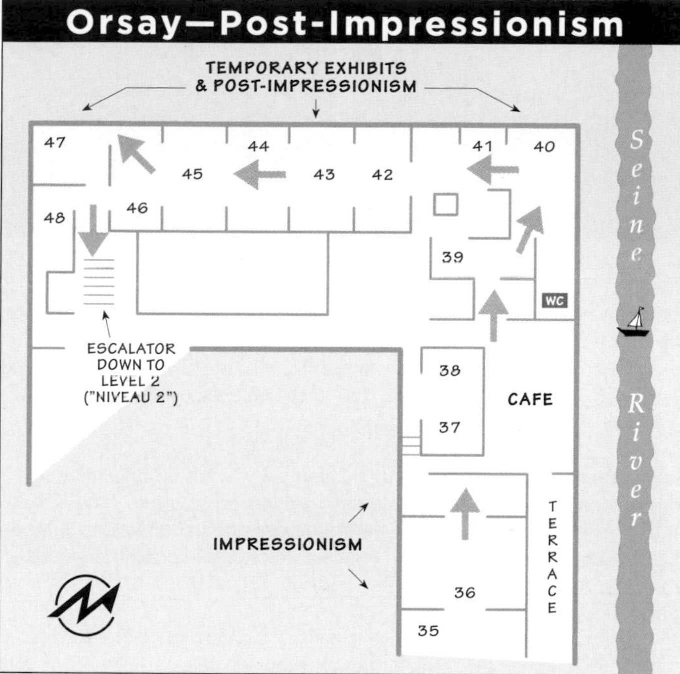

revolutionary young artists who understood his efforts. Cézanne's brush was a blunt instrument. With it, he'd bludgeon reality into submission, drag it across a canvas, and leave it there to dry. But Cézanne, the mediocre painter, was a great innovator. His work spoke for itself—which is good because, as you can see here, he had no mouth.

Paul Cézanne—*Landscape*
(*Rochers près des Grottes au-dessus de Château-Noir,* 1904)

Cézanne used chunks of green, tan, and blue paint as building blocks to construct this rocky brown cliff. Whereas the Impressionists built a figure out of a mosaic of individual brushstrokes, Cézanne used blocks of paint to give it a more solid, geometrical shape. A block of paint forming part of a

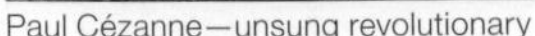

Paul Cézanne—unsung revolutionary

Card Players built from patches of paint

rock in the foreground is the same size as one in the background, flattening the scene into a wall of brushstrokes.

These chunks are like little "cubes." It's no coincidence that his experiments in reducing forms to their geometric basics influenced the... Cubists.

Paul Cézanne—*The Card Players* (*Les Joueurs de Cartes,* c. 1890–1895)

These aren't people. They're studies in color and pattern. The subject matter—two guys playing cards—is less important than the pleasingly balanced pattern they make on the canvas, two sloping forms framing a cylinder (a bottle) in the center. Later, abstract artists would focus solely on the shapes and colors.

The jacket of the player to the right is a patchwork of tans, greens, and browns. Even the "empty" space between the men—painted with fragmented chunks of color—is almost as tangible as they are. As one art scholar puts it: "Cézanne confused intermingled forms and colors, achieving an extraordinarily luminous density in which lyricism is controlled by a rigorously constructed rhythm." Just what I said—chunks of color.

Vincent van Gogh

Impressionists have been accused of being "light"-weights. The colorful style lends itself to bright country scenes, gardens, sunlight on the water, and happy crowds of simple people. It took a remarkable genius to add profound emotion to the Impressionist style.

Like Michelangelo, Beethoven, Rembrandt, Wayne Newton, and a select handful of others, Vincent van Gogh (1853–1890, van-go, or van-HOCK by the Dutch and the snooty) put so much of himself into his work

Van Gogh—*Self-Portrait, St. Rémy*

that art and life became one. In the Orsay's collection of paintings, you'll see both Van Gogh's painting style and his life unfold.

Vincent van Gogh—*Peasant Woman near the Hearth* (*Paysanne près de l'Atre,* 1885)

As the son of a Dutch minister, Van Gogh feels drawn to a religious vocation, and he spreads the gospel among the poorest of the poor—peasants and miners in overcast Holland and Belgium. He paints these hardworking, dignified folks in a crude, dark style that reflects the oppressiveness of their lives...and the loneliness of his own as he roams northern Europe in search of a calling.

Vincent van Gogh—*Self-Portrait, Paris* (*Portrait de l'Artiste,* 1887)

Encouraged by his art-dealer brother, Van Gogh moves to Paris, and *voilà!* The color! He meets Monet, drinks with Paul Gauguin and Henri de Toulouse-Lautrec, and soaks up the Impressionist style. (See how he builds a bristling brown beard using thick strokes of red, yellow, and green side by side.)

At first, he paints like the others, but soon he develops his own style. By using thick, swirling brushstrokes, he even infuses life into inanimate objects. Van Gogh's brushstrokes curve and thrash like a garden hose pumped full of wine.

Vincent van Gogh—*Midday*
(*La Méridienne,* 1890, based on a painting by Millet)

The social life of Paris becomes too much for the solitary Van Gogh. He moves to the South of France. At first, in the glow of the bright spring sunshine, he has a period of incredible creativity and happiness, as he is overwhelmed by the bright colors, landscape vistas, and common people—an Impressionist's dream.

Vincent van Gogh—*Van Gogh's Room at Arles*
(*La Chambre de van Gogh à Arles,* 1889)

But being alone in a strange country begins to wear on him. An ugly man, he finds it hard to get a date. The close-up perspective of this painting makes his tiny rented room look even more cramped. He invites his friend Gauguin to join him, but after two months together arguing passionately about art, nerves get raw. Van Gogh threatens Gauguin with a knife, and in crazed despair, mutilates his own ear.

The people of Arles realize they have a madman on their hands and convince Van Gogh to seek help. He enters a mental hospital.

Van Gogh's Room at Arles

The mysterious *Church at Auvers-sur-Oise*

Vincent van Gogh—*The Church at Auvers-sur-Oise* (*L'Eglise d'Auvers-sur-Oise*, 1890)

Van Gogh's paintings done in the peace of the mental hospital are more meditative—fewer bright landscapes, more closed-in scenes with deeper and almost surreal colors. Van Gogh, the preacher's son, saw painting as a calling, and he approached it with a spiritual intensity.

The sky is cobalt blue and the church's windows are also blue, as if we're looking right through the building to an infinite sky. There's a road that leads from us to the church, then splits to go behind it. A choice must be made: which way?

Vincent van Gogh—*Self-Portrait, St. Rémy* (1889)

Van Gogh wavers between happiness and madness. He despairs of ever being sane enough to continue painting.

This self-portrait shows a man engulfed in a confused background of brushstrokes that swirl and rave, setting in motion the waves of the jacket. But in the midst of this rippling sea of mystery floats a still, detached island of a face with a probing, questioning, wise expression.

Do his troubled eyes know that only a few months on, he will take a pistol and put a bullet through his chest? Vincent van Gone.

Primitives

Some artists, rejecting the harried, scientific, and rational world, remembered a time before "isms," when works of art weren't scholarly "studies in form and color," but voodoo dolls full of mystery and magic power. They learned from the art of primitive tribes in Africa and the South Seas, trying to re-create a primal Garden of Eden of peace and wholeness. In doing so, they created another "ism": Primitivism.

Henri Rousseau—*War* (*La Guerre, or La Chevauchée de la Discorde*, 1894)

War, in the form of a woman with a sword, flies on horseback across the battlefield, leaving destruction in her wake: broken bare trees, burning clouds in the background, and heaps of corpses picked at by the birds.

Henri Rousseau (1844–1910), a man who painted like a child, was an amateur artist who palled around with all the great painters, though they never took his naive style of art seriously. Like a child's drawing of a nightmare, the images are primitive—flat and simple, with unreal colors—but the effect is both beautiful and terrifying.

Rousseau's *War*

Paul Gauguin—*Arearea, or Joyousness* (*Joyeusetés*, 1892)

Paul Gauguin (1848–1903, go-gan) got the travel bug early in childhood and grew up wanting to be a sailor. Instead, he became a stockbroker. In his spare time, he painted, and he was introduced to the Impressionist circle. At 35, he quit his job, abandoned his wife (her stern portrait bust may be nearby), and traveled to the South Seas in search of the exotic.

In Tahiti, Gauguin found his Garden of Eden. He simplified his life into a routine of eating, sleeping, and painting. He painted the native girls in their naked innocence (so different from Cabanel's seductive *Venus*). His simple paintings feature flat images with heavy black outlines filled with bright, pure colors. But this simple style had a deep undercurrent of symbolic meaning.

Arearea shows native women and a dog. In the "distance" (there's no attempt at traditional 3-D here), a procession goes by with a large pagan idol. What's the connection between the idol and the foreground figures, who are apparently unaware of it? In primitive societies, religion permeates life. Idols, dogs, and women are holy.

Gauguin paints his primitive paradise.

Pointillist Paintings (Lots of Dots)

Pointillism, as illustrated by many paintings in the next rooms, brings Impressionism to its logical conclusion—little dabs of different colors placed side by side to blend in the viewer's eye. In works such as *The Circus* (*Le Cirque,* 1891), Georges Seurat (1859–1891) uses only red, yellow, blue, and green points of paint to create a mosaic of colors that shimmers at a distance, capturing the wonder of the dawn of electric light.

Toulouse-Lautrec

Henri de Toulouse-Lautrec (1864–1901) was the black sheep of a noble family. At age 15 he broke both legs, which left him disabled. Shunned by his family, a freak to society, he felt more at home in the underworld of other outcasts—prostitutes, drunks, thieves, dancers, and actors. He painted the Montmartre lowlife in the bars, cafés, dance halls, and brothels he frequented. Toulouse-Lautrec died young of alcoholism.

Henri de Toulouse-Lautrec—*The Clownesse Cha-U-Kao* (1895)

This is one of his fellow freaks, a fat lady clown who made her living by being laughed at. She slumps wearily after a performance, indifferent to the applause, and adjusts her dress to prepare for the curtain call. Like Degas, Toulouse-Lautrec was a true Impressionist, catching his models in snapshot poses and working spontaneously.

Henri de Toulouse-Lautrec—*Jane Avril Dancing* (*Jane Avril dansant*, 1891)

One of the most popular dancers at the Moulin Rouge was this slim, graceful, elegant, and melancholy woman, who stood out above the rabble. Her legs keep dancing while her mind is far away. Toulouse-Lautrec, the artistocrat, might have identified with her noble face—sad and weary of the nightlife, but immersed in it.

▸ *The essential Orsay includes one final artist—the sculptor Rodin, whose work is located on Level 2* (niveau 2). *Along the way there, take a peek at an "other" Orsay I think you'll find entertaining.*

THE "OTHER" ORSAY—LEVEL 2

The beauty of the Orsay is that it combines all the art from 1848 to 1914, both modern and classical, in one building. See a slice of opulent, *fin de siècle* Paris at the still-functioning "Le Restaurant." Next, find the chandeliered Salle des Fêtes (Grand Ballroom, Room 51), once one of Paris' poshest nightspots. Along the mezzanine, pop into Rooms 55 and 59 to see some non-Impressionist art—so popular in the 19th century and now so unpopular. Rooms 61–66 are a curvaceous IKEA of Art Nouveau furniture.

▸ *Find Rodin's statues at the far end of the Level 2 mezzanine. Start with the man missing everything but his legs.*

Auguste Rodin—*The Walking Man* (*L'Homme Qui Marche*, c. 1900)

Like this statue, Auguste Rodin (1840–1917) had one foot in the past, while the other was stepping into the future. Rodin combined classical solidity with Impressionist surfaces to become the greatest sculptor since Michelangelo.

This muscular, forcefully striding man could be a symbol of Renaissance Man with his classical power. With no mouth or hands, he speaks with his body. Get close and look at the statue's surface. This rough, "unfinished" look reflects light in the same way the rough Impressionist brushwork does, making the statue come alive, never quite at rest in the viewer's eye.

The "Other" Orsay—Level 2

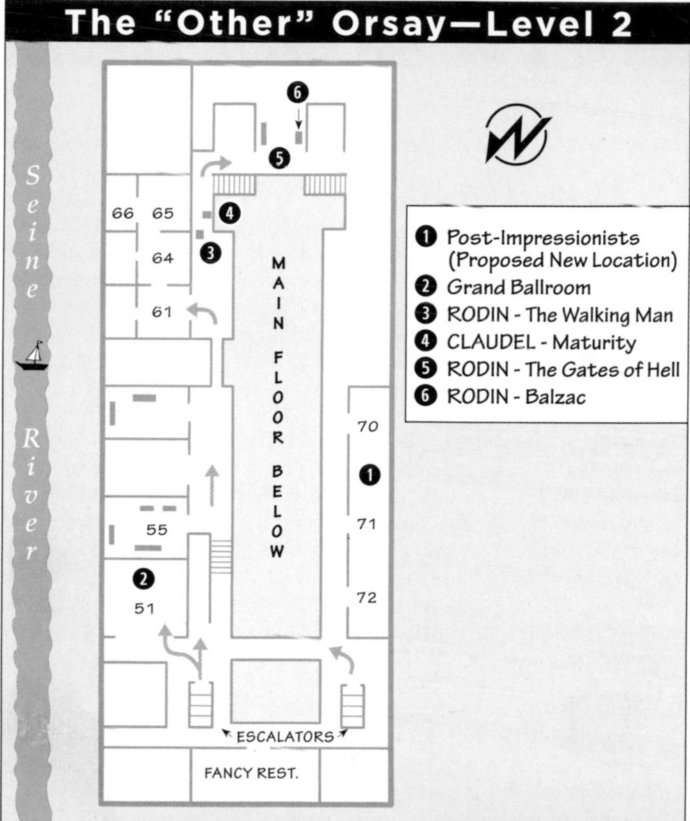

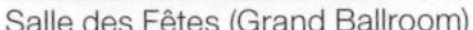
Salle des Fêtes (Grand Ballroom)

Claudel was dumped by Rodin.

► *Near the far end of the mezzanine, you'll see a small bronze statue of a couple.*

Camille Claudel—*Maturity* (*L'Age Mûr,* 1899–1903)
Camille Claudel, Rodin's student and mistress, may have portrayed their doomed love affair here. A young girl desperately reaches out to an older man, who is led away reluctantly by an older woman. The center of the composition is the empty space left when their hands separate. In real life, Rodin refused to leave his wife, and Claudel (see her head sticking up from a block of marble nearby) ended up in an insane asylum.

Auguste Rodin—*The Gates of Hell* (*La Porte de l'Enfer,* 1880–1917)
Rodin worked for decades on these doors depicting Dante's hell, and they contain some of his greatest hits—small statues that he later executed in full size. Find *The Thinker* squatting above the doorway, contemplating Man's fate. And in the lower left is the same kneeling man eating his children *(Ugolin)* that you'll see in full size nearby. Rodin paid models to run, squat, leap, and spin around his studio however they wanted. When he saw an interesting pose, he'd yell, "freeze" (or "statue maker") and get out his sketch pad.

Auguste Rodin—*Honoré de Balzac* (1897)
The great French novelist is given a heroic, monumental ugliness. Wrapped in a long cloak, he thrusts his head out at a defiant angle, showing the strong individualism and egoism of this pioneer of Modernism.

From this perch, look over the main floor at the classical statues below—beautiful, smooth, balanced, and idealized—and realize how far

Looking back over the main floor

we've come. Rodin's powerful, haunting works are a good place to end this tour. With a stable base of 19th-century stone, he launched art into the 20th century.

Eiffel Tower Tour

La Tour Eiffel

It's crowded, expensive, and there are probably better views in Paris, but visiting this 1,000-foot-tall ornament is worth the trouble. Visitors to Paris may find *Mona Lisa* to be less than expected, but the Eiffel Tower rarely disappoints, even in an era of skyscrapers. This is a once-in-a-lifetime, I've-been-there experience. Making the trip gives you membership in the exclusive society of the quarter of a billion other humans who have made the Eiffel Tower the most visited monument in the modern world.

ORIENTATION

Cost: €13.10 all the way to the top, €8.10 if you're only going up to the two lower levels, not covered by Museum Pass. You can skip the elevator line and climb the stairs to the first and second level for €4.50; it's another €5 to take the elevator from the second level to the top.

Hours: Open daily mid-June–Aug 9:00–24:00, last ascent to top at 23:00 and to lower levels at 23:30. From Sept–mid-June 9:30–23:00, last ascent to top at 22:00 and to lower levels at 22:30 (elevator) or 18:00 (stairs).

Reservations and Avoiding Lines: There are generally one- to two-hour waits to get in—weekends and holidays are worst.

At www.toureiffel.fr, you can book an entry time (e.g., June 12 at 16:30) and skip the line—at no extra cost. You pay online and print your own ticket (or have a confirmation sent to your mobile phone). Arrive 10 minutes before your entry time, and go to the entrance for *visitors with reservation,* where attendants scan your ticket and put you on the first available elevator. Note that, even with a pre-paid reservation, to catch the elevator from the second level to the summit, you'll still have to wait in line like everybody else (and show your ticket again).

If you don't have a reservation, try arriving first thing in the morning or after dark, or take the (less-crowded) stairs. A reservation at either of the tower's view restaurants lets you skip the worst lines (see "Cuisine Art" below).

When to Go: For the best of both worlds, arrive with enough light to see the views, then stay as it gets dark to see the lights.

Getting There: The Bir-Hakeim and Trocadéro Métro stops, and the Champ de Mars-Tour Eiffel RER stop, are each about a 10-minute walk away. The Ecole Militaire Métro stop in the rue Cler area is 20 minutes away. Buses #69 and #87 stop nearby.

Information: An information office is at the base between the north and east pillars. Tel. 01 44 11 23 23, www.toureiffel.fr.

Length of This Tour: With a reservation and minimal crowds, figure 90 minutes to the top and back. It takes three or four hours with crowds and lines.

Pickpockets: In crowded elevators and lines, *en garde.*

Security Check: Bags larger than 19" × 8" × 12" are not allowed and there

is no baggage check. All bags are subject to a security search. No knives, glass bottles, or cans are allowed.

Services: There are free WCs at the base of the tower behind the east pillar. Inside the tower itself, WCs are on all levels, but they have long lines.

Photography: All photos and videos are allowed.

Cuisine Art: The first and second levels have small sandwich-and-pizza-type cafés (€5). The tower's two classy restaurants offer great views, and a reservation at either restaurant lets you skip the initial elevator line. Reserve weeks in advance for a view table.

On the first level is 58 Tour Eiffel. Dinner reservations only; lunch is first come, first served (€20 lunches, €65 dinners, open daily, tel. 01 72 76 18 46, www.restaurants-toureiffel.com).

The expensive Jules Verne Restaurant is on the second level (€85 lunch *menu,* €200 dinner *menu,* open daily, tel. 01 45 55 61 44, www.lejulesverne-paris.com).

At the tower's base, there's not much besides the burger-and-fries stands. Rue Cler, with many options, is a 20-minute walk away (✪ see pages 196–197). Avenue de la Bourdonnais, a mere block east of the tower, has a few eateries and sandwich shops, including Pâtisserie de la Tour Eiffel, which offers inexpensive salads, quiche, sandwiches, and tower views (closed Mon, 21 avenue de la Bourdonnais, tel. 01 47 05 59 81).

Your tastiest option may be to assemble a picnic beforehand to eat alongside the Champ de Mars park. The center of the park is off-limits to picnickers.

Starring: All of Paris...and beyond.

OVERVIEW

There are three observation platforms, at 200, 400, and 900 feet. Although being on the windy top of the Eiffel Tower is a thrill you'll never forget, the view is better from the first and second levels, where you can actually see Paris' monuments. All three levels have some displays, WCs (usually with

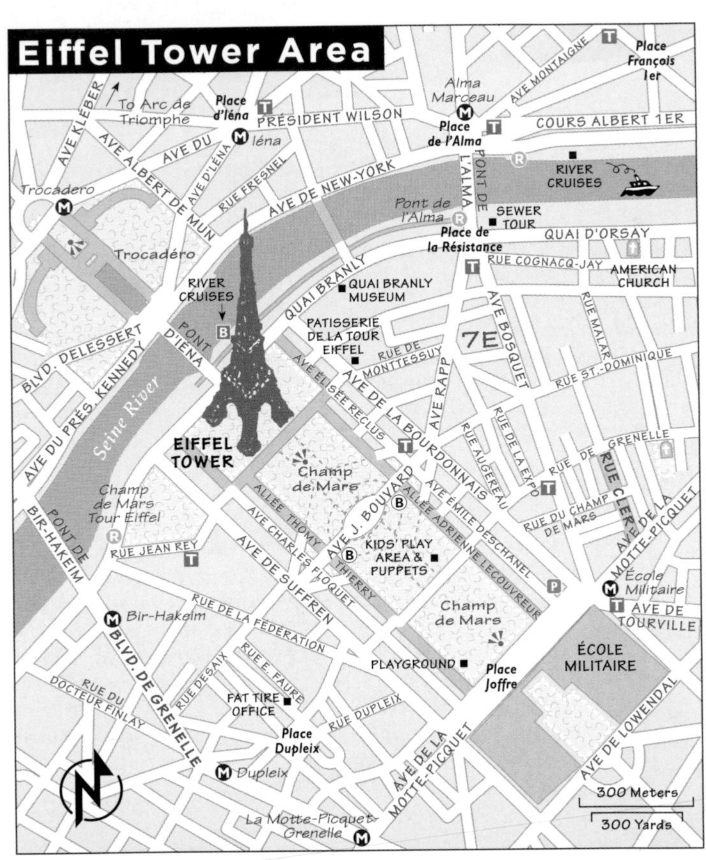

long lines), souvenir stores, and a few other services.

To get to the top, you need to ride one elevator to the second level (it bypasses the first level on the way up), then catch a second elevator to the top. For the hardy, stairs lead from the ground level up to the first level (360 steps) and second level (another 360 steps). The staircase is enclosed with a wire cage, so you can't fall, but those with vertigo issues may still find them dizzying.

If you want to see the entire tower, from top to bottom, then see it... from top to bottom. Ride the elevator to the second level, then immediately line up for the other elevator to the top. Enjoy the views on top, then ride back down to the second level. Frolic there for a while, then descend to the first level by the stairs (no line) or elevator. After more views, shops, exhibits, and a snack, take the elevator or stairs back down to earth.

View from Trocadéro

THE TOUR BEGINS

Find the various entrances at the base of the tower's four *piliers* (pillars), named for their compass points: *nord, sud, est,* and *ouest.* Make sure you get in the right line. If you have a reservation, look for signs saying *visitors with reservation.* Otherwise, follow signs for *individuels* or *visiteurs sans*

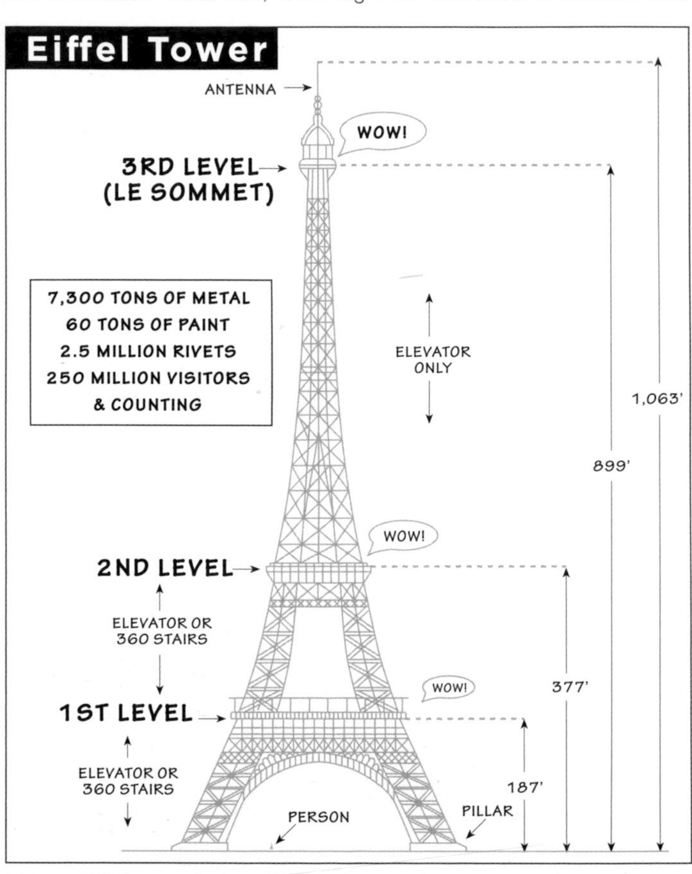

tickets. (Avoid lines selling tickets only for *groupes.*) To climb the stairs, enter at the south pillar, next to the Jules Verne Restaurant entrance. As you wait to enter, look up at the tower towering above you, and don't even think about what would happen if someone dropped a coin from the top.

Exterior

Delicate and graceful when seen from afar, the Eiffel Tower is massive—even a bit scary—close up. You don't appreciate its size until you walk toward it; like a mountain, it seems so close but takes forever to reach.

The tower, including its antenna, stands 1,063 feet tall, or slightly higher than the 77-story Chrysler Building in New York. Its four support pillars straddle an area of 3.5 acres. Despite the tower's 7,300 tons of metal and 60 tons of paint, it is so well-engineered that it weighs no more per square inch at its base than a linebacker on tiptoes.

Once the world's tallest structure, it's now eclipsed by a number of towers (e.g., the CN Tower, Toronto, 1,815 feet), radio antennae (KVLY-TV Mast, North Dakota, 2,063 feet), and skyscrapers (the Burj Khalifa in Dubai, UAE, 2,717 feet).

The long green lawn stretching south of the tower is the Champ de Mars, originally the training ground for troops and students of the nearby Military School (Ecole Militaire) and now a park. On the north side, across the Seine, is the curved palace colonnade framing a square called the Trocadéro, site of numerous world's fairs.

History

In 1889, the first visitor to Paris' Universal Exposition walked beneath the "arch" formed by the newly built Eiffel Tower and entered the fairgrounds.

Eiffel—designer, financier, and builder

Wheel lifting the elevator

Building the Tower

An 18,000-piece Erector set

As you ascend through the metal beams, imagine being a worker, perched high above nothing, riveting this thing together. It was a massive project, and it took all the ingenuity of the Industrial Age—including mass production, cutting-edge technology, and capitalist funding.

The tower went up like an 18,000-piece erector set, made of 15-foot iron beams held together with 2.5 million rivets. For two years, 300 workers assembled the pieces, the tower rising as they went.

First, they sank massive iron pillars into the ground at an angle, surrounded by cement 20 feet thick and capped with stone. They erected wooden scaffolding to support the lower (angled) sections,

The World's Fair celebrated both the centennial of the French Revolution and France's position as a global superpower. Bridge-builder Gustave Eiffel (1832–1923) won the contest to build the fair's centerpiece by beating out such rival proposals as a giant guillotine.

Gustave deserved to have the tower named for him. He not only designed it, he financed it, his factory produced the iron beams, he invented special cranes and apparatus, he paid the workers, and—working on a deadline for the World's Fair—he brought in the project on time and under budget.

The tower was nothing but a showpiece, with no functional purpose except to demonstrate to the world that France had the wealth, knowledge, and can-do spirit to erect a structure far taller than anything the world had ever seen. The original plan was to dismantle the tower as quickly as it was built after the celebration ended, but it was kept by popular demand.

until the pillars came together and the tower could support itself. Then the iron beams were lifted up with steam-powered cranes, including cranes on tracks (creeper cranes) that inched up the pillars as the tower progressed. There, daring workers dangled from rope ladders, balanced on beams, and tightrope-walked their way across them as they put the pieces in place. The workers then hammered in red-hot rivets which, as they cooled, locked the structure in place.

After a mere year and a half of work, the tower already surpassed the previous tallest building in the world—the Washington Monument (555 feet)—which had taken 36 years to build.

The tower was painted a rusty red. Since then, it's sported several colors, including mustard and the current brown-gray. It is repainted every seven years, a process that takes 25 full-time painters 18 months to apply 60 tons of paint by hand—no spraying allowed.

Two years, two months, and five days after construction began, the tower was done. On May 15, 1889, a red, white, and blue beacon was lit on the top, the World's Fair began, and the tower carried its first astounded visitor to the top.

To a generation hooked on technology, the tower was the marvel of the age, a symbol of progress and human ingenuity. Not all were so impressed, however; many found it a monstrosity. The writer Guy de Maupassant (1850–1893) routinely ate lunch in the tower just so he wouldn't have to look at it.

In subsequent years, the tower has come to serve many functions: as a radio transmitter (1909–present), a cosmic-ray observatory (1910), a billboard (spelling "Citroën" in lights, 1925–1934), a broadcaster of Nazi TV programs (1940–1944), a fireworks launch pad (numerous times), and as a framework for dazzling lighting displays, including the current arrangement, designed in 2000 for the celebration of the millennium.

► *To reach the top, ride the elevator to the second level. From there, get in line for the next elevator and continue to the top. Pop out 900 feet above the ground.*

Third Level (Le Sommet, or Summit)

The top level is tiny. All you'll find here are wind and grand, sweeping views. The city lies before you, with a panorama guide. On a good day, you can see for 40 miles. Do a 360-degree tour of Paris. (Note that the following compass points are only approximate; in fact, what the tower's displays call "west" is more like southwest, etc.) Feeling proud you made it this high? You can celebrate your accomplishment with a €10 glass of champagne.

Looking West *(Ouest)*: The Seine runs east to west (though at this point it's flowing more southwest). At the far end of the skinny "island" in the river, find the tiny copy of the Statue of Liberty, looking 3,633 miles away to her big sister in New York. Gustave Eiffel, a man of many talents, also designed the internal supports of New York's Statue of Liberty, which was cast in copper by fellow Frenchman Frederic Bartholdi (1886).

Looking North *(Nord)*: At your feet is the curved arcade of the Trocadéro. Beyond that is the vast, forested expanse of the Bois de Bolougne, the three-square-mile park that hosts joggers and *boules* players by day and prostitutes by night. In the far distance are the skyscrapers of La Défense and, to the right of the Trocadéro, is the Arc de Triomphe.

Looking East *(Est)*: At your feet are the Seine and its many bridges, including the pont Alexandre bridge, with its four golden statues. Looking farther upstream, find the Orsay Museum, the Louvre, pont Neuf, and the twin towers of Notre-Dame.

In the far distance on the Right Bank is the bullet-shaped dome of Sacré-Cœur, atop Butte Montmartre.

Looking South *(Sud)*: In a line, find the Champ de Mars, the Ecole Militaire, the Y-shaped UNESCO building, and the 689-foot Montparnasse Tower skyscraper. To the left is the golden dome of Les Invalides.

Looking west—next stop, New York

Looking north—Place Trocadéro

The Tippy Top: Ascend another short staircase to the open-air top, beneath satellite dishes. You'll see the tiny apartment given to the builder of the tower. The mannequins re-create the moment during the 1889 Exhibition when the American Thomas Edison paid a visit to his fellow techie, Gustave Eiffel (the one with the beard) and Gustave's daughter Claire, presenting them with his new invention, a phonograph. (Then they cranked it up and blasted The Who's "I Can See for Miles.")

▸ *Catch the elevator down to the...*

Second Level

The second level (400 feet) has the best views because you're closer to the sights, and the monuments are more recognizable. This level has souvenir shops, public telephones to call home, and a small stand-up café.

The famous Jules Verne Restaurant on this level is currently run by celebrity chef Alain Ducasse. One would hope his three-star brand of haute cuisine matches the 400-foot haute of the restaurant.

▸ *Catch the elevator or take the stairs (5 minutes, 360 steps, free) down to the...*

First Level

The first level (200 feet) has more great views, all well-described by the tower's panorama displays. There are a number of photo exhibits on the tower's history, WCs, a conference hall (closed to tourists), an ATM, and souvenirs. A small café sells pizza and sandwiches (outdoor tables in summer). The 58 Tour Eiffel restaurant has more *accessible* prices than the Jules Verne Restaurant above, and is also run by Alain Ducasse. In winter,

Looking east—the Seine River

Looking south—Champ de Mars

part of the first level is set up for winter activities (most recently as an ice-skating rink).

Videos shown in the small theater (some permanent, some rotating) document the tower's construction, paint job, fireworks displays, and place in pop culture.

A display on how weather impacts the tower shows how the sun warms the metal, causing the top to expand and lean about five inches away from the sun. Nearby, a small model of the tower oscillates slightly, simulating the tower's real-time movement in the wind and sun. Because of its lacy design, even the strongest of winds could never blow the tower down, only cause it to sway back and forth a few inches. In fact, Eiffel designed the tower primarily with wind resistance in mind, and many modern skyscrapers follow his mathematics.

Watch the original hydraulic pump (1889) at work. It once pumped water from this level to the second level to feed the machinery powering the upper elevator. Then look at the big wheels that wind and unwind heavy cables to lift the elevators.

Up and Down

The tower—which was designed from the start to accommodate hordes of visitors—has always had elevators. Back in the late 19th century, elevator technology was so new that they needed a special design to accommodate the angle of the tower's pillars. Today's elevators (modern replacements) make about 100 round-trip journeys a day.

There are 1,665 stairs up to the top level, though tourists can only climb 720 of them, up as far as the second level. During a race in 1905, a gentleman climbed from the ground to the second floor—elevation gain 400 feet—in 3 minutes, 12 seconds.

Light display at the top of the hour

▸ *Consider a drink or a sandwich while overlooking all of Paris, then take the elevator or stairs (5 minutes, 360 steps, free) to the ground.*

The Tour Ends

Welcome back to earth.

For a final look, stroll to place du Trocadéro or to the end of the Champ de Mars and look back for great views. However impressive it may be by day, the tower is an awesome thing to see at twilight, when it becomes engorged with light, and virile Paris lies back and lets night be on top. When darkness fully envelops the city, the tower seems to climax with a spectacular light show at the top of each hour...for five minutes.

Rue Cler Walk

The Art of Parisian Living

Paris is changing quickly, but a stroll down this open-air-market street introduces you to a thriving, traditional Parisian neighborhood and its local culture. Though somewhat upscale, rue Cler retains the workaday charm of village Paris.

In food-crazy Paris, shopping for groceries is an integral part of everyday life. Rue Cler, traffic-free since 1984, is lined with the essential shops—wine, cheese, bread, chocolate—as well as a bank, a post office, and pleasant cafés.

To learn the fine art of living Parisian-style, there's no better classroom than rue Cler. And you can assemble the ultimate French picnic. The Rue Cler Walk is the only tour in this guidebook you should start while hungry.

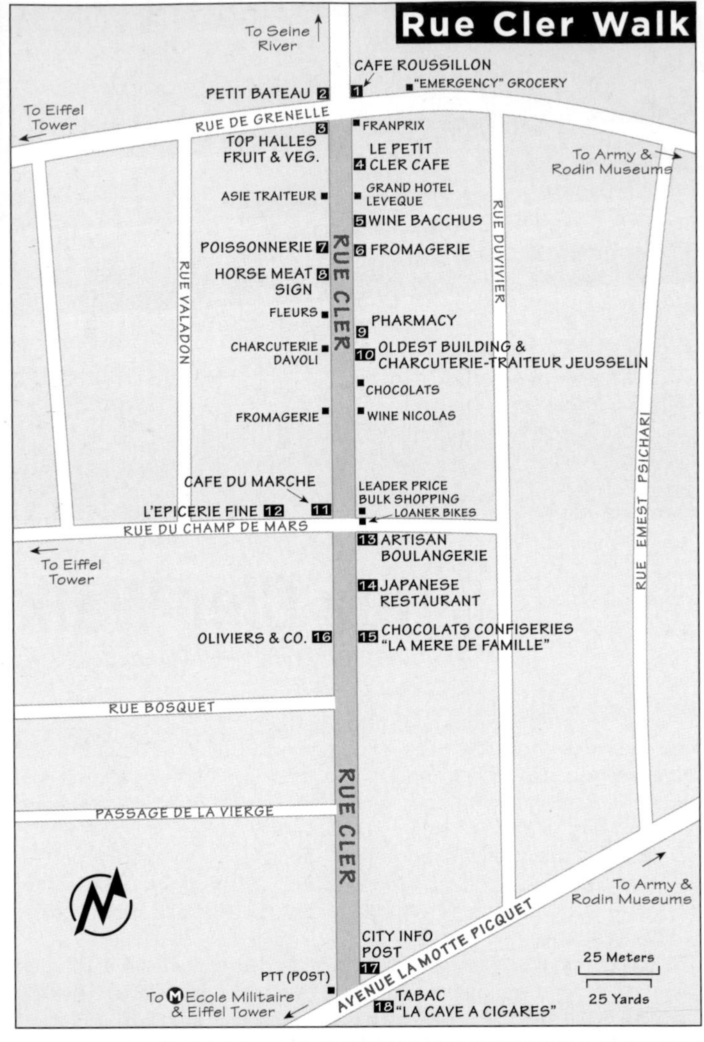

Rue Cler Walk
To Seine River
CAFE ROUSSILLON
"EMERGENCY" GROCERY
PETIT BATEAU 2
1
To Eiffel Tower
RUE DE GRENELLE
3
TOP HALLES FRUIT & VEG.
FRANPRIX
LE PETIT
4 CLER CAFE
To Army & Rodin Museums
ASIE TRAITEUR
GRAND HOTEL LEVEQUE
5 WINE BACCHUS
RUE DUVIVIER
POISSONNERIE 7
RUE CLER
6 FROMAGERIE
HORSE MEAT SIGN 8
RUE VALADON
FLEURS
9 PHARMACY
CHARCUTERIE DAVOLI
10 OLDEST BUILDING & CHARCUTERIE-TRAITEUR JEUSSELIN
CHOCOLATS
FROMAGERIE
WINE NICOLAS
RUE EMEST PSICHARI
CAFE DU MARCHE
LEADER PRICE BULK SHOPPING
L'EPICERIE FINE 12
11
LOANER BIKES
RUE DU CHAMP DE MARS
13 ARTISAN BOULANGERIE
To Eiffel Tower
14 JAPANESE RESTAURANT
OLIVIERS & CO. 16
15 CHOCOLATS CONFISERIES "LA MERE DE FAMILLE"
RUE BOSQUET
PASSAGE DE LA VIERGE
RUE CLER
To Army & Rodin Museums
AVENUE LA MOTTE PICQUET
CITY INFO POST
17
25 Meters
25 Yards
PTT (POST)
To M Ecole Militaire & Eiffel Tower
TABAC
18 "LA CAVE A CIGARES"

ORIENTATION

Length of This Walk: Allow an hour to browse and café-hop along this short walk of two or three blocks.

When to Go: Visit rue Cler when its markets are open and lively (Tue–Sat 8:30–13:00 or 15:00–19:30, Sun 8:30–12:00, dead on Mon).

Etiquette: Greet the store owner with *"Bonjour, Madame or Monsieur* or *Mademoiselle"* as you enter and *"Au revoir, Madame* or *Monsieur* or *Mademoiselle"* when you leave. If you really want to win a clerk over, follow up your greeting with *"Excusez-moi de vous déranger"* (ek-skew-zay-mwah duh voo day-rahn-zhay)—Pardon me for bothering you—then ask for what you need. Remember that these shops are busy serving regular customers; don't get in the way.

Getting There: Start your walk where the pedestrian section of rue Cler begins, at rue de Grenelle (Mo: Ecole Militaire or bus #69 stop).

THE WALK BEGINS

❶ Café Roussillon

This neighborhood fixture recently dumped its old-fashioned, characteristic look for the latest café style—warm, natural wood tones, easy lighting, and music. To the right of the door, you'll see the *Consommations* sign required by French law, making the pricing clear: Drinks served at the bar *(comptoir)* are cheaper than drinks served at the tables *(salles).* Inside, the bar is always busy. The blackboard lists wines sold by the little, 7-centiliter glass (about 2.5 ounces), along with other drinks.

The little **late-night grocery** next door is one of countless corner shops nicknamed *dépanneurs* ("to help you out of difficulty"). Open nightly until midnight, these stores are often run by hardworking North Africans willing to keep long hours. Locals happily pay the higher prices for the convenience *dépanneurs* provide.

► *If you're shopping for designer baby clothes, you'll find them across the street at...*

❷ Petit Bateau

The French spend at least as much on their babies as they do on their dogs—dolling them up with designer jammies. This store is one in a popular chain. Babies-in-the-know just aren't comfortable unless they're making a fashion statement (such as underwear with sailor stripes). In the last generation, an aging and shrinking population has been a serious problem for Europe's wealthier nations. But France now has one of Europe's biggest baby populations—the fertile French average two children per family, compared to 1.6 for the rest of Europe. Babies are trendy today, and the government rewards parents with substantial tax deductions for their first two children—and then doubles the deductions after that. Making babies is good business.

► *Cross rue de Grenelle to find...*

❸ Top Halles Fruits and Vegetables

Each morning, fresh produce is trucked in from farmers' fields to Paris' huge Rungis market—Europe's largest, near Orly Airport—and then dispatched to merchants with FedEx-like speed and precision. Good luck finding a shopping bag—locals bring their own two-wheeled carts or reusable bags. Also, notice how the earth-friendly French resist excessive packaging.

Parisians—who know they eat best by being tuned in to the seasons—shop with their noses. Try it. Smell the cheap foreign strawberries, which locals call "plastic strawberries"—red on the outside, white on the inside. One sniff of the torpedo-shaped French ones *(garriguettes)* in June, and you know which is better.

Find the herbs in the back—is today's delivery in? Check the price of those melons and their country of origin—it must be posted. If they're from Guadeloupe, they're out of season, and many locals won't buy them.

The **Franprix** across the street is a small outpost of a nationwide supermarket chain. Opposite Grand Hôtel Lévêque is **Asie Traiteur.** Fast Asian food to go—about as common as bakeries now—has had an impact on traditional Parisian eating habits.

❹ Le Petit Cler

This small café is a good example of how life is changing on rue Cler. Formerly a working-class bar with a *tabac* (tobacco shop) inside, it has recently joined the ranks of the trendy outdoor cafés.

▸ *Just past Grand Hôtel Lévêque is...*

❺ Wine Bacchus

After they've assembled their meal at other stores, shoppers come here to pick the appropriate wine. The clerk is a counselor who works with your needs and budget, and he can put a bottle of white in the fridge for you to pick up later. The wine is classified by region. Most "Parisians" (born elsewhere) have an affinity for the wines of their home region. Check out the great prices: wines of the month (in the center) for as little as €8-12 (open until 20:00 except Sun).

▸ *Next door, smell the...*

❻ *Fromagerie*

Spilling outside into the street, this cheese shop offers more than 200 types of French cheese, both cow *(vache)* and goat *(chèvre)* cheese. The place is lab-coat-serious but friendly. Known as a "BOF," it's where people buy *beurre, oeuf,* and *fromage*—butter, eggs, and cheese.

Notice the many cheese shapes—wedges, cylinders, balls, and miniature hockey pucks, all powdered white, gray, and burnt marshmallow. It's

A cheese for every day of the year

Parisians often shop daily.

a festival of mold. The shape tells the buyer where the cheese is from—e.g., a pyramid is from the Loire region. This information is crucial. The region creates the *terroir* (the physical and magical union of sun, soil, and generations of farmer love) that gives the cheese its personality. *Ooh la la* means you're impressed. More *la*s means you're more impressed. *Ooh la la la la.* A Parisian friend once held the stinkiest glob close to her nose, took an orgasmic breath, and exhaled, "Yes, it smells like zee feet of angels." Go ahead...inhale.

In the back room, they store *les meules,* the big, 170-pound wheels of cheese, made from 250 gallons of milk. Don't eat the skin of the "hard" cheeses cut from these...they're rolled on the floor. But the skin on most smaller cheeses—the Brie, the Camembert—is part of the taste. "It completes the package," says my local friend.

At dinner tonight you can take the cheese course just before or instead of dessert. On a good cheese plate you have a hard cheese (like Emmentaler—a.k.a. "Swiss cheese"), a flowery cheese (maybe Brie or Camembert), a bleu cheese, and a goat cheese—ideally from different regions. Because it's strongest, the goat cheese is usually eaten last.

► *Across the street, find the fish shop, known as the...*

❼ Poissonnerie

Fresh fish is brought into Paris daily from ports on the English Channel, 110 miles away. In fact, fish here is likely fresher than in many towns closer to the sea, because Paris is a commerce hub (from here, it's shipped to outlying towns). Anything wiggling? This *poissonnerie,* like all such shops, recently was upgraded to meet the new Europewide hygiene standards.

Next door at Crêperie Ulysée en Gaule (under the awning—get close to see) is a particularly tempting rue Cler storefront.

❽ No More Horse Meat

The stones and glass set over the doorway advertise horse meat: *Boucherie Chevaline.* While today this store serves souvlaki and crêpes, the classy 1930s storefront survives from the previous occupant. Signed by the artist, it's a work of art fit for a museum—but it belongs right here.

The door is decorated with lunch coupon decals (like *chèque déjeuner*) for local workers. In France, an employee lunch subsidy program is an expected perk. Employers—responding to strong tax incentives designed to keep the café culture vital—issue voucher checks (worth about €8 each) for each day an employee works in a month. Sack lunches are rare, since a good lunch is sacred.

A few steps farther along is a flower shop. When visiting friends, French people give a gift of flowers. It's classiest to have them delivered before you show up. Across the street is the...

❾ Pharmacy

In France, as in much of Europe, the pharmacist makes the first diagnosis and has the authority to prescribe certain drugs. If it's out of his league, he'll recommend a doctor. Pharmacies are also the only place to get many basic medical items, such as aspirin and simple reading glasses.

❿ Oldest Building and Charcuterie-Traiteur Jeusselin

Next to the pharmacy is rue Cler's oldest building (with the two garret windows on the roof). It's from the early 1800s, when this street was part of a village near Paris, and was lined with structures like this.

Occupying the ground floor of this house is Charcuterie-Traiteur Jeusselin. Charcuteries sell mouthwatering deli food to go. Because Parisian kitchens are so small, these gourmet delis are handy, even for those who cook. It lets the hosts concentrate on creating the main course, and then buy beautifully prepared side dishes to complete a fine dinner.

The charcuterie business is fiercely competitive in France. Jeusselin proudly displays its hard-won cooking-contest awards by the entrance. One reads: *Medaille d'Or du Fromage de Tête du Jambon blanc 2009*—gold medal for head cheese with white ham. Head cheese is a meat jelly made from the head of a pig or cow. Who would brag about that?? The French.

The other award—*Meilleur Traiteur de Paris, Gault & Millau 2008*—is for the "best deli," determined by the prestigious food-rating organization Gault Millau. The prominently posted *Diplôme de Cordon Bleu* is a diploma from the most famous cooking school in France, which used to be in the neighborhood.

Even with such credentials, many of these charcuteries (cold-cut delis) have had to add *traiteur* (restaurant-type) services to survive. They're now selling cooked dishes, pastries, and wines-to-go, and often have a few tables where customers can sit and eat.

Notice the Italian charcuterie **Davoli** right across rue Cler. Each day these charcuteries go *mano a mano,* cooking up *plats du jour* (specials of the day), advertised on boards outside and inside, and sometimes on their websites. Note the system: Order, take your ticket to the cashier to pay, and return with the receipt to pick up your food.

► *A few doors down is...*

⓫ Café du Marché and More

Café du Marché, on the corner, is *the* place to sit and enjoy the action (✪ see page 196). It's rue Cler's living room, where locals gather before heading home, many staying for a relaxed and affordable dinner. The owner priced his menu so that locals could afford to dine out on a regular basis, and it worked—many patrons eat here five days a week. For a reasonable meal, grab a chair and check the chalk menu listing the *plat du jour.* Notice how the new no-smoking-indoors laws have made outdoor seating and propane heaters a huge hit.

The shiny, sterile **Leader Price grocery store** (across the street) is a Parisian Costco, selling bulk items. Because storage space is so limited in most Parisian apartments, bulk purchases are unlikely to become a big deal here. Most locals buy nonperishables online, shop for produce three times a week on rue Cler, and buy fresh bread daily. The ugly exterior of this store suggests a sneaky bending of rue Cler's normally rigorous design review for building permits.

► *From Café du Marché, hook right and side-trip a couple doors down rue du Champ de Mars to visit...*

⓬ L'Epicerie Fine

This fine-foods boutique stands out from the rest because of its gentle owners, Pascal and Joanna. Their mission in life is to explain to travelers, in fluent English, what the French fuss over food is all about. Say *bonjour* to Pascal and company. Let them help you assemble a picnic and tempt you with fine gourmet treats, Berthillon ice cream, and generous tastes of caramel, balsamic vinegar, and French and Italian olive oil (Tue–Fri 9:30–13:00 & 15:00–19:30, Sat 10:00–13:30, Sun 10:00–13:00, closed Mon, tel. 01 47 05 98 18).

► *Return to rue Cler. The neighborhood bakery on the corner is often marked by a line of people waiting to pick up their daily baguette.*

⓭ Artisan Boulangerie

Since the French Revolution, the government has regulated the cost of a basic baguette. Locals debate the merits of Paris' many *boulangeries*. Some like their baguette a tad well-done while others prefer it more doughy. It's said that a baker cannot be both good at bread and good at pastry—at cooking school they major in one or the other. So a baker either bakes

Give us this day our daily bread.

bread or makes pastries and has the other done elsewhere. But here, the baker does both, and nobody's complaining.

► *Next door is a strangely out-of-place...*

⑭ Japanese Restaurant

Sushi is for sale everywhere in Paris these days. Locals explain that the phenomenon is the same as when Chinese restaurants were spreading like gastronomic weeds. Real French restaurants found it so hard to compete with these inexpensive places that in some areas, local authorities actually forbid business permits for Chinese restaurants.

► *A bit farther along is...*

⑮ La Mère de Famille Gourmand Chocolats Confiseries

This shop has been in the neighborhood for 30 years. The wholesalers try to pressure the owner to push newer candies, but the owner has kept the old traditional ones, too. "The old ladies, they want the same sweets that made them so happy 80 years ago," she says. You can buy "naked bonbons" right out of the jar and chocolate by the piece (about €0.75 each). You're welcome to assemble a small assortment.

Until a few years ago, the chocolate was dipped and decorated right on the premises. As was the tradition in rue Cler shops, the merchants resided and produced in the back and sold in the front.

► *Across the street, you'll find...*

⑯ Oliviers & Co. Olive Oils

This shop, typical of an upscale neighborhood like this, sells fine gourmet goodies from the south of France and olive oil from around the Mediterranean. They are happy to give visitors a taste test. Find the ancient stone mill wheel that was once used to press olives. Use their tiny spoons to sample three distinct oils.

► *Walk on to the end of rue Cler (where it hits a busy street).*

⑰ City Info Post

This electronic signpost directs residents to websites for local information—transportation changes, surveys, employment opportunities, community events, and so on. Also notice the big, green recycling stations and see-through green garbage sacks. In the 1990s, Paris suffered a rash of trash-can bombings. Bad guys hid rigged-up camp stove canisters in metal garbage cans, which broke into deadly "shrapnel" when they exploded. Local authorities solved this by replacing the metal cans with these see-through plastic bags.

▶ *Across the busy street is a* tabac.

⑱ Tabac La Cave à Cigares

Just as the US has liquor stores licensed to sell booze, the only place for people over 16 to buy tobacco legally in France is at a *tabac* (tah-bah) counter. Notice how European laws require a bold warning sign on cigarettes (about half the size of the package) that says, bluntly, *fumer tue*—smoking kills.

A *tabac* sells more than just tobacco, and is a much-appreciated fixture of Parisian neighborhoods. It's a kind of government cash desk, selling stamps and public-transit tickets (plus a five percent markup). Locals pay for parking meters by buying a card...or pay their fines here if they don't. Like back home, the LOTO is a big deal—and a lucrative way for the government to tax poor and less-educated people.

American smokers may not be able to resist the temptation to pick up a *petit Corona*—your chance to buy a fine Cuban cigar for €6 without breaking US law.

▶ *Rue Cler ends at the post office. The Ecole Militaire Métro stop is just down the street. If you bought a picnic along this walk, there are two fine parks nearby—turn left down avenue de la Motte-Picquet for the Army Museum, or right for the Eiffel Tower. Or make a U-turn and dive back into neighborhood Paris.*

Versailles

Château de Versailles

If you've ever wondered why your American passport has French writing in it, you'll find the answer at Versailles (vehr-"sigh")—every king's dream palace. The powerful court of Louis XIV at Versailles set the standard of culture for all of Europe, right up to modern times.

Versailles has three blockbuster sights. The palace itself, the **Château,** features the lavish, chandeliered living rooms of France's kings. The expansive **Gardens** are a landscaped wonderland of statues and fountains. Finally, the **Trianon Palaces and Domaine de Marie-Antoinette** offer a pastoral getaway of small palaces, including Marie's faux-peasant Hamlet.

Versailles is big and crowded, so arm yourself with a pass to skip ticket-buying lines. Arrive early or late to avoid crowds.

ORIENTATION

Cost: I recommend buying either a Paris Museum Pass or Versailles' combo-ticket called "Le Passeport," both of which cover your entrance to the most important parts of the complex. If you don't get a pass, you can buy individual tickets for each of the three different sections:

• **The Château,** the main palace, costs €15 (€13 after 15:00, free on first Sun Nov–March).

• **The Trianon Palaces and Domaine de Marie-Antoinette**—the small palaces in the far corner of the Gardens—cost €10 (€6 after 16:00 and Nov–March).

• **The Gardens** are free, except on certain days (generally weekends April–Oct) when the fountains blast and the price is €8.

The Le Passeport one-day combo-ticket covers all three sections. It costs €18, or €25 on Fountain Spectacle days. The handy Paris Museum Pass covers the Château and the Trianon/Domaine area (a €25 value), but you'll have to buy an additional ticket for any Fountain Spectacles.

Hours: The **Château** is open Tue–Sun April–Oct 9:00–18:30, Nov–March 9:00–17:30, closed Mon year-round.

The **Trianon Palaces and Domaine de Marie-Antoinette** are open Tue–Sun April–Oct 12:00–18:30, Nov–March 12:00–17:30, closed Mon year-round (off-season only the two Trianon Palaces are open, not the Hamlet or other outlying buildings).

The **Gardens** are open April–Oct daily 9:00–20:30; Nov–March Tue–Sun 8:00–18:00, closed Mon.

Last entry to all of these areas is 30 minutes before closing.

Crowd-Beating Strategies: Versailles is a zoo May–Sept 10:00–13:00, with especially big crowds all day Tue and Sun. Lines to buy tickets and go through security are long, and the Château is a slow shuffle of shoulder-to-shoulder tourists.

You can skip the ticket-buying line by using a Paris Museum Pass or Le Passeport, by buying tickets in advance, or by booking a guided tour. Everyone—including advance ticket and passholders—must wait in line to go through security (longest lines 10:00–12:00).

To avoid the long lines at the Château box office (to the left as you face the palace), buy tickets in advance at the Versailles city TI. They're also available at any Paris FNAC department store, or online at www.chateauversailles.fr (print out your pass/ticket or pick it up near the entrance). If you do wait to buy tickets at the Château, walk straight to the back of the box office to use the ticket machines (cash only).

For fewer crowds, arrive by 9:00 (when the palace opens), and tour the Château first, then the Gardens. If you arrive later, tour the Gardens first, then visit the Château after 13:00 when crowds dissipate.

Here's how I'd spend the day at Versailles: Leave Paris by 8:00 to beat the crowds. Tour the Château, then break for lunch in the Gardens. Spend the afternoon touring the Gardens and the Trianon/Domaine. Have dinner in Versailles town, then head back to Paris.

Pickpockets: Assume pickpockets are working the packed-in tourist crowds.

Getting There: The town of Versailles is 30 minutes southwest of Paris. Take the RER-C train (4/hour, 30–40 minutes one-way, €6.20 round-trip) from any of these Paris RER stops: Gare d'Austerlitz, St. Michel, Musée d'Orsay, Invalides, Pont de l'Alma, and Champ de Mars. Scan the list of departing trains. Any train whose name starts with a V (e.g., "Vick") goes to Versailles; don't board other trains. Get off at the last stop (Versailles R.G., or "Rive Gauche"). Exit through the turnstiles by inserting your ticket. To reach the palace, turn right out of the train station, then left at the first boulevard, and walk 10 minutes. To return to Paris, all trains serve all downtown Paris RER stops on the C line. Taxis for the 30-minute ride (without traffic) cost about €55.

Information: Tel. 01 30 83 78 00. The excellent website has the latest changes and calendar of special events—www.chateauversailles.fr. The uncrowded and helpful Versailles city TI (daily April–Sept 9:00–19:00, Oct–March 9:00–18:00, tel. 01 39 24 88 88) is in town on your walk from the RER station to the palace—it's just past the Pullman Hôtel. The Château's information office (long lines) is on the left side of the courtyard as you face the Château (toll tel. 08 10 81 16 14).

Guided Tours: Ninety-minute English tours of the Château often sell out; book immediately upon arrival at the guided-tours office in the Château courtyard, just to the right as you approach the palace (€14.50, or €7.50 if you already have Château admission or pass).

Audioguides: A free audioguide to the Château is included in admission. Other podcasts and digital tours are available in the "multimedia" section at www.chateauversailles.fr. A free Rick Steves audio tour is

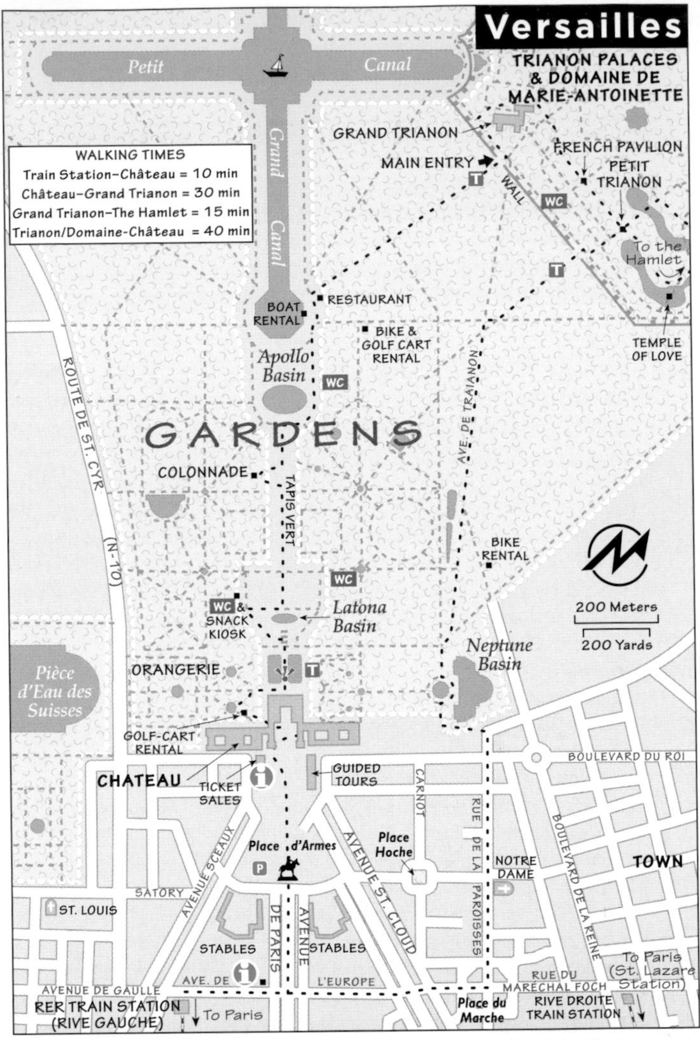

Versailles
TRIANON PALACES & DOMAINE DE MARIE-ANTOINETTE
Petit
Canal
Grand
Canal
WALKING TIMES
Train Station–Château = 10 min
Château–Grand Trianon = 30 min
Grand Trianon–The Hamlet = 15 min
Trianon/Domaine-Château = 40 min
GRAND TRIANON
MAIN ENTRY
WALL
WC
FRENCH PAVILION
PETIT TRIANON
To the Hamlet
TEMPLE OF LOVE
RESTAURANT
BOAT RENTAL
BIKE & GOLF CART RENTAL
Apollo Basin
AVE. DE TRAIANON
ROUTE DE ST. CYR
(N-10)
GARDENS
COLONNADE
TAPIS VERT
BIKE RENTAL
200 Meters
200 Yards
WC & SNACK KIOSK
Latona Basin
Neptune Basin
ORANGERIE
Pièce d'Eau des Suisses
GOLF-CART RENTAL
CHATEAU
TICKET SALES
GUIDED TOURS
BOULEVARD DU ROI
CARNOT
RUE DE LA PAROISSES
BOULEVARD DE LA REINE
Place d'Armes
Place Hoche
AVENUE SCEAUX
AVENUE ST. CLOUD
NOTRE DAME
TOWN
SATORY
ST. LOUIS
DE PARIS
AVENUE
STABLES
STABLES
AVE. DE
L'EUROPE
AVENUE DE GAULLE
RER TRAIN STATION (RIVE GAUCHE)
To Paris
RUE DU MARÉCHAL FOCH
To Paris (St. Lazare Station)
Place du Marche
RIVE DROITE TRAIN STATION

available on iTunes (search for "Rick Steves Audio Tours") or at www.ricksteves.com.

Length of This Day Trip: With the usual lines, allow 1.5 hours each for the Château, the Gardens, and the Trianon/Domaine. Add another two hours for round-trip transit, plus another hour for lunch...and, at around eight hours, Versailles is a full day trip from Paris.

Baggage Check: To enter the Château and the two Trianons, you must use the free baggage check for large bags.

Services: Reminiscent of the days when dukes urinated behind the potted palm trees, WCs at the Château are few and far between. There are WCs immediately upon entering the Château (Entrance H); near the Grand Café d'Orléans; in the Gardens near the Latona Basin; at the Grand Canal; in the Grand Trianon and Petit Trianon; and several others.

Cuisine Art: The Grand Café d'Orléans, to the left of the Château's entrance, has a restaurant (€13 salads, €20 *plats*) and a take-out bar (€5 sandwiches, great for picnicking in the Gardens). In the Gardens, you'll find several restaurants, cafés, and snack stands. Most are clustered near the Latona Fountain (less crowded) and the Grand Canal (more crowds and more choices, including two restaurants).

In the town, restaurants are on the street to the right (as you face the Château). A handy McDonald's (with WC) is immediately across from the train station (Internet café next door). Several places line rue de Satory between the station and the palace. The town center has many colorful eateries near lively place du Marché Notre-Dame, including traditional crêpes at the friendly a la Côte Bretonne (€4–10 crêpes, Tue–Sun 12:00–14:30 & 19:00–22:30, closed Mon, rue des Deux Portes 12, tel. 01 39 51 18 24).

Photography: Allowed, but no flash indoors.

Fountain Spectacles in the Gardens: On spring and summer weekends, loud classical music accompanies impressive fountain displays. The fountains run April–Oct Sat–Sun 11:00–12:00 & 15:30–17:30, (finale 17:20–17:30). They also run some Tue late May–late June 11:00–12:00 & 14:30–16:00. On these spray days, the Gardens cost €8. Also, elaborate sound-and-light displays are staged Saturday nights June–Aug at 21:00 (€21)—see calendar at www.chateauversailles.fr.

Starring: Luxurious palaces, endless gardens, Louis XIV, Marie-Antoinette, and the *ancien régime*.

THE TOUR BEGINS

► *Stand in the huge courtyard and face the palace, or Château. The ticket-buying office is to the left. The entrance to the Château (once you have your ticket or pass) is through the modern concrete-and-glass security checkpoint, marked Entrance A.*

On this self-guided tour, we'll see the Château, the landscaped Gardens in the "backyard," and the Trianon Palaces and Domaine de Marie-Antoinette, located at the far end of the Gardens.

Exterior—The Original Château and the Courtyard

The section of the palace with the clock is the original château, once a small hunting lodge where little Louis XIV spent his happiest boyhood years. Naturally, the Sun King's private bedroom (the three arched windows beneath the clock) faced the rising sun. The palace and grounds are laid out on an east–west axis.

Once king, Louis XIV expanded the lodge by attaching wings, creating the present U-shape. Later, the long north and south wings were built. The total cost of the project has been estimated at half of France's entire GNP for one year.

Think how busy this courtyard must have been 300 years ago. As many as 5,000 nobles were here at any one time, each with an entourage. They'd buzz from games to parties to amorous rendezvous in sedan-chair taxis. Servants ran about delivering secret messages and roast legs of lamb. Horse-drawn carriages arrived at the fancy gate with their finely dressed passengers, having driven up the broad boulevard that ran

Entrance A—security checkpoint

Original Château and courtyard

We Three Kings

Versailles was the residence of the king and the seat of France's government for a hundred years. With 18 million people united under one king (England had only 5.5 million), a booming economy, and a powerful military, France was Europe's number-one power. Versailles was the cultural heartbeat of Europe. Everyone learned French. French taste in clothes, hairstyles, table manners, theater, music, art, and kissing spread across the Continent.

Three kings lived in Versailles during its century of glory:

Louis XIV (reigned 1643–1715), Europe's greatest king, built Versailles and established French dominance.

Louis XV (r. 1715–1774) was his great grandson. (Louis XIV had reigned for 72 years, outliving several heirs.) Louis XV carried on the tradition and policies, but without the Sun King's flair. France's power abroad was weakening, and there were rumblings of rebellion from within.

Louis XVI (r. 1774–1792)—a shy, meek bookworm—inherited a nation in crisis. He married a sweet girl from the Austrian royal family, Marie-Antoinette, and together they retreated into the idyllic gardens of Versailles while Revolutionary fires smoldered.

directly from Paris. Incredible as it seems, both the grounds and most of the palace were public territory, where even the lowliest peasants could come to gawk. Then, as now, there were hordes of tourists, pickpockets, palace workers, and men selling wind-up children's toys.

▶ *After passing through security at Entrance A, you spill out into the open-air courtyard inside the golden Royal Gate. Enter the Château at Entrance H—the State Apartments. Once inside, there's an info desk (get a free map), WCs, and free audioguides. Glance through a doorway at the impressive Royal Chapel, which we'll see again upstairs.*

Just follow the flow of crowds through a number of rooms (the route and exhibits change frequently). Climb the stairs and pass through more exhibits. Finally, you reach a palatial golden-brown room, with a doorway that overlooks the Royal Chapel.

Royal Chapel

Dut-dutta-dah! Every morning at 10:00, the musicians struck up the music, these big golden doors opened, and Louis XIV and his family stepped onto the balcony to attend Mass. While Louis looked down on the golden altar, the lowly nobles on the ground floor knelt with their backs to the altar and looked up—worshipping Louis worshipping God. Important religious ceremonies took place here, including the marriage of young Louis XVI to Marie-Antoinette.

In the vast pagan "temple" that is Versailles—built to glorify one man, Louis XIV—this Royal Chapel is a paltry tip of the hat to that "other" god... the Christian one.

► *Enter the next room, an even more sumptuous space with a fireplace and a colorful painting on the ceiling.*

Royal Chapel

Versailles Château— Ground Floor & Entrances

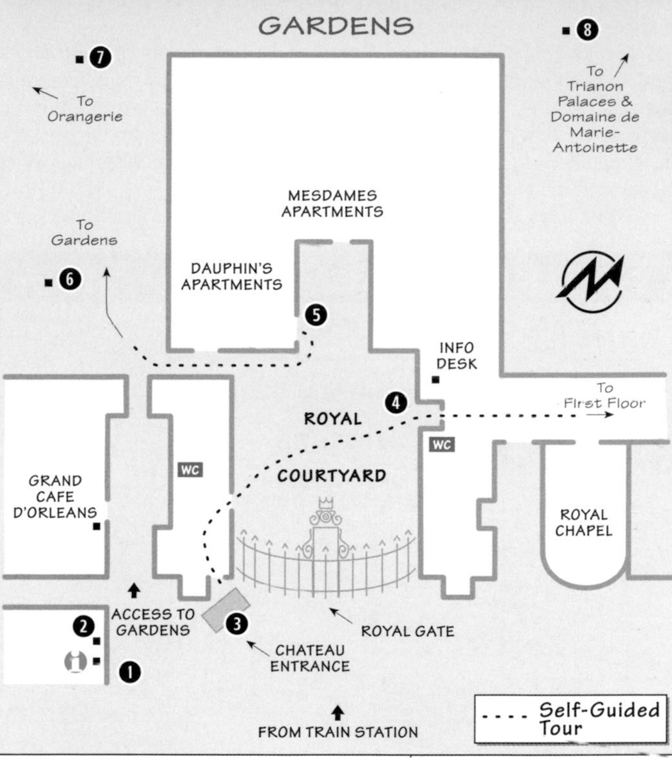

1. Chateau Ticket & Pass Sales
2. Guided Tour Reservations & Departure Point
3. Entrance A
4. Entrance H
5. Exit from State Apartments
6. Fountain Spectacles Tickets (weekends only)
7. Golf-Cart Rental
8. Petit Train (Tram)

Hercules Drawing Room

Pleasure ruled. The main suppers, balls, and receptions were held in this room. Picture elegant partygoers in fine silks, wigs, rouge, lipstick, and fake moles (and that's just the men), as they dance to the strains of a string quartet.

On the wall opposite the fireplace is an appropriate painting showing Christ in the middle of a Venetian party. The work by Paolo Veronese was one of Louis XIV's favorites, so they decorated the room around it. Stand by the fireplace for the full effect: The room's columns, arches, and frieze match the height and style of Veronese's painted architecture, which makes the painting an extension of the room.

The ceiling painting creates the effect of a sunroof opening up to

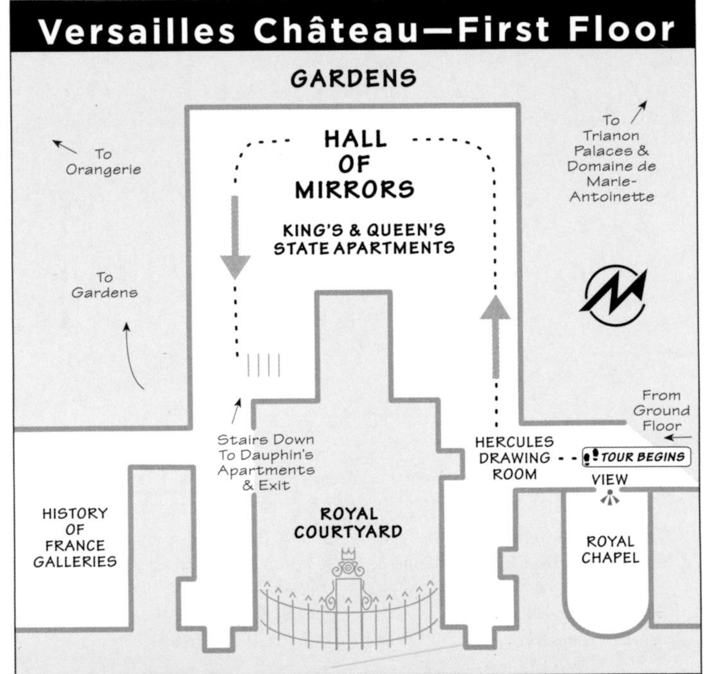

Louis XIV—The Sun King

Louis XIV, age 63, by Hyacinth Rigaud

Louis XIV was a true Renaissance man, a century after the Renaissance: athletic, good-looking, a musician, dancer, horseman, statesman, art-lover, lover. He was a good listener who could put even commoners at ease.

Louis had grown up in the previous royal residence—the Louvre in Paris. When he became king, he moved the government to the forests of Versailles, where he'd hunted as a kid. There, he could concentrate power around himself. He invited France's nobles—who in other countries were the center of power—to live at Versailles. They became virtual slaves of pleasure, dependent on Louis' generosity, while he made the important decisions.

Louis called himself the Sun King because he gave life and warmth to all he touched. He was also thought of as Apollo, the Greek god of the sun. Versailles became the personal temple of this god on earth, decorated with statues and symbols of Apollo, the sun, and Louis XIV himself.

For 70 years he was the perfect embodiment of the absolute monarch. He summed it up best himself with his famous rhyme—*"L'état, c'est moi!"* (lay-tah say-mwah): "The state, that's me!"

heaven. Hercules (with his club) hurries up to heaven on a chariot, late for his wedding to the king of the gods' daughter. The scene echoes real life—Louis XIV built the room for his own daughter's wedding reception.

► *From here on it's a one-way tour—getting lost is not allowed. Follow the crowds into the small green room with a ceiling painting showing a goddess in pink showering riches on invited guests. The names of the rooms generally come from the paintings on the ceilings.*

Salon of Abundance

If the party in the Hercules Room got too intense, you could always step in here for some refreshments. Silver trays were loaded up with liqueurs, exotic stimulants (coffee), juice, chocolates, and, on really special occasions, three-bean salad.

Louis XIV was a gracious host who enjoyed letting his hair down at night. If he took a liking to you, he might sneak you through those doors there (in the middle of the wall) and into his own private study, where he'd show off his collection of dishes, medals, jewels, or...the *Mona Lisa,* which hung on his wall.

Venus Room

Love ruled at Versailles. In this room, couples would cavort beneath the goddess of love, floating on the ceiling. Venus sends down a canopy of golden garlands to ensnare mortals in delicious *amour.* Notice how a painted garland goes "out" the bottom of the central painting, becomes a golden garland held by a satyr, transforms into a gilded wood garland, and then turns back into a painting again. Baroque artists loved to mix their media to fool the eye.

Don't let the statue of a confident Louis XIV as a Roman emperor fool you. He started out as a poor little rich kid with a chip on his shoulder. The French *parlements* treated little Louis and his mother as virtual prisoners in their home, the Royal Palace in Paris (today's Louvre). There they eked by with bland meals, hand-me-down leotards, and pointed shoes. After Louis XIV attained power, he made Versailles a pleasure palace—his way of saying that "Living well is the best revenge."

Hercules among the gods

Venus Room ceiling painting

Diana Room

Here in the billiards room, Louis and his men played on a table that stood in the center of the room, while ladies sat surrounding them on Persian-carpet cushions, and music wafted in from next door. Louis was a good pool player, a sore loser, and a king—thus, he rarely lost.

The famous bust of Louis by Giovanni Lorenzo Bernini (in the center) shows a handsome, dashing, 27-year-old playboy-king. His gaze is steady amid his windblown cloak and hair. Young Louis loved life. He hunted animals by day (notice Diana the Huntress, with her bow, on the ceiling) and chased beautiful women at night.

Games were actually an important part of Louis' political strategy, known as "the domestication of the nobility." By distracting the nobles with the pleasures of courtly life, he was free to run the government his way. Gambling was popular (especially a blackjack-type card game), and Louis lent money to the losers, making them even more indebted to him. The good life was an addiction, and Louis kept the medicine cabinet well-stocked.

As you move into the next room, notice the fat walls that hid thin servants, who were to be at their master's constant call—but out of sight when not needed.

Mars Room

This red room, home to Louis' Swiss bodyguards, has a military flair. On the ceiling there's Mars, the Greek god of war, in a chariot pulled by wolves. As you wander, remember that the carpets, mirrors, furniture, and tapestries we see today are (generally) not original, but are from the same period.

Mercury Room

Louis' life was a work of art. Everything he did was a public event designed to show his subjects how it should be done. This room may have served as Louis' official (not actual) bedroom, where the Sun King would ritually rise each morning to warm his subjects.

From a canopied bed (like this 18th-century one), Louis would get up, dress, and take a seat for morning prayer. Meanwhile, the nobles would stand behind a balustrade, in awe of his piety, nobility, and clean socks. At breakfast they murmured with delight as he deftly decapitated his boiled egg with a knife. And when Louis went to bed at night, the dukes and

Venus Room—Louis XIV as emperor

Mercury Room—the king's official bedroom

barons would fight over who got to hold the candle while he slipped into his royal jammies. Bedtime, wakeup, and meals were all public rituals.

Apollo Room

This was the grand throne room. Louis held court from a 10-foot-tall, silver-and-gold, canopied throne on a raised platform placed in the center of the room.

Everything in here reminds us of Louis XIV's glory. On the ceiling the sun god Apollo (representing Louis) drives his chariot, dragging the sun across the heavens to warm the four corners of the world—including good ol' America, symbolized by an Indian maiden with a crocodile.

The famous portrait by Hyacinthe Rigaud over the fireplace gives a more human look at Louis XIV, age 63. He's shown in a dancer's pose, displaying the legs that made him one of the all-time dancing fools of kingery. At night they often held parties in this room, actually dancing around the throne. Louis had more than 300 wigs like this one. The fashion sprouted all over Europe, even spreading to the American colonies.

Louis XIV may have been treated like a god, but his subjects adored him as a symbol of everything a man could be, the fullest expression of the Renaissance Man.

► *Continue into the final room of the King's Wing.*

The War Room

"Louis Quatorze was addicted to wars," and the room depicts his victories over the rest of Europe—in marble, gilding, stucco, and paint. On the ceiling, Lady France hurls down thunderbolts at her enemies. The stucco relief on the wall shows Louis XIV on horseback, triumphing over his fallen enemies. But Louis' greatest triumph may be the next room, the one that everybody wrote home about.

The Hall of Mirrors

No one had ever seen anything like this hall when it was opened. Mirrors were still a great luxury at the time, and the number and size of these monsters was astounding. The hall is nearly 250 feet long. There are 17 arched mirrors, matched by 17 windows letting in that breathtaking view of the Gardens. Lining the hall are 24 gilded candelabra, eight busts of Roman emperors, and eight classical-style statues (seven of them ancient). The ceiling shows Louis in the central panel doing what he did best—triumphing.

Imagine this place lit by the flames of thousands of candles, filled with ambassadors, nobles, and guests dressed in silks and powdered wigs. At the far end of the room sits the king, on the canopied throne moved in temporarily from the Apollo Room. Servants glide by with silver trays of hors d'oeuvres, and an orchestra fuels the festivities. The mirrors reflect an age when beautiful people loved to look at themselves. It was no longer a sin to be proud of good looks or to enjoy the good things in life: laughing, dancing, eating, drinking, flirting, and watching the sun set into the distant canal.

From the center of the hall you can fully appreciate the epic scale of Versailles. The huge palace (by architect Louis Le Vau), the fantasy interior (by Charles Le Brun), and the endless Gardens (by André Le Nôtre) made Versailles *le* best. In 1919, Germany and the Allies signed the Treaty of Versailles, ending World War I (and, some say, starting World War II) right here, in the Hall of Mirrors.

The War Room—Louis triumphant

The Hall of Mirrors—chandeliered grandeur

► *From the Hall of Mirrors, a short detour to the left takes you to the center of the palace...*

King's Bedroom and Council Rooms

Pass through a first large room to find Louis XIV's bedroom. With an impressive bed and balustrade, it's elaborately decorated. The decor changed with the season.

Look out the window and notice how this small room is at the exact center of the immense horseshoe-shaped building, overlooking the main courtyard and—naturally—facing the rising sun in the east. It symbolized the exact center of power in France. Imagine the humiliation on that day in 1789 when Louis' great-great-great-grandson, Louis XVI, was forced to stand here and acknowledge the angry crowds that filled the square demanding the end of the divine monarchy.

► *Return to the Hall of Mirrors. At the far end is the...*

Peace Room

By the end of the Sun King's long life, he was tired of fighting. In this sequel to the War Room, peace is granted to Europe as cupids play with the discarded cannons, and swords are transformed into violins. Louis XIV advised his great-grandson—the future Louis XV—to "be a peaceful king." The oval painting above the fireplace shows 19-year-old Louis XV, with his wife and twins, bestowing an olive branch on Europe.

► *The Peace Room marks the beginning of the queen's half of the palace. Enter the first room of the Queen's Wing, with its canopied bed.*

The Queen's Bedchamber

It was here that the queen rendezvoused with her husband. Two queens died here, and this is where 19 princes were born. Royal babies were delivered in public to prove their blue-bloodedness. (The large canopied bed is a reconstruction.)

True, Louis XIV was not the most faithful husband. The Sun King warmed more than one bed, for he was above the rules of mere mortals. Adultery became acceptable—even fashionable—in court circles. Some of Louis XIV's (and XV's) mistresses became more famous and powerful than their queens. But Louis XIV made a point of sleeping with the queen as often as possible—the secret-looking door on the left side of the bed led straight to his rooms.

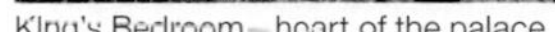
King's Bedroom—heart of the palace

Napoleon—revolutionary with a crown

This room looks just like it did in the days of the final queen, Marie-Antoinette, who substantially redecorated the entire wing. That's her bust over the fireplace, and the double eagle of her native Austria in the corners. The big mahogany chest to the left of the bed held her jewels.

Salon of the Nobles

Here, in this mint-green room, the wife of Louis XV and her circle of friends met, under paintings by Boucher—popular with the queen for their pink-cheeked Rococo exuberance. Discussions ranged from politics to gossip, food to literature, fashion to philosophy. All three of Versailles' rulers considered themselves enlightened monarchs who promoted the arts and new ideas. Louis XIV laughed at the anti-authoritarian plays of Molière, and Louis XV gave free room and board here to the political radical Voltaire. Ironically, these discussions planted the seeds of liberal thought that would grow into the Revolution.

Queen's Antechamber (Grand Couvert)

The royal family dined here publicly, while servants and nobles fluttered around them, admired their table manners, and laughed at the king's jokes like courtly Paul Shaffers. A typical dinner consisted of four different soups, two whole birds stuffed with truffles, mutton, ham slices, fruit, pastries, compotes, and preserves.

The central portrait is of luxury-loving, "let-them-eat-cake" Marie-Antoinette, who became a symbol of decadence to the peasants. The portrait at the far end is a public-relations attempt to soften her image by showing her with three of her children.

Queen's Guard Room

On October 5, 1789, a mob of Revolutionaries stormed the palace. They were fed up with the ruling class leading a life of luxury in the countryside while they were starving in the grimy streets of Paris.

King Louis XVI and his queen Marie-Antoinette locked themselves in. The Revolutionaries burst into this room where Marie-Antoinette was hiding, overcame her bodyguards, ransacked the palace, and dragged her off with her husband. (Some claim that, as they carried her away, she sang, "Louis, Louis, oh-oh...we gotta go now.") Eventually, the king and queen were brought to the place de la Concorde in Paris, where they knelt under the guillotine and were made a foot shorter at the top.

Coronation Room

No sooner did the French throw out a king than they got an emperor. The Revolution established a shaky democracy, but it was usurped by the upstart general Napoleon Bonaparte, who soon conquered Europe. The huge canvas on the left-hand wall (a copy of the Louvre's version) captures Napoleon's "crowning" moment—making himself and his kneeling wife, Josephine, emperor and empress.

► *This ends our tour of the Château, but there is more—the History of France rooms (on this floor) and the modestly furnished Dauphin's and Mesdames Apartments (downstairs).*

When you're ready to exit, stairs lead from the Coronation Room down to the ground floor. Exit the palace into the central courtyard. From there, follow signs to the Gardens (les Jardins), located behind the Château.

Now might be a good time to break for lunch. Then explore the Gardens.

THE GARDENS

Controlling Nature

Louis XIV was a divine-right ruler. One way he proved it was by controlling nature like a god. These lavish grounds—elaborately planned, pruned, and decorated—showed everyone that Louis was in total command.

▶ *Entering the Gardens, go to the far left to reach the stone railing which overlooks...*

The Orangerie

The warmth from the Sun King was so great that he could even grow orange trees in chilly France. Louis XIV had a thousand of these to amaze his visitors. In winter they were kept in the greenhouses (beneath your feet) that surround the courtyard. On sunny days, they were wheeled out in their silver planters and scattered around the grounds.

▶ *Make an about-face and walk back toward the palace. Sit on the top stairs and look away from the palace.*

View Down the Royal Drive

This, to me, is the most stunning spot in all of Versailles. With the palace behind you, it seems as if the grounds stretch out forever. Versailles was laid out along an eight-mile axis that included the grounds, the palace, and the town of Versailles itself, one of the first instances of urban planning since Roman times and a model for future capitals, such as Washington, D.C., and Brasilia.

Looking down the Royal Drive, you see the round Apollo fountain far in the distance. Just beyond that is the Grand Canal. The groves on either

The Orangerie—gardens and greenhouses

Latona Basin—violators will be toad

View down the Royal Drive—eight-mile axis

side of the Royal Drive were planted with trees from all over, laid out in an elaborate grid, and dotted with statues and fountains. Of the original 1,500 fountains, 300 remain.

► *Stroll down the steps to get a good look at the frogs and lizards that fill the round...*

Latona Basin

Atop the fountain stands Apollo (the sun god) as a child, with his sister and mom, Latona. Latona, an unwed mother, was insulted by the local peasants, so Zeus swooped down and turned them into toads and newts.

► *As you walk down past the basin toward the Royal Drive, you'll pass by "ancient" statues done by 17th-century French sculptors. The Colonnade is hidden in the woods on the left-hand side of the Royal Drive, about three-fourths of the way to the Apollo Basin (you'll spot it off the main path through an opening).*

Getting Around the Gardens

On Foot: It's a 40-minute walk (plus sightseeing) from the palace, down to the Grand Canal, past the two Trianon palaces, to the Hamlet at the far end of Domaine de Marie-Antoinette.

By Bike: There's a bike rental station by the Grand Canal (€6.50/hour). You can't take your bike inside the grounds of the Trianon/Domaine, but you can park it outside an entrance.

By *Petit Train:* The fast-looking, slow-moving tram travels from the Château, with stops at the Grand Canal, and at the Grand and Petit Trianon entrance points to the Trianon/Domaine (€7 day pass, €3.50 single trip).

By Golf Cart: This makes for a fun drive through the Gardens, but you can't take it inside the Trainon/Domaine. You can't diverge from the prescribed route or the cart shuts off automatically (€30/hour, steep late fees, rent at Château or Grand Canal).

The Colonnade

Versailles had no prestigious ancient ruins, so the king built this prefab Roman ruin—a 100-foot circle of 64 marble columns supporting arches. Nobles could picnic in the shade, watching the birdbath fountains spout, listening to a string quartet, and pretending they were enlightened citizens of the ancient world.

The Apollo Basin

The fountains of Versailles were its most famous attraction, and this one—of the sun god—was the centerpiece. Apollo, in his sunny chariot, starts his journey across the sky. The horses are half-submerged, giving the impression, when the fountains play, of the sun rising out of the mists of dawn.

All of Versailles' fountains are gravity-powered. They work on the same principle as blocking a hose with your finger to make it squirt. Underground streams (pumped into Versailles by Seine River pressure) feed into smaller pipes at the fountains, which shoot the water high into the air.

Looking back at the palace from here, realize that the distance you just walked is only a fraction of this vast complex of buildings, gardens, and waterways. Be glad you don't have to mow the lawn.

The Apollo Basin—sun god rises from the mist

The Grand Canal

In an era before virtual reality, this was the next best thing to an actual trip to Venice. Imported Venetian gondoliers would pole along the waters accompanied by barges with orchestras playing "O Sole Mio." The canal is one mile from end to end.

The Grand Canal hosts eateries, rental boats, bike and golf-cart rentals, and a *Petit Train* tram stop.

► *The area called the Trianon Palaces and Domaine de Marie-Antoinette is a 10-minute walk from the Grand Canal. There are three entrances to the walled enclosure: near the Grand Trianon palace (where we'll enter), near the Petit Trianon palace, or near the Hamlet.*

To get to the Grand Trianon, start walking up the Grand Canal (✪ see the map on page 130). About 70 yards past the boat rental (and immediately past the restaurant), veer right. You'll find twin dirt paths flanking a lo-o-ong strip of lawn. This leads uphill 500 yards to the Grand Trianon.

THE TRIANON PALACES AND DOMAINE DE MARIE-ANTOINETTE

Versailles began as an escape from the pressures of kingship. But in a short time, the Château had become as stressful as Paris ever was—sniping politics, strict etiquette, and 24/7 scrutiny. Louis XIV and his successors needed an escape from their escape. They built this fantasy world

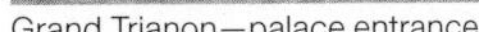

Grand Trianon—palace entrance

Louis XIV's bedroom—wake up with the king

of palaces and pleasure gardens and retreated further and further from everyday life.

Grand Trianon

Delicate, pink, and set amid gardens, the Grand Trianon was the perfect summer getaway. Louis XIV built it for his mistress. They spent a couple of nights a week here, near the tiny peasant village of Trianon—hence the name.

Inside, the rooms are a complex overlay of furnishings from many different kings, dauphins, and nobles that have lived here over the centuries. Louis XIV alone had three different bedrooms. Concentrate on the illustrious time of Louis XIV (1688–1715) and Napoleon Bonaparte (1810–1814).

The spacious Mirror Room (Room 3) has the original white walls and mirrors of Louis XIV, and the Empire-style furniture of Napoleon (unornamented, high-polished wood, with classical motifs). In Louis XIV's Bedchamber (Room 4), imagine waking up in this big bed with your lover,

Grand Trianon's Peristyle

Grand Trianon—gardens in back

throwing back the curtain, and looking out the windows at the gardens. Exit into the open-air colonnade (Peristyle) that connects the two wings and admire the gardens. The flowers were changed daily for the king's pleasure—for new color combinations and new "nasal cocktails."

French Pavilion

This small, white building with rooms fanning out from the center has big French doors to let in a cool breeze. Here Marie-Antoinette spent summer evenings with family and friends, listening to music or playing parlor games, exploring all avenues of *la douceur de vivre*—the sweetness of living.

Marie-Antoinette's Theater (Le Théâtre de la Reine)

Marie-Antoinette was an aspiring performer. In this plush, fully-functioning, 100-seat doll-house theater, she and her friends acted out plays for a select audience.

Belvedere, Rock, and Grotto

A pond graced with a tiny palace flanked by a fake mountain—how bucolic. The octagonal Belvedere palace is as much windows as it is walls. When the doors were open, it could serve as a gazebo for musicians, serenading nobles in this man-made alpine setting. To the right of the Belvedere (you'll have to find it) is the secret Grotto.

The Hamlet (Le Village du Hameau)

Continue frolicking along the paths till you spy a round, fanciful tower and a smattering of rustic, half-timbered buildings fronting a lake—the Hansel-and-Gretel-like hamlet. Marie-Antoinette longed for the simple life of a

French Pavilion

Belvedere—tiny palace above a pond

The Hamlet—Marie Antoinette's fantasy

peasant—not the hard labor of real peasants, who sweated and starved around her—but the fairytale world of simple country pleasures.

This was an actual working farm with a dairy (by the tower), a water mill, a pigeon coop (Le Colombier), and a menagerie where her servants kept cows, goats, and chickens. The Queen's House—two buildings connected by a wooden skywalk—was like any typical peasant farmhouse, with a billiard room, library, dining hall, and two living rooms.

Temple of Love

A circle of 12 white marble Corinthian columns supports a dome, decorating a path where lovers could stroll. It's a delightful monument to a society where the rich could afford that ultimate luxury, romantic love.

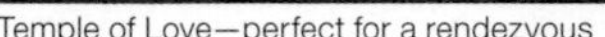

Temple of Love—perfect for a rendezvous

Petit Trianon—four-faced palace

Petit Trianon

Louis XV's first mistress, Madame de Pompadour, built the Petit Trianon ("Small Trianon"), and it later became home to his next mistress, Madame du Barry.

The gray, cubical building is a masterpiece of Neoclassical architecture. It has four distinct facades, each a perfect and harmonious combination of Greek-style columns, windows, and railings. You can tour the handsome interior. The Baroque WC was a head of its time.

When Louis XVI became king, he gave the building to his new bride, Marie-Antoinette. She made it her home and installed a carousel on the lawn outside. Here she played, while in the cafés of faraway Paris, revolutionaries plotted the end of the *ancien régime.*

▸ *The real world and the main Château are a 45-minute walk to the southeast. Or catch the Petit Train from here (€3.50 one-way, buy from driver).*

Sights

Paris is blessed with world-class museums and monuments—more than anyone could see in a single visit. To help you prioritize your limited time and money, I've chosen only the best of Paris' many sights—admittedly, a tough call. I've clustered them into walkable neighborhoods for more efficient sightseeing. In the Historic Core, for example, you could string together a number of great sights, from Notre-Dame to Ste. Chapelle to the Pont Neuf, in a single day of sightseeing. You'll find a full day's worth of sights on the Left Bank, near the Eiffel Tower, and more.

Note that some of Paris' biggest sights—the Louvre, the Eiffel Tower, and others—are described in much more detail in the individual walks and tours chapters. There you'll find self-guided tours, plus crucial info on how to avoid lines, save money, and get a decent bite to eat nearby. If there's more information on a sight elsewhere, it's marked with a ✪.

HISTORIC CORE OF PARIS: NOTRE-DAME, SAINTE-CHAPELLE, AND MORE

The Historic Core consists of the island in the center of Paris named Ile de la Cité, and spills onto the neighboring river banks. Here you'll find sights from Paris' 2,000-year history, with an emphasis on its medieval glory days. (Mo: Cité, Hôtel de Ville, or St. Michel.)

▲▲▲Notre-Dame Cathedral (Cathédrale Notre-Dame de Paris)

✪ See page 18 in the Historic Paris Walk chapter.

▲▲▲Sainte-Chapelle

✪ See page 33 in the Historic Paris Walk chapter.

▲Conciergerie

✪ See page 39 in the Historic Paris Walk chapter.

▲Deportation Memorial (Mémorial de la Déportation)

✪ See page 27 in the Historic Paris Walk chapter.

Paris Archaeological Crypt

Visit Roman ruins, trace the street plan of the medieval village, and see models of how early Paris grew. The ruins are a confusing mix of foundations from every time period. Press the buttons on the display cases to light up a particular section, such as the oldest rampart, a medieval hospital, or a Roman building with a heated floor. Worthwhile if you have a Museum Pass.

- *€4, covered by Museum Pass, Tue–Sun 10:00–18:00, closed Mon, enter 100 yards in front of Notre-Dame, tel. 01 55 42 50 10.*

▲Paris Plage (Beach)

This fanciful faux beach is assembled every summer along a two-mile stretch of the Right Bank of the Seine. They truck in 2,000 tons of sand, potted palm trees, lounge chairs, volleyball nets, prefab pools, and "beach cafés" for a drink. The Riviera it's not, but it's a fun place to stroll, play, and watch Parisians at play.

- *Free, mid-July–mid-Aug daily 7:00–24:00, between pont des Arts and pont de Sully.*

MAJOR MUSEUMS NEIGHBORHOOD

Paris' grandest park, the Tuileries Garden, links Paris' grandest museums. All these are less than a 20-minute walk apart. Key Métro stops are Palais Royal–Musée du Louvre, Concorde, and the RER-C stop called Musée d'Orsay.

▲▲▲Louvre (Musée du Louvre)

✪ See the Louvre Tour on page 45.

▲▲▲Orsay Museum (Musée d'Orsay)

✪ See the Orsay Museum Tour chapter on page 71.

▲▲Orangerie Museum (Musée de l'Orangerie)

Step out of the tree-lined, sun-dappled Impressionist painting that is the Tuileries Garden, and into the Orangerie (oh-rahn-zheh-ree), a little bijou of select works by Claude Monet and his contemporaries. Start with the museum's claim to fame: Monet's water lilies. These eight mammoth-scale paintings are displayed exactly as Monet intended them—surrounding you in oval-shaped rooms—so you feel as though you're immersed in his garden at Giverny.

Working from his home there, Monet built a special studio with skylights and wheeled easels to accommodate the canvases—1,950 square feet in all. Each canvas features a different part of the pond, painted from varying angles at distinct times of day—but the true subject of these works is the play of reflected light off the surface of the pond. The Monet rooms are considered the first art installation, and the blurry canvases signaled the abstract art to come.

Downstairs you'll see artists that bridge the Impressionist and Modernist worlds—Renoir, Cézanne, Utrillo, Matisse, and Picasso. Together they provide a snapshot of what was hot in the world of art collecting, circa 1920.

▸ *€7.50, more for temporary exhibitions, €13 combo-ticket with Orsay Museum, covered by Museum Pass. Open Wed–Mon 9:00–18:00, closed Tue. It's located in the Tuileries Garden near place de la Concorde, Mo: Concorde. Tel. 01 44 77 80 07, www.musee-orangerie.fr.*

Major Museums Neighborhood

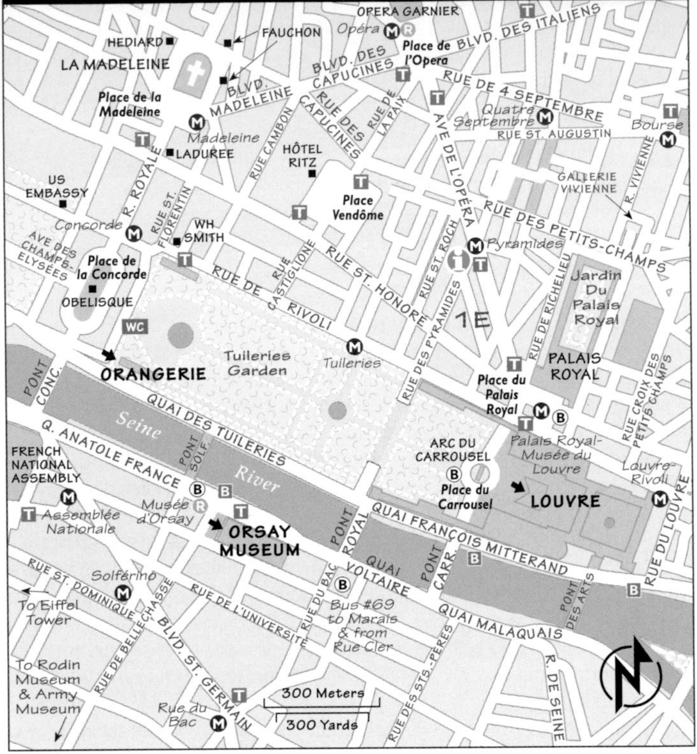

Palais Royal Courtyards

Just steps from noisy rue de Rivoli is this peaceful, perfectly Parisian scene—a courtyard of whimsical modern columns, flowers, and outdoor cafés. This is where in-the-know Parisians take a quiet break, walk their poodles and kids, or enjoy a rendezvous. Bring a picnic and create your own quiet break. At the far end, exit the courtyard to find early-1900s shopping arcades, which still bustle with shoppers.

► *Free and always open. It's directly north of the Louvre on rue de Rivoli (Mo: Palais Royal–Musée du Louvre).*

EIFFEL TOWER AND NEARBY

From the Eiffel Tower to the golden dome of Invalides, this area has fine museums and the refined ambience of the rue Cler. A number of Métro stops serve this area, but you may find the RER more useful.

▲▲▲Eiffel Tower (La Tour Eiffel)

✪ See the Eiffel Tower Tour chapter on page 101.

▲▲Rodin Museum (Musée Rodin)

This user-friendly museum is filled with passionate works by the greatest sculptor since Michelangelo. You'll see *The Kiss, The Thinker,* the *Burghers of Calais, The Gates of Hell,* and many more. However, some rooms may be closed until the museum's renovation is complete in 2014.

Auguste Rodin (1840–1917) sculpted human figures on an epic scale, revealing through the body their deepest thoughts and feelings. Like many of Michelangelo's unfinished works, Rodin's statues rise from the raw stone around them, driven by the life force. With missing limbs and scarred skin, these are prefab classics, making ugliness noble. Rodin's people are always moving restlessly. Even the famous *Thinker* is moving. While he's plopped down solidly, his mind is a million miles away.

Rodin worked with many materials—he chiseled marble (though not often), modeled clay, cast bronze, worked plaster, painted, and sketched. He often created different versions of the same subject in different media.

Rodin lived and worked in this mansion, renting rooms alongside Henri Matisse, the poet Rainer Maria Rilke (Rodin's secretary), and the dancer Isadora Duncan. The well-displayed exhibits trace Rodin's artistic development and explain how his bronze statues were cast. Learn about Rodin's tumultuous relationship with his apprentice and lover, Camille Claudel, and see some of her passionate works done in a Rodin-esque style. And stroll the leafy gardens, dappled with many of his greatest works.

► *€6, covered by Museum Pass, free on first Sun of the month, €12 combo-ticket with Orsay, €1 for gardens only. Open Tue–Sun 10:00–17:45,*

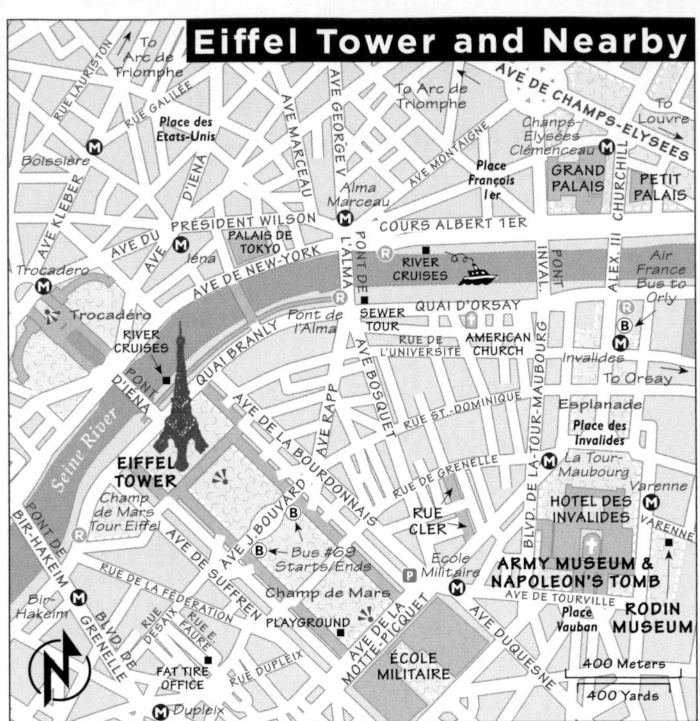

gardens close at 18:00, last entry 30 minutes before closing, closed Mon. It's near the golden dome of Invalides, 79 rue de Varenne, Mo: Varenne. Tel. 01 44 18 61 10, www.musee-rodin.fr.

▲▲Army Museum and Napoleon's Tomb (Musée de l'Armée)

The Hôtel des Invalides—a former veterans' hospital topped by a golden dome—houses Napoleon's over-the-top-ornate tomb, as well as Europe's greatest military museum. Visiting the Army Museum's different sections, you can watch the art of war unfold from stone axes to Axis powers.

At the center of the complex, Napoleon Bonaparte lies majestically dead inside several coffins under a grand dome—a goose-bumping pilgrimage for historians. Your visit continues through an impressive range of museums filled with medieval armor, cannons and muskets, Louis XIV-era uniforms and weapons, and Napoleon's horse—stuffed and mounted.

The best section is dedicated to the two World Wars. Walk chronologically through displays on the trench warfare of WWI, France's horrendous losses, the victory parades, and the humiliating Treaty of Versailles that led to WWII. The WWII rooms use black-and-white photos, maps, videos, and a few artifacts to trace Hitler's rise, the Blitzkrieg that overran France, the concentration camps, America's entry into the war, D-Day, the atomic bomb, and the eventual Allied victory. There's special insight into France's role (the French Resistance), and how it was Charles de Gaulle that actually won the war.

▸ *€9 covers all museums, covered by the Museum Pass, price drops to €7 an hour before closing time, audioguide €6.*

Open daily April–Sept 10:00–18:00, Sun until 18:30 and Tue until 21:00, July–Aug tomb stays open until 19:00; daily Oct–March 10:00–17:00, Sun until 17:30; last tickets sold 30 minutes before closing; Oct–June closed first Mon of every month.

The Hôtel des Invalides is at 129 rue de Grenelle; Mo: La Tour Maubourg, Varenne, or Invalides. Tel. 01 44 42 38 77 or toll 08 10 11 33 99, www.invalides.org.

▲Paris Sewer Tour (Les Egouts de Paris)

Discover what happens after you flush. This quick, interesting, and slightly stinky visit takes you along a few hundred yards of water tunnels in the world's first and longest underground sewer system. With good English information, you'll trace the sewer's evolution: from Roman times to medieval (washed straight into the river), to Victor Hugo's fictional hero Jean Valjean (who hid here in *Les Misérables*), to today's 1,500 miles of tunnels carrying 317 million gallons of water a day. The sight has WCs.

▸ *€4.30, covered by Museum Pass. Open Sat–Wed May–Sept 11:00–17:00, Oct–April 11:00–16:00, closed Thu–Fri. Located at the south end of pont de l'Alma, Mo: Alma-Marceau, RER: Pont de l'Alma. Tel. 01 53 68 27 81.*

▲▲Marmottan Museum (Musée Marmottan Monet)

This intimate, less-touristed mansion on the southwest fringe of urban Paris has the best collection of works by the father of Impressionism, Claude Monet (1840–1926). Fiercely independent and dedicated to his

Best Views Over the City of Light

Eiffel Tower: The ultimate. Period.

Arc de Triomphe: Best at night when the Champs-Elysées positively glitters.

Notre-Dame's Tower: You're right in the thick of it all, among the gargoyles.

Steps of Sacré-Cœur: Join the guitar-strumming partiers on Paris' only hilltop (free).

Galeries Lafayette or Printemps: Both department stores have a stunning overlook of the old Opéra district (free).

Montparnasse Tower: This solitary skyscraper's views are best by day.

Pompidou Center: Great views plus exciting modern art (free with Museum Pass).

Place du Trocadéro: It's at street level, but is *the* place to see the Eiffel Tower (free). The Café de l'Homme is great for a drink.

Bar at Hôtel Concorde-Lafayette: This otherwise unappealing hotel has a 33rd-floor bar with a stunning night-time panorama (free elevator but pricey drinks, 3 place du Général Koenig, Mo: Porte Maillot, tel. 01 40 68 50 68, www.concorde-lafayette.com).

craft, Monet gave courage to the other Impressionists in the face of harsh criticism.

Though the museum is not arranged chronologically, you can trace his life. You'll see black-and-white sketches from his youth, his discovery of open-air painting, and the canvas—*Impression: Sunrise*—that gave Impressionism its name. There are portraits of his wives and kids, and his well-known "series" paintings (done at different times of day) of London, Gare St. Lazare, and the Cathedral of Rouen. The museum's highlight is scenes from his garden at Giverny—the rose trellis, the Japanese bridge, and the larger-than-life water lilies.

In addition, the Marmottan features a world-class collection of works by Berthe Morisot and other Impressionists; an eclectic collection of non-

Monet objects (furniture, illuminated manuscript drawings); and temporary exhibits.

► *€9, not covered by Museum Pass. Open Tue 11:00–21:00, Wed–Sun 11:00–18:00, last entry 30 minutes before closing, closed Mon. Located at 2 rue Louis-Boilly, Mo: La Muette. Tel. 01 44 96 50 33, www.marmottan.com.*

LEFT BANK

The Left Bank is as much an attitude as an actual neighborhood. There are fewer busy boulevards, businessmen in suits, and modern buildings, and more quiet lanes, students, and intimate cafés. The sightseeing core stretches roughly from the Panthéon to St. Germain-des-Prés, and from the river to Luxembourg Garden. Lively nighttime hotspots include areas around St. Germain-des-Prés Church, rue de Buci, rue des Canettes (near St. Sulpice), and the Latin Quarter.

▲Latin Quarter (Quartier Latin)

This Left Bank neighborhood, just opposite Notre-Dame, was medieval Paris' university district, where scholars spoke Latin. It developed a reputation for artsy, bohemian character. Although still youthful and artsy, much of it has become a tourist ghetto filled with cheap North African eateries. The neighborhood's main boulevards (St. Michel and St. Germain) are lined with cafés—once the haunts of great poets and philosophers, and still popular today.

▲▲Cluny Museum (Musée National du Moyen Age)

This treasure trove of art from the Middle Ages *(Moyen Age)* fills old Roman baths. You'll see the baths' cavernous cool-down room, plus displays of fine medieval objects: stained glass, swords, jewels, and the decapitated heads of Notre-Dame statues (✪ see page 22).

The star here is the exquisite *Lady and the Unicorn* series of six tapestries: A delicate, as-medieval-as-can-be noble lady introduces a delighted unicorn to the senses of taste, hearing, sight, smell, and touch. The sixth is the most talked-about tapestry, called *A Mon Seul Désir* (To My Sole Desire). What *is* the lady's only desire? Is it that jewel box, or is it something—or someone—inside that tent? Middle Age Europe was awakening

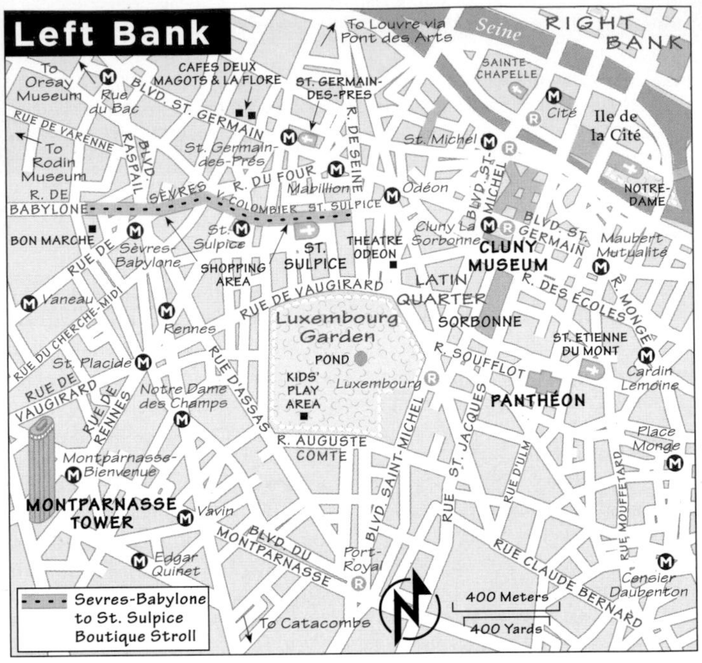

from a thousand-year slumber, Paris was emerging on the world stage, and the Renaissance was moving in like a warm front from Italy.

▸ *€8, free on first Sun of month, covered by Museum Pass. Open Wed–Mon 9:15–17:45, last entry at 17:15, closed Tue. Located at 6 place Paul Painlevé, Mo: Cluny-La Sorbonne. Tel. 01 53 73 78 16, www.musee-moyenage.fr.*

▲St. Sulpice Church and Organ Concert

Sitting amid a colorful neighborhood of boutiques and cafés, this big but unremarkable church has several delights inside. Three murals of fighting angels by Delacroix (in the first chapel on the right) were completed during his final years, while fighting illness. They sum up his long career, from meticulously drawn Renaissance roots to furious Romanticism to messy-paint proto-Impressionism.

The Egyptian-style obelisk (on the wall of the north transept) is used as a sundial. The sun shines into the church through a tiny hole opposite the obelisk (high up on the south wall) and strikes a mark on the obelisk that indicates the date. (The sundial was featured in the novel *The Da Vinci Code*—a fanciful book that St. Sulpice's caretakers disdain.)

The church's 7,000-pipe organ is famous, and St. Sulpice's 300-year tradition of great organists continues today. Notice the unmarked door next to the Delacroix chapel. On Sundays, just after noon, this door opens, and organ fans scurry like sixteenth notes up to the organ loft. There visitors can meet renowned organist Daniel Roth, and watch him up close as he operates five keyboards to play for the next Mass.

▸ *Free, open daily 7:30–19:30, Mo: St. Sulpice or Mabillon. For organ schedule and details, see www.stsulpice.com.*

▲Luxembourg Garden (Jardin du Luxembourg)

Slip into a green chair by the pond and take in the Impressionist scene around you—the radiant flower-beds, the old men playing chess, kids sailing toy boats... the joggers on cell phones. The 60-acre gardens are dotted with fountains and statues and anchored by the Renaissance-style Luxembourg Palace, where the French Senate meets. The brilliant flower beds are completely changed three times a year, and the boxed trees are brought out of the *orangerie* in May. Children enjoy pony rides and marionette shows (Les Guignols, or Punch and Judy). There's no better place to watch Parisians at play.

▸ *Open daily dawn until dusk, Mo: Odéon, RER: Luxembourg.*

▲Panthéon

This state-capitol-style Neoclassical monument celebrates France's illustrious history. Built to be a church, it was converted during the Revolution (1791) into a secular mausoleum honoring "the great men of the Fatherland."

Inside the vast building (36" by 280' by 270') are monuments tracing the triumphs of the French people. Foucault's pendulum (first placed here in 1851) still swings gracefully at the end of a 220-foot cable, demonstrating how the earth rotates beneath it. Downstairs in the crypt lie a pantheon of greats—the tombs of philosophers Rousseau and Voltaire, scientist Marie

Curie, writers Victor Hugo and Alexandre Dumas, and Louis Braille, who invented the script for the blind. You can climb 206 steps up the dome for fine views.

- *€8, covered by Museum Pass. Open daily 10:00–18:30 in summer, until 18:00 in winter, last entry 45 minutes before closing. Escorted dome visits leave hourly. Mo: Cardinal Lemoine. Tel. 01 44 32 18 00, www.monum.fr.*

St. Germain-des-Prés

This church, built in 1163, has a colorful interior reminding us that medieval churches were originally painted in bright colors. The surrounding area hops at night with venerable cafés, mimes, and scads of artists.

- *Free, daily 8:00–20:00, Mo: St. Germain-des-Prés.*

Montparnasse Tower (La Tour Montparnasse)

This ugly, out-of-place, 59-story superscraper has one virtue—its view. It's cheaper and easier to visit than the Eiffel Tower, and the view includes the Eiffel Tower... and you can't see the Montparnasse Tower at all. Sunset is great, but views are disappointing after dark. The 56th floor has a restaurant (reasonable for drinks or light lunch), dioramas identifying the monuments below, and a worthwhile 12-minute video. Then climb to the 59th-floor heli-pad—690 feet above Paris—and scan the city with the wind in your hair.

- *€11, not covered by Museum Pass. April–Sept daily 9:30–23:30, Oct–March daily 9:30–22:30, Fri–Sat until 23:00, last entry 30 minutes before closing. Enter on rue de l'Arrivée, Mo: Montparnasse-Bienvenüe (follow signs for La Tour). Tel. 01 45 38 52 56, www.tourmontparnasse56.com.*

▲Catacombs

Descend 60 feet below the street and walk a one-mile, one-hour route through tunnels containing the anonymous bones of six million permanent Parisians.

In 1786, a health-conscious city emptied the church cemeteries and moved the bones here, to former limestone quarries. The bones are stacked in piles five feet high and as much as 80 feet deep. Ignore the sign announcing, "Halt, this is the empire of the dead," and walk through passageways of skull-studded tibiae, past more cheery signs: "Happy is he who is forever faced with the hour of his death and prepares himself for the end every day." You emerge far from where you entered, with white-limestone-covered toes, telling everyone you've been underground gawking at bones. Note to wannabe Hamlets: An attendant checks your bag at the exit for stolen souvenirs.

▸ *€8, not covered by Museum Pass. Open Tue–Sun 10:00–17:00, last entry at 16:00, closed Mon. Located at 1 place Denfert-Rochereau, Mo: Denfert-Rochereau. You'll exit at 36 rue Remy Dumoncel; turn right and walk several blocks to either Mo: Alésia or Mouton Duvernet. Tel. 01 43 22 47 63.*

Expect a one-hour wait in line—arrive by 14:30 or risk not getting in. A flashlight is handy. Being under 6'2" is helpful.

CHAMPS-ELYSÉES AND NEARBY

This famous boulevard is Paris' backbone, stretching from the Arc de Triomphe downhill to place de la Concorde. The surrounding area features more broad boulevards lined with big, classy 19th-century buildings. These days, the boulevards are choked with cars, and the buildings house the glitzy businesses of globalized Paris.

▲▲Champs-Elysées

The Champs-Elysées is as international as it is Parisian, and a walk down the two-mile boulevard is a must.

In 1667, Louis XIV opened the first section of the street, and it soon became *the* place to cruise in your carriage. (It still is today.) By the 1920s, this boulevard was pure elegance—fancy residences, rich hotels, and cafés. Today it's home to big business, celebrity cafés, glitzy nightclubs, high-fashion shopping, and international people-watching. People gather here to celebrate Bastille Day (July 14), World Cup triumphs, the finale of the Tour de France, and the ends of wars.

Start at the Arc de Triomphe (Mo: Charles de Gaulle-Etoile) and head downhill on the left-hand side. The arrival of McDonald's (at #140) was an unthinkable horror, but these days dining *chez MacDo* has become typically Parisian, and this branch is the most profitable McDonald's in the world.

Fancy car showrooms abound, including Peugeot (#136) and Mercedes-Benz (#118). The Lido (#116) is Paris' largest burlesque-type cabaret (and a multiplex cinema). The flagship store of leather-bag makers

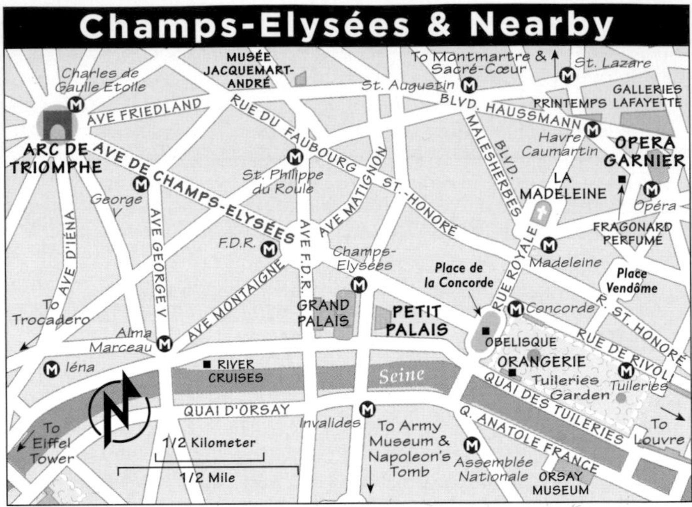

Louis Vuitton is at #101. Fouquet's café (across the street, #99), is a popular spot among French celebrities, especially movie stars—note the names in the sidewalk in front. Enter if you dare for an €8 espresso. Ladurée café (#75) is also classy but has a welcoming and affordable take-out bakery.

Continuing on, you pass international-brand stores, such as Sephora perfume, Virgin, Disney, the Gap, etc. You can end your walk at the round Rond Point intersection (Mo: Franklin D. Roosevelt) or continue to obelisk-studded place de la Concorde, Paris' largest square.

▲▲▲Arc de Triomphe

Napoleon built the magnificent Arc de Triomphe to commemorate his victory at the battle of Austerlitz. There's no triumphal arch bigger—165 feet high, 130 feet wide. The carvings show a toga-clad Napoleon (left pillar) and an excitable Lady Liberty leading the people (right).

Beneath the Arch is the Tomb of the Unknown Soldier where, every day at 18:30, the flame is rekindled and new flowers set in place. The foot of the arch is a stage on which the last two centuries of Parisian history have played out—from the funeral of Napoleon to the goose-stepping arrival of the Nazis to the triumphant return of Charles de Gaulle after the Allied liberation. Today, national parades start and end here with one minute of silence.

Enter and climb the 284 steps to the observation deck up top, with sweeping skyline panoramas. You're at the center of a grand axis of city planning, stretching from the Louvre, up the Champs-Elysées to the Arc de Triomphe, then continuing west to the huge rectangular, modern Grande Arche de la Défense.

Looking down you see 12 converging boulevards forming a star *(etoile)*. What a traffic mess! Or is it? Cars entering the circle have the right of way, blending in smoothly while others jockey to the perimeter to exit. Still, there are plenty of accidents, and insurance companies—tired of the disputes—routinely split the damages 50/50.

▸ *€9 to climb, free on first Sun of month Oct–March, covered by Museum Pass. Open daily April–Sept 10:00–23:00, Oct–March 10:00–22:30, last entry 30 minutes before closing. Use the underpass to reach the arch. Mo: Charles de Gaulle-Etoile. Tel. 01 55 37 73 77, www.arc-de-triomphe.monuments-nationaux.fr.*

▲Opéra Garnier

This grand theater (1875) of France's beautiful age—the *belle époque*—still anchors a neighborhood filled with Paris' most fashionable haunts.

The building is huge, though the auditorium itself seats only 2,000. There's a cavernous backstage to accommodate elaborate sets, as well as the extravagant lobbies out front. That's where the real show took place, between acts, when the elite of Paris—out to see and be seen—strutted their elegant stuff. The massive foundations straddle an underground lake, inspiring the mysterious world of the *Phantom of the Opera*.

Visitors can explore the lobbies, the grand marble staircase, and the Salon du Glacier, iced with decor typical of 1900. The small museum will interest opera buffs. The highlight of the visit is a view from the upper seats into the actual red-velvet performance hall. There you can see Marc Chagall's colorful ceiling (1964) playfully dancing around the eight-ton chandelier. (To go inside the hall, you must take a guided tour.)

These days, most opera is performed across town at the modern and functional Bastille Opera House. But the Garnier still hosts ballets and concerts, and attending a performance—dressed in the cleanest clothes you can find in your rucksack—can transport you back to the belle époque.

▸ *€9, not covered by Museum Pass. The opening hours are erratic due* *to performances and rehearsals, but generally daily 10:00–17:00, mid-July–Aug until 18:00. Located at 8 rue Scribe, Mo: Opéra. €12.50 English tours run daily during summer and off-season on weekends and Wed, usually at 11:30 and 14:30. Tel. 01 40 01 17 89 or 08 25 05 44 05.*

For performances (generally Oct–June), check the schedule and buy tickets at the box office; by phone at tel. 08 92 89 90 90 or (from the US) tel. 011 33 1 71 25 24 23; or online at www.operadeparis.fr.

Note: Near the Opéra are the Fragonard Perfume Museum (free, 9 rue Scribe, www.fragonard.com), the venerable Galeries Lafayette department store (40 Boulevard Haussmann), and the glitterati-flecked Café de la Paix (place de l'Opéra).

▲Petit Palais (and its Musée des Beaux-Arts)

This free museum displays a broad collection of second-choice paintings and sculpture from the 1600s to the 1900s.

Enter the museum, ask for a ticket to the permanent collection (free but required), and head toward the left wing, filled with turn-of-the-century vases and portraits. The main hall has Courbet's soft-porn *The Sleepers* (*Le Sommeil,* 1866) capturing two women nestled in post-climactic bliss. At the end of the main hall, enter the smaller room to find Claude Monet's hazy, moody *Sunset on the Seine at Lavacourt* (1880), painted the winter after his wife died. Nearby are works by the American painter Mary Cassatt and other Impressionists. The Palais also has a pleasant garden courtyard and café.

▸ *Free for permanent collection, but temporary exhibits charge admission. Open Tue–Sun 10:00–18:00, Thu until 20:00 for temporary exhibits, closed Mon. Located on avenue Winston Churchill, Mo: Champs-Elysées-Clemenceau. Tel. 01 53 43 40 00, www.petitpalais.paris.fr.*

Grand Palais

This grand exhibition hall built for the 1900 World's Fair is now used for temporary exhibits.

▸ *Admission prices and hours vary with each exhibition. Located on avenue Winston Churchill, Mo: Rond Point or Champs-Elysées. Tel. 01 44 13 17 17, www.grandpalais.fr.*

▲▲Jacquemart-André Museum (Musée Jacquemart-André)

This thoroughly enjoyable museum certainly has some nice art, but its star is the lavish mansion itself. After wandering the grand boulevards, get inside for an intimate look at the lifestyle of a wealthy, art-loving 19th century couple. Edouard André and his wife Nélie Jacquemart had no children. They spent their lives and fortunes designing, building, and then decorating this sumptuous mansion. What makes the visit so rewarding is the excellent audioguide (included with admission). The place is strewn with paintings by Rembrandt, Botticelli, Uccello, Mantegna, Bellini, Boucher, and Fragonard—enough to make a painting gallery famous.

After your visit, enjoy the museum's sumptuous tearoom, serving delicious cakes and tea. A few blocks north is Paris' most beautiful park, Parc Monceau.

▸ *€10, not covered by Museum Pass, daily 10:00–18:00. Located at 158 boulevard Haussmann, Mo: Miromesnil or Saint-Philippe de Roule. Tel. 01 45 62 11 59, www.musee-jacquemart-andre.com.*

MARAIS NEIGHBORHOOD AND NEARBY

The Marais neighborhood extends along the Right Bank of the Seine, from the Pompidou Center to the Bastille. There's a main west–east axis formed by rue Ste. Croix de la Bretonnerie, rue des Rosiers (heart of Paris' Jewish community), and rue St. Antoine. The centerpiece of the neighborhood is the elegant place des Vosges.

▲Strolling the Marais

With more pre-Revolutionary lanes and mansions than anywhere else in town, the Marais is more atmospheric than touristy. In the 1600s, this former swamp *(marais)* became home to artistocrats' private mansions *(hôtels),* located close to the king's townhouse on stylish place des Vosges. With the Revolution, the Marais turned working-class, filled with artisans and immigrants, and became home to Paris' Jewish community.

Today the area is trending upward, full of young professionals. You'll find nightlife (especially around place de la Bastille), fashion boutiques (along rue des Francs Bourgeois), the Jewish neighborhood (rue des Rosiers), and gay Paree's LGBT community (along rue Ste. Croix de la Bretonnerie). On Sunday afternoons, the area pulses with shoppers and café crowds.

▲Place des Vosges

Henry IV (r. 1589–1610) built this centerpiece of the Marais in 1605, instantly turning the Marais into Paris' most exclusive neighborhood. In the center, a statue of Louis XIII on horseback gestures, "Look at this wonderful square my dad built." He's surrounded by locals in the shade of trees, children frolicking in the sandbox, lovers warming benches, and pigeons guarding their fountains. Around the square, arcades shade cafés and art galleries.

Study the architecture: nine pavilions (houses) per side. The two highest—at the front and back—were intended for the king and queen, but were never used. Warm red brickwork—some real, some fake—is topped

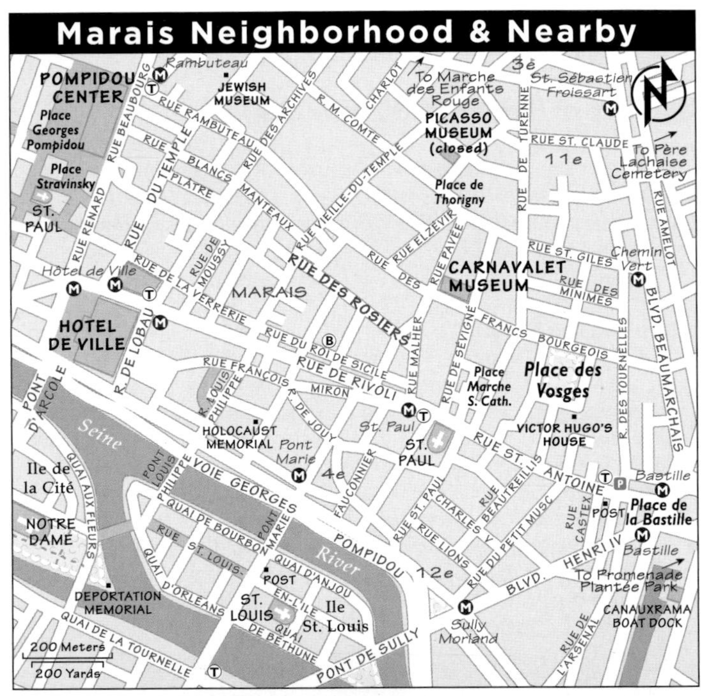

with sloped slate roofs, chimneys, and another quaint relic of a bygone era: TV antennas.

▸ *Mo: Bastille or St. Paul.*

Victor Hugo's House

France's literary giant (1802–1885) lived here after the phenomenal success of *The Hunchback of Notre-Dame* and while he was writing *Les Misérables.* You'll see well-decorated rooms adorned with paintings of Hugo and his family, and of some of his character creations.

▸ *Free, temporary exhibits are optional. Open Tue–Sun 10:00–18:00, last entry at 17:40, closed Mon. 6 place des Vosges. Tel. 01 42 72 10 16, www.musee-hugo.paris.fr.*

The Bastille

Don't waste time looking for the famous prison that was stormed on July 14, 1789, sparking the French Revolution. The building is long gone and just the square (place de la Bastille) remains.

▲Rue des Rosiers—Jewish Quarter

Once the largest in Western Europe, Paris' Jewish Quarter is still colorful. The intersection of rue des Rosiers and rue des Ecouffes marks the heart of the small neighborhood that Jews call the Pletzl ("little place").

Rue des Rosiers features kosher *(cascher)* restaurants and fast-food places selling falafel, *shawarma, kefta,* and other Mediterranean dishes. Bakeries specialize in braided challah, bagels, and strudels. Delis offer gefilte fish, piroshkis, and blintzes. Art galleries exhibit Jewish-themed works, and store windows post flyers for community events. Need a menorah? This is a great place to buy one. You may see Jewish men in yarmulkes, a few bearded Orthodox Jews, and Hasidic Jews with black coat and hat, beard, and earlocks.

▸ *Most shops close on Saturday, the Jewish Sabbath.*

▲▲Pompidou Center (Centre Pompidou)

Some people hate Modern art. But Paris was the cradle of Modernism, and the Pompidou houses one of Europe's greatest collections. In addition, the Pompidou Center always has lively temporary exhibitions, the rooftop has a great view, and outside there's a perpetual street fair of performers and crepe stands.

The colorful building is exoskeletal (like a crab or Notre-Dame), with its functional parts—the pipes, heating ducts, and escalator—on the outside, and the meaty art inside. It's the epitome of Modern architecture, where "form follows function."

The permanent collection (on the fourth and fifth floors) features all the big names of the early 20th century—Matisse, Picasso, Chagall, Kandinsky, Dalí—and continues with post-1960 art. This art was ahead of its time and is still waiting for the world to catch up. After so many Madonnas-and-children in Paris' older museums, a piano smashed to bits and glued to the wall is refreshing. Once you've seen the permanent collection, explore the temporary exhibits to connect with what is "now" from around the globe.

▸ *€10–12 depending on current exhibits, free on first Sun of month. The Museum Pass covers the permanent collection and view escalators but not special exhibitions. €3 for view only.*

Open Wed–Mon 11:00–21:00, closed Tue, ticket counters close at 20:00. Located at Mo: Rambuteau or Hôtel de Ville. Tel. 01 44 78 12 33, www.centrepompidou.fr.

▲Jewish Art and History Museum (Musée d'Art et Histoire du Judaïsme)

This fine museum in a Marais mansion tells the story of Judaism in Europe and the traditions that helped the dispersed population maintain cultural unity. Besides learning about bar mitzvahs and menorahs, you'll see exquisite traditional costumes and objects, and paintings by Jewish artists such as Chagall, Modigliani, and Soutine.

▸ *€7, more during special exhibits, includes audioguide, covered by Museum Pass. Open Mon–Fri 11:00–18:00, Sun 10:00–18:00, last entry 45 minutes before closing, closed Sat. 71 rue du Temple, Mo: Rambuteau. Tel. 01 53 01 86 60, www.mahj.org.*

▲▲Picasso Museum (Musée Picasso)

The world's largest collection of Picasso's art is currently closed for a major renovation that will last several years.

▲Carnavalet Museum (Musée Carnavalet)

At the Carnavalet Museum, French history unfolds in a series of stills—like a Ken Burns documentary, except you have to walk. The Revolution is the highlight, but you get a good overview of everything—from Louis XIV–period rooms to Napoleon to the belle époque.

The Revolution section is the best. No period of history is as charged with the full range of human drama: bloodshed, martyrdom, daring speeches, murdered priests, emancipated women, backstabbing former friends—all in the name of government "by, for, and of the people."

You'll see paintings of the Estates General assembly that planted the seeds of democracy. Then comes a model of the Bastille, the hated prison that was the symbol of oppression. Read the "Declaration of the Rights of Man." See pictures of ill-fated King Louis XVI and Queen Marie-Antoinette, and the fate that awaited them—the guillotine. You'll see portraits of all the major players—Robespierre, Danton, Charlotte Corday—as well as the dashing general who would inherit democracy and turn it into dictatorship... Napoleon Bonaparte.

▸ *Free. Open Tue–Sun 10:00–18:00, closed Mon. Located at 23 rue de Sévigné, Mo: St. Paul. Tel. 01 44 59 58 58, www.carnavalet.paris.fr.*

Promenade Plantée Park (Viaduc des Arts)

This two-mile-long garden sits atop a narrow, elevated viaduct once used for train tracks. It's now a fine place for a refreshing stroll. It runs from near place de la Bastille (Mo: Bastille) along avenue Daumesnil to Saint-Mandé (Mo: Michel Bizot).

▸ *Free, open daily until sunset. The entry point near place Bastille is located a loooong walk down rue de Lyon.*

▲Père Lachaise Cemetery (Cimetière du Père Lachaise)

This 100-acre cemetery is big and confusing, but it's a pleasant park-like setting for a stroll. You can also find the graves of illustrious people who have called Paris home: Frédéric Chopin (the Polish pianist), Molière (playwright to Louis XIV), Edith Piaf (warbling singer who regretted nothing), Oscar Wilde (controversial figure who died in Paris), Jim Morrison (ditto), Gertrude Stein (American writer), Héloïse and Abélard (illicit medieval lovers), and many more.

▸ *Free, open Mon–Fri 8:00–18:00, Sat 8:30–18:00, Sun 9:00–18:00, closes at 17:30 in winter, last entry 15 minutes before closing. Buy grave-locator maps from shops near the entrance. The best entrance is Porte Gambetta near Mo: Gambetta (not Mo: Père Lachaise) and bus #69's last stop. Tel. 01 55 25 82 10, www.pere-lachaise.com.*

MONTMARTRE

Paris' highest hill, topped by Sacré-Cœur Basilica, is best known as the home of cabaret nightlife and bohemian artists. Struggling painters, poets, dreamers, and drunkards came here for cheap rent, untaxed booze, rustic landscapes, and views of the underwear of high-kicking cancan girls at the Moulin Rouge.

These days, the hill is equal parts charm and kitsch—still vaguely village-like but mobbed with tourists on sunny weekends. Come for a bit of history, a get-away from Paris' noisy boulevards, a meal, and the view.

▸ *Métro stop Anvers takes you to the base of the hill, where you can climb stairs up or ride a funicular. The Abbesses stop is closer but less scenic. A taxi to the top costs about €15 from Notre-Dame.*

▲▲Sacré-Cœur

The Sacré-Cœur (Sacred Heart) Basilica's exterior, with its onion domes and bleached-bone pallor, looks ancient, but was finished only a century ago. Inside, a mosaic shows Jesus with his sacred heart burning with love for mankind. For an unobstructed panoramic view of Paris, climb 260 feet (300 steps) up the tight and claustrophobic spiral stairs to the top of the dome. The ground-level view from the front steps is also spectacular.

▸ *Church interior is free, open daily 6:00–22:30, last entry at 22:15. €5 to climb the dome, not covered by Museum Pass, daily June–Sept 9:00–19:00, Oct–May 10:00–18:00.*

▲The Heart of Montmartre

The leafy place du Tertre—lined with restaurants and filled with draw-your-portrait artists—was once the haunt of Toulouse-Lautrec and the original bohemians. Today, it's mobbed with tourists and unoriginal bohemians, but it's still fun. A block west is a *boulangerie* made famous in a painting by Utrillo. Head downhill past a vineyard to the Montmartre Museum, housed in a mansion that both Renoir and Utrillo once called home. The museum re-creates the cabaret scene, with paintings, original posters, and memorabilia.

A few blocks away are the Au Lapin Agile cabaret (still in business) and the Moulin de la Galette, a dance-hall featured in a famous Renoir painting (✪ see page 85). Wandering the neighborhood, you can see the boring exteriors of former homes of Picasso, Toulouse-Lautrec, Van Gogh, and Erik Satie.

At the base of the hill, the Moulin Rouge ("Red Windmill") nightclub still offers glitzy, pricey shows to busloads of tourists. The neighborhood around it, called Pigalle, is pretty rough and raunchy, with sex shops and bars where a €150 bottle of cheap champagne comes with a friend.

► *The Montmartre Museum costs €8, not covered by Museum Pass. Open Tue–Sun 11:00–18:00, closed Mon. 12 rue Cortot. Tel. 01 49 25 89 39, www.museedemontmartre.fr.*

DAY TRIPS FROM PARIS

Though there's plenty to see within Paris' ring-road, efficient public transportation expands your sightseeing horizons.

▲▲▲Versailles

✪ See the Versailles chapter on page 127.

▲▲Chartres: The Town and the Cathedral

One of Europe's greatest Gothic cathedrals soars above the pleasant town of Chartres, an hour southwest of Paris.

► *Catch the train from Paris' Gare Montparnasse (10/day, about €13 one-way). The church is open daily 8:30–19:30.*

▲Giverny

Claude Monet's garden still looks like it did when he painted it. Wander among the flowers, the rose trellis, the Japanese Bridge, and the pond filled with lily pads.

► *Big bus tours are the easiest way to get there (about €70, ask your hotelier). On your own, take the Rouen-bound train from Gare St. Lazare to Vernon (about €21 round-trip, 45 minutes). From there, take a taxi (€12), the public bus, or rent a bike at the café opposite the train station (€12). Monet's Garden and House are open daily April–Oct 9:30–18:00, last entry 17:30, closed Nov–March (€8, not covered by Paris Museum Pass, tel. 02 32 51 90 31, www.fondation-monet.fr).*

Sleeping

In Paris, choosing the right neighborhood is as important as choosing the right hotel. I've focused most of my recommendations in three safe, handy, and colorful neighborhoods: the village-like rue Cler (near the Eiffel Tower), the artsy and trendy Marais (near place de la Bastille), and the lively yet classy Luxembourg (on the Left Bank). I like hotels that are clean, central, good-value, friendly, run with a respect for French traditions, and small enough to have a hands-on owner and stable staff. Four of these six virtues means it's a keeper.

Double rooms listed in this book average around €150 (including a private bathroom). They range from a low of roughly €70 (very simple, with toilet and shower down the hall) to €480 (maximum plumbing and more).

$$$ Most rooms are €150 or more.

$$ Most rooms between €100–150.

$ Most rooms €100 or less.

These rates are for a standard double room with bath during high season. Asterisks (*) are for the French hotel rating system, ranging from zero to four stars. All hotels listed have an elevator and air-conditioning (A/C) unless otherwise noted.

A Typical Parisian Hotel Room

A typical €150 double room will be small by American standards. It will have one double bed (either queen-sized or slightly narrower) or two twins. There's probably a bathroom in the room with a toilet, sink, and bathtub or shower. The room has a telephone and TV, and may have a safe. Most hotels at this price will have air-conditioning—cheaper places may not. Single rooms, triples, and quads will have similar features.

Breakfast is rarely included in the room price, but is usually offered for an additional €8–15. It's normally a self-service buffet of cereal, cheese, yogurt, fruit, and juice, while a waitress takes your coffee order.

The hotel will likely have some form of Internet access, either free or pay-as-you-go. It may be Wi-Fi in your room (assuming you have your own laptop) or a public terminal in the lobby. The staff speaks at least enough English to get by. Night clerks aren't paid enough to care deeply about problems that arise.

Note that the French hotel rating system (zero to four stars) only reflects the number of amenities (e.g. fancier lobbies, more elaborately designed rooms), and does not necessarily rate quality.

Making Reservations

Reserve at least a few weeks in advance in peak season (April–October, especially May, June, September, and October) or for a major holiday. Do it by email (the best way), phone, fax, or through the hotel's website. Your hotelier will want to know:

- the type of room you want (e.g., "one double room with bath")
- how many nights ("three nights")
- dates (using European format: "arriving 22/7/12, departing 25/7/12")
- any special requests ("with twin beds, air-conditioning, quiet, view")

If you prefer a double or queen bed (instead of twins) and a shower (instead of a tub), you should ask for it or risk getting whatever's available.

If they require your credit-card number for a deposit, you can send it by email (I do), but it's safer via phone, fax, or the hotel's secure website. Once your room is booked, print out the confirmation, and reconfirm your reservation with a phone call a day or two in advance. If you must cancel your reservation, some hotels require advance notice or you'll be billed, but even if there's no penalty, give at least three days' notice.

Budget Tips

Some of my listed hotels offer a 5–10 percent discount and/or free breakfast for readers of this book—it's worth asking when you book your room. (Look for "RS discount" in these listings.)

To get the best deals, email several hotels to comparison shop, and check hotel websites for promo deals. You may get a cheaper rate if you stay at least three nights, get a double bed and shower rather than twin beds and a bathtub, or simply ask if there are any cheaper rooms. Rates can drop 10–35 percent off-season—roughly November through mid-March, and mid-July through August.

Besides hotels, there are cheaper alternatives. I list a few all-ages hostels, which offer €25–50 dorm beds (and a few inexpensive doubles) and come with curfews and other rules. Bed-and-breakfasts (B&Bs) offer a private room in someone's home—try www.bed-and-breakfast-in-paris.com. Apartment rentals can save money if you're traveling as a family, staying more than a week, and planning to cook your own meals.

Don't be too cheap when picking a hotel. In summer, pay a little more for air-conditioning. And remember that cheaper places in nondescript neighborhoods can be depressing. Your Paris experience will be more memorable with a welcoming oasis to call home.

	Price		
RUE CLER AREA—A safe, tidy, upscale area near the Eiffel Tower			
Hôtel Relais Bosquet***	$$$	Excellent value with generous public spaces and large, comfortable rooms, RS discount	
Hôtel du Cadran***	$$$	Perfectly located, daringly modern with stylish rooms, RS discount	
Hôtel Valadon**	$$$	Cute and quiet with 12 pleasing rooms, near rue Cler, RS discount	
Hôtel Beaugency***	$$	Good value on quiet street near rue Cler, small rooms, RS discount	
Grand Hôtel Lévêque**	$$	Busy hotel with average rooms right on rue Cler	
Hôtel du Champ de Mars**	$	Plush little hotel with serious owners, snug but lovingly kept rooms, no A/C	
Hôtel Duquesne Eiffel***	$$$	Hospitable and expertly run with handsome rooms and welcoming lobby, RS discount	
Hôtel La Bourdonnais***	$$$	Très Parisian, with creaky, comfortable rooms and a nice lobby	
Hôtel de Turenne**	$	Humble but well-situated with adequate rooms and several true single rooms	
Hôtel de Londres Eiffel***	$$$	Close to Eiffel Tower with immaculate, warmly decorated rooms and helpful staff	
Hôtel de la Tour Eiffel**	$	Fair value, quiet street, modest rooms, thin walls, no A/C, no breakfast	
Hôtel Kensington**	$	Good budget hotel near Eiffel Tower, small rooms, no A/C, no Wi-Fi	
Hôtel Les Jardins d'Eiffel***	$$$	Modern hotel with spacious and peaceful rooms and comfortable lobby, RS discount	
Hôtel Muguet***	$$	Peaceful refuge with tasteful rooms and a small garden courtyard	
Hôtel de l'Empereur**	$$	Smashing views of Invalides from plush rooms, some with small balconies	

Address/Phone/Website/Email
19 rue du Champ de Mars, tel. 01 47 05 25 45, fax 01 45 55 08 24, www.hotel-paris-bosquet.com, hotel@relaisbosquet.com
10 rue du Champ de Mars, tel. 01 40 62 67 00, www.cadranhotel.com, resa@cadranhotel.com
16 rue Valadon, tel. 01 47 53 89 85, www.hotelvaladon.com, info@hotelvaladon.com
21 rue Duvivier, tel. 01 47 05 01 63, fax 01 45 51 04 96, www.hotel-beaugency.com, infos@hotel-beaugency.com
29 rue Cler, tel. 01 47 05 49 15, fax 01 45 50 49 36, www.hotel-leveque.com, info@hotel-leveque.com
7 rue du Champ de Mars, tel. 01 45 51 52 30, fax 01 45 51 64 36, www.hotelduchampdemars.com, reservation@hotelduchampdemars.com
23 avenue Duquesne, tel. 01 44 42 09 09, fax 01 44 42 09 08, www.hde.fr, hotel@hde.fr
111 avenue de la Bourdonnais, tel. 01 47 05 45 42, fax 01 45 55 75 54, www.hotellabourdonnais.fr, hlb@hotellabourdonnais.fr
20 avenue de Tourville, tel. 01 47 05 99 92, fax 01 45 56 06 04, www.hotel-turenne-paris.com, info@hotel-turenne-paris.com
1 rue Augereau, tel. 01 45 51 63 02, fax 01 47 05 28 96, www.londres-eiffel.com, info@londres-eiffel.com
17 rue de l'Exposition, tel. 01 47 05 14 75, fax 01 47 53 99 46, www.hotel-toureiffel.com, hte7@wanadoo.fr
79 avenue de la Bourdonnais, tel. 01 47 05 74 00, fax 01 47 05 25 81, www.hotel-kensington.com, hk@hotel-kensington.com
8 rue Amélie, tel. 01 47 05 46 21, fax 01 45 55 28 08, www.hoteljardinseiffel.com, reservations@hoteljardinseiffel.com
11 rue Chevert, tel. 01 47 05 05 93, fax 01 45 50 25 37, www.hotelmuguet.com, muguet@wanadoo.fr
2 rue Chevert, tel. 01 45 55 88 02, fax 01 45 51 88 54, www.hotelempereurparis.com, contact@hotelempereur.com

	Price		
MARAIS AREA—Classy mansions alongside trendy boutiques create a Greenwich Village vibe			
Hôtel Castex***	$$$	Quiet street, narrow, tile-floored rooms and many family suites	
Hôtel Bastille Spéria***	$$$	Ideally located business-class hotel with modern, well-configured rooms	
Hôtel du 7ème Art**	$$	Carefree with spacious, good-value rooms and 1970s decor, no elevator	
Grand Hôtel Jeanne d'Arc**	$	Lovely little hotel with thoughtfully appointed rooms, great location, no A/C	
Hôtel Lyon-Mulhouse**	$	On a busy street near the Bastille with less character but good value rooms	
Hôtel Daval**	$	Tiny rooms, narrow halls, and good rates; streetside rooms can be loud	
Hôtel Sévigné**	$	Well-situated with small, comfy rooms and strict cancellation policy	
MIJE Fourcy	$	Hostel, all-ages welcome, well-located, clean dorm rooms, prices per person	
MIJE Maubisson	$	Small, quiet hostel with same rates as MIJE Fourcy	
Hôtel de la Bretonnerie***	$$	Warm lobby, well-appointed, good-value rooms with character, no A/C	
Hôtel Beaubourg***	$$	Good value on a quiet street in the shadow of the Pompidou Center	
Hôtel de Nice**	$$	On busy road; colorful decor, thoughtful touches, and tight bathrooms	
Hôtel du Loiret*	$	Dingy lobby, noisy but sharp rooms, no A/C, no Wi-Fi	
ILE ST. LOUIS AREA—Island in the Seine near Notre-Dame: peaceful, residential, and pricey			
Hôtel du Jeu de Paume****	$$$	Wonderful location, magnificent place with half-timbered lobby and plush rooms	
Hôtel de Lutèce***	$$$	Cozy lobby with a real fireplace, warmly appointed rooms	
Hôtel des Deux-Iles***	$$$	Bright and colorful, with small but well-configured rooms	

	Address/Phone/Website/Email
	5 rue Castex, Mo: Bastille, tel. 01 42 72 31 52, fax 01 42 72 57 91, www.castexhotel.com, info@castexhotel.com
	1 rue de la Bastille, Mo: Bastille, tel. 01 42 72 04 01, fax 01 42 72 56 38, www.hotelsperia.com, info@hotelsperia.com
	20 rue St. Paul, Mo: St. Paul, tel. 01 44 54 85 00, fax 01 42 77 69 10, www.paris-hotel-7art.com, hotel7art@wanadoo.fr
	3 rue de Jarente, Mo: St. Paul, tel. 01 48 87 62 11, fax 01 48 87 37 31, www.hoteljeannedarc.com, information@hoteljeannedarc.com
	8 boulevard Beaumarchais, Mo: Bastille, tel. 01 47 00 91 50, fax 01 47 00 06 31, www.1-hotel-paris.com, hotelyonmulhouse@wanadoo.fr
	21 rue Daval, Mo: Bastille, tel. 01 47 00 51 23, fax 01 40 21 80 26, www.hoteldaval.com, info@hoteldaval.com
	2 rue Malher, Mo: St. Paul, tel. 01 42 72 76 17, fax 01 42 78 68 26, www.le-sevigne.com, message.le-sevigne@wanadoo.fr
	6 rue de Fourcy, tel. 01 42 74 23 45, fax 01 40 27 81 64, www.mije.com, info@mije.com
	12 rue des Barres, tel. 01 42 74 23 45, fax 01 40 27 81 64, www.mije.com, info@mije.com
	22 rue Ste. Croix de la Bretonnerie, tel. 01 48 87 77 63, fax 01 42 77 26 78, www.bretonnerie.com, hotel@bretonnerie.com
	11 rue Simon Le Franc, Mo: Rambuteau, tel. 01 42 74 34 24, fax 01 42 78 68 11, www.beaubourg-paris-hotel.com, reservation@hotelbeaubourg.com
	42 bis rue de Rivoli, tel. 01 42 78 55 29, fax 01 42 78 36 07, www.hoteldenice.com, contact@hoteldenice.com
	8 rue des Mauvais Garçons, tel. 01 48 87 77 00, fax 01 48 04 96 56, www.hotel-du-loiret.fr, hotelduloiret@hotmail.com
	54 rue St. Louis-en-l'Ile, tel. 01 43 26 14 18, fax 01 40 46 02 76, www.jeudepaumehotel.com, info@jeudepaumehotel.com
	65 rue St. Louis-en-l'Ile, tel. 01 43 26 23 52, fax 01 43 29 60 25, www.paris-hotel-lutece.com, info@hoteldelutece.com
	59 rue St. Louis-en-l'Ile, tel. 01 43 26 13 35, fax 01 43 29 60 25, www.deuxiles-paris-hotel.com, info@hoteldesdeuxiles.com

Sleeping

	Price		
LUXEMBOURG GARDEN AREA—Left Bank energy with shops, cafés, and the park			
Hôtel le Récamier***	$$$	Boutique hotel on place St. Sulpice, snazzy rooms and public spaces	
Hôtel de l'Abbaye****	$$$	Refuge with sumptuous rooms and public spaces, includes breakfast	
Hôtel Bonaparte**	$$	Unpretentious, welcoming place with Old World rooms at good prices	
Hôtel Jean Bart**	$	Basic hotel near Luxembourg Garden, no A/C, cash only	
Hôtel Relais Médicis***	$$$	Refuge with Old World charm near Odéon Theater, includes breakfast	
Hôtel des Grandes Ecoles***	$$	Lovely rooms around a peaceful, flowery courtyard, no A/C	
Hôtel des 3 Collèges**	$$	Bright lobby, narrow hallways, and unimaginative rooms, fair rates	
Hôtel Cujas Panthéon**	$	Traditional comfort at fair prices, no A/C	
Hôtel Cluny Sorbonne**	$	Modest, warmly run place across from the Sorbonne, thin walls, no A/C	
Hôtel des Mines**	$$$	Less central but a good value, comfortable rooms at fair prices	
BOTTOM OF RUE MOUFFETARD—Blue-collar by day, bohemian at night; not so central, but a good value			
Young & Happy Hostel	$	Easygoing hostel with kitchen facilities, acceptable conditions, no A/C, rates per person	
Port-Royal-Hôtel*	$	Immaculate hotel on busy street with comfortable rooms, cash only	
Hôtel de L'Espérance**	$	Terrific value with quiet, cushy rooms, and pleasing public spaces	

Address/Phone/Website/Email
3 bis place St. Sulpice, tel. 01 43 26 04 89, fax 01 43 26 35 76, www.hotelrecamier.com, contact@hotelrecamier.com
10 rue Cassette, tel. 01 45 44 38 11, fax 01 45 48 07 86, www.hotelabbayeparis.com, hotel.abbaye@wanadoo.fr
61 rue Bonaparte, tel. 01 43 26 97 37, fax 01 46 33 57 67, www.hotelbonaparte.fr, reservation@hotelbonaparte.fr
9 rue Jean-Bart, tel. 01 45 48 29 13, fax 01 45 48 10 79, hotel.jean.bart@gmail.com
23 rue Racine, tel. 01 43 26 00 60, fax 01 40 46 83 39, www.relaismedicis.com, reservation@relaismedicis.com
75 rue du Cardinal Lemoine, Mo: Cardinal Lemoine, tel. 01 43 26 79 23, fax 01 43 25 28 15, www.hotel-grandes-ecoles.com, hotel.grandes.ecoles@free.fr
16 rue Cujas, tel. 01 43 54 67 30, fax 01 46 34 02 99, www.3colleges.com, hotel@3colleges.com
18 rue Cujas, tel. 01 43 54 58 10, fax 01 43 25 88 02, www.cujas-pantheon-paris-hotel.com, hotel-cujas-pantheon@wanadoo.fr.
8 rue Victor Cousin, tel. 01 43 54 66 66, fax 01 43 29 68 07, www.hotel-cluny.fr, cluny@club-internet.fr
125 boulevard St. Michel, tel. 01 43 54 32 78, fax 01 46 33 72 52, www.hoteldesminesparis.com, hotel@hoteldesminesparis.com
80 rue Mouffetard, Mo: Place Monge, tel. 01 47 07 47 07, fax 01 47 07 22 24, www.youngandhappy.fr, smile@youngandhappy.fr
8 boulevard de Port-Royal, Mo: Les Gobelins, tel. 01 43 31 70 06, fax 01 43 31 33 67, www.hotelportroyal.fr, portroyalhotel@wanadoo.fr
15 rue Pascal, Mo: Censier-Daubenton, tel. 01 47 07 10 99, fax 01 43 37 56 19, www.hoteldelesperance.fr, hotel.esperance@wanadoo.fr

	Price	
MONTMARTRE AREA—Lively, un-touristy base of the hill, great for young and budget travelers		
Hôtel Regyn's**	$$	Small, comfortable rooms with mediocre bathrooms at good rates, no A/C
My Hôtel in France Montmartre	$	Basic hotel with well-maintained rooms, free breakfast, no A/C, no elevator
Plug-Inn Boutique Hostel	$	Hostel-like hotel, free breakfast, kitchen facilities, rates per person
Hôtel Bonséjour Montmartre	$	Old, worn place with shared bathrooms, and dirt-cheap prices, no A/C, no elevator
APARTMENT RENTALS—Furnished apartments for longer-term stays		
Paris Perfect	$$$	Offers top-quality places, most have A/C, washers and dryers, RS discount
Paris Appartements Services	$$$	Rents studios and one-bedroom apartments in central neighborhoods
France Homestyle	$$$	Offers personal service and hand-picks every apartment
Home Rental Service	$$$	Offers a big selection of apartments throughout Paris with no agency fees
Locaflat	$$$	Rents accommodations ranging from studios to five-room apartments
Immo Marais	$$$	Has over 100 apartments in all sizes in the Marais
Paris For Rent	$$$	San Francisco–based group with top-end apartments in Paris
VRBO	$$$	Cuts out the middleman by putting you directly in touch with the owners

	Address/Phone/Website/Email
	18 place des Abbesses, tel. 01 42 54 45 21, fax 01 42 23 76 69, www.paris-hotels-montmartre.com, hrm18@club-internet.fr
	57 rue des Abbesses, tel. 01 42 51 50 00, fax 01 42 51 08 68, www.myhotelinfrance-montmartre.com, montmartre@my-hotel-in-france.com
	7 rue Aristide Bruant, tel. 01 42 58 42 58, fax 01 42 23 93 88, www.plug-inn.fr, bonjour@plug-inn.fr
	11 rue Burq, tel. 01 42 54 22 53, fax 01 42 54 25 92, www.hotel-bonsejour-montmartre.fr, hotel-bonsejour-montmartre@wanadoo.fr
	Toll-free US tel. 888-520-2087, www.parisperfect.com
	20 rue Bachaumont, tel. 01 40 28 01 28, fax 01 40 28 92 01, www.paris-appartements-services.com
	US tel. 206/325-0132, www.francehomestyle.com, info@francehomestyle.com
	120 Champs-Elysées, tel. 01 42 25 65 40, fax 01 42 25 65 45, www.homerental.fr
	63 avenue de la Motte-Picquet, tel. 01 43 06 78 79, fax 01 40 56 99 69, www.locaflat.com
	60 rue Roi de Sicile, tel. 01 42 74 06 17, www.parislocationsmeublees.com
	US tel. 415/642-1111, www.parisforrent.com
	Several hundred rentals available in Paris, organized by arrondissement, www.vrbo.com

Eating

The Parisian eating scene is kept at a rolling boil. Entire books (and lives) are dedicated to the subject. Parisians eat long and well. Relaxed lunches, three-hour dinners, and endless hours of sitting in outdoor cafés are the norm. Budget some time and money to sightseeing for your palate. Even if the rest of you is sleeping in a cheap hotel, let your taste buds travel first-class in Paris.

I list a full range of restaurants and eateries, from budget options for a quick bite to multi-course splurges with maximum ambience. My listings are in Paris' atmospheric neighborhoods, handy to recommended hotels and sights.

When in Paris, I eat on the Parisian schedule. For breakfast, I eat at the hotel or belly up to a café counter for a quick café au lait with a croissant or *une tartine* (a baguette slathered with butter or jam). Lunch (12:00–14:00) may be a big salad or *plat du jour,* or an atmospheric picnic.

$$$ Most main courses €25 or more

$$ Most main courses €15–25.

$ Most main courses €15 or less.

Based on the average price of a meat or seafood dish on the menu. Salads and appetizers are several euros cheaper. So a typical meal at a $$ restaurant—including appetizer, main dish, house wine, water, and service—would cost about €40. The circled numbers in the restaurant listings indicate locations on the maps on pages 202–205.

In the afternoon and evening, Parisians enjoy a beverage at a sidewalk table. Dinner is the time for slowing down and savoring a multi-course restaurant meal.

Restaurants

Restaurants and bistros start serving dinner to tourists around 19:00, to locals after 20:00, and can be packed by 21:00. Many restaurants close Sunday and Monday. In 2008, a new law mandated that all café and restaurant interiors be smoke-free. (Outdoor tables can be smoky.)

A full restaurant meal comes in courses. It might include an *apéritif* (before-dinner drink), an *entrée* (appetizer), a *plat* (main dish), the cheese course, dessert, coffee, liqueurs, several different wines, and so on.

It's not obligatory to order every course—in fact, many Parisians these days consider two courses (e.g. *plat* and dessert) a "full" meal. Ordering as little as a single main dish as your entire meal is acceptable, and couples can share a starter or dessert. If you want to eat lighter than that, try a café or brasserie instead. Since even a two- or three-course restaurant meal can take hours, and the costs can add up quickly, plan your strategy before sitting down to a full meal.

For a full meal at a predictable price, consider a fixed-price meal. Most restaurants offer a *"menu"*—a multi-course meal where you can choose from a list of select items. It includes the service charge, and is usually a good value. Many places serve a daily special *plat du jour* (a main dish plus a side, on a single plate), though it may only be offered at lunch.

Parisians are willing to pay for bottled water with their meal (*eau mi-*

nérale), but a free carafe of tap water *(une carafe d'eau)* is always available upon request, and more bread is also free.

The service charge is automatically built into your bill's total. For exceptional service, you could tip up to 5 percent, though Parisians rarely do. Waiters probably won't overwhelm you with friendliness or attention—they're invariably overworked, and besides, the tip is already included in the price. To get a waiter's attention, say, *"S'il vous plaît."*

To get the most out of your Parisian restaurant—slow down. Allow ample time for the meal, engage the waiter, show you're serious about food, consider his or her recommendations, and enjoy the experience as much as the food itself.

Cafés and Brasseries

Less formal than restaurants, these places serve user-friendly meals, as well as coffee and drinks. They're not necessarily less expensive than restaurants, but they serve food throughout the day, and you're welcome to order just a single dish (even for dinner), rather than a several-course meal.

Feel free to order a *plat* (main course), a *plat du jour* (daily special), a salad (they're usually big), a sandwich (e.g. a *croque monsieur*, or grilled ham and cheese sandwich), an omelet, an *entrée* (appetizer), or a bowl of soup. It's also fine to split starters and desserts, though not main courses. Many cafés and brasseries have outdoor tables (with braziers in winter) perfect for nursing a glass of wine or cafe au lait, and watching the parade of passersby. A crêperie is another less formal, budget alternative.

Be aware that the price of drinks may be 20–40 percent more if you consume them while sitting at a table *(salle)* instead of standing at the bar *(comptoir)*. Outdoor tables can sometimes be more expensive still. The prices will always be clearly posted. Don't sit without first checking out the financial consequences.

Picnicking

Parisian picnics can be first-class affairs and adventures in high cuisine. Take-out delis (a *charcuterie* or *traiteur*, as well as some bakeries) sell high-quality cooked dishes, quiches, pâtés, and salads you can build a meal around. The deli can warm it up for you (*chauffé* = heated up) and pack it in a take-out box *(une barquette)*, along with a plastic fork.

You'll also find bakeries and small stands selling baguette sandwiches, quiche, and pizza-like items to-go for €4–6. For your side dishes, a generic *supermarché* is easy for one-stop shopping, but you'll do better browsing a *boulangerie* for your baguette, a *fromagerie* for cheese, and an open-air market for the freshest produce.

Be daring. Try the smelly cheeses, ugly pâtés, and sissy quiches. Some good picnic spots in the heart of Paris are the Palais Royal courtyard, the place des Vosges, the west tip of Ile de la Cité, and the Tuileries Garden.

Parisian Cuisine

There is no "Parisian cuisine" to speak of. Rather, Paris is France's melting-pot. You'll find dishes from every French region, and many restaurants specialize in a particular regional cuisine.

From Burgundy (among France's best cuisines), try *coq au vin* (chicken with wine sauce), *bœuf bourguignon* (beef stew), or *escargots.* From Normandy and Brittany you'll find mussels and oysters, crepes, and cider. Any dish prepared *à la provençale* features that region's garlic, olive oil, herbs, and tomatoes. You'll find *bouillabaisse* from the Côte d'Azur, *pâté de foie gras* (goose-liver pâté) from the southwest, and even Alsatian *choucroute*—sauerkraut.

Paris has a particular fondness for steak, including steak tartare—raw ground beef. Duck from the southwest *(confit de canard),* leg of lamb *(gigot d'agneau),* roasted chicken *(poulet roti)* and salmon *(saumon)* are also popular. Raw oysters *(huîtres)* from Brittany are a tradition at Christmas and New Year's, when every café seems to have overflowing baskets lining the storefront.

Commonly served cheeses are Brie de Meaux (mild and creamy, from just outside Paris), Camembert (semicreamy and pungent, from Normandy), *chèvre* (goat cheese with a sharp taste, usually from the Loire), and Roquefort (strong and blue-veined, from south-central France). For dessert, try a *café gourmand,* an assortment of small desserts selected by the restaurant. Other classic desserts include crème bruleé, *tarte-tatin,* and *mousse au chocolat.*

No meal in France is complete without wine. Even the basic house wine (*vin ordinaire,* or *vin du maison*) is fine with a meal—order it by the pitcher, or *pichet*. For good-but-inexpensive wines by the bottle, look for reds from Côtes du Rhone or Languedoc, and whites from Burgundy or

Alsace. In summer, everyone should try an inexpensive rosé. Those willing to pay more can get a good (but not cheap) pinot noir from Burgundy, or a heavier red from Bordeaux.

The French do not drink wine as *apéritifs*. Champagne, beer, a Kir (a dash of crème de Cassis with white wine) or Pastis (an anise-flavored liquor from Provence) are most common. France's best beer is Alsatian; try Kronenbourg or the heavier Pelfort. *Une panaché* is a refreshing French shandy (7-Up and beer).

For coffee, Parisians like *une café* (shot of espresso), a *café au lait* (coffee plus steamed milk, aka *un café creme*), or *une noisette* (espresso with a shot of milk).

A fun, bright, nonalcoholic drink is *un diablo,* featuring 7-Up with various flavored syrups (mint or fruit flavors). If you're ordering a Coke, remember that Paris' last ice cubes melted after the last Yankee tour group left.

	Price		
RUE CLER AREA—Eateries catering to upscale residents near the Eiffel Tower (see map, pages 202–203)			
❶ Café du Marché	$	High-energy, great outdoor seating and low prices right on rue Cler	
❷ Tribeca Italian Restaurant	$	Same owners as Café du Marché, similar formula with Italian theme	
❸ Le Petit Cler	$	Tiny, traditional café with leather booths, fine food, and a few outdoor tables	
❹ Crêperie Ulysée en Gaule	$	Cheapest seats on rue Cler with crêpes to go	
❺ Le Florimond	$$	Intimate and welcoming, with classic French cuisine	
❻ Restaurant Pasco	$$	Tasty Mediterranean cuisine, good indoor and outdoor seating	
❼ Café le Bosquet	$$	Modern brasserie with dressy waiters, mod inside or outside seating.	
❽ La Terrasse du 7ème	$$	Sprawling café with grand outdoor seating and a living-room interior	
❾ Le Petit Niçois	$$	Delicious seafood at fair prices—try the *marmite du pêcheur*	
❿ Chez Pierrot	$$	Inviting bistro specializing in Lyonnaise cuisine with large portions	
⓫ 58 Tour Eiffel	$$$	Snazzy place in the Eiffel Tower (ticket required), reserve ahead for view tables	
⓬ Le P'tit Troquet	$$	Soft, intimate, and welcoming bistro with fragile elegance and wonderful meals	
⓭ Café Constant	$$	Cool, two-level place with delicious and affordable dishes	
⓮ Le Violon d'Ingres	$$$	Famous chef Christian Constant serves top cuisine in a modern setting	
⓯ Pâtisserie de la Tour Eiffel	$	Inexpensive salads, quiches, sandwiches, and Eiffel Tower views	
⓰ La Varangue	$	Friendly, entertaining one-man show with simple and cheap meals	

Operating Hours and Days	Address/Phone
Mon–Sat 11:00–23:00, Sun 11:00–17:00	38 rue Cler, tel. 01 47 05 51 27
Open daily	Next to Café du Marché
Closed Mon	29 rue Cler, tel. 01 45 50 17 50
Open daily	28 rue Cler, tel. 01 47 05 61 82
Closed Sun	19 avenue de la Motte-Picquet, tel. 01 45 55 40 38
Open daily	74 boulevard de la Tour Maubourg, Mo: La Tour Maubourg, tel. 01 44 18 33 26
Closed Sun	46 avenue Bosquet, tel. 01 45 51 38 13
Open daily until at least 24:00 and sometimes until 2:00 in the morning	2 Place de L'Ecole Militaire, tel. 01 45 55 00 02
Open daily	10 rue Amélie, Mo: La Tour Maubourg, tel. 01 45 51 83 65
Open daily	9 rue Amélie, Mo: La Tour Maubourg, tel. 01 45 51 50 08
Open daily	Mo: Bir-Hakeim or Trocadéro, tel. 08 25 56 66 62 or 01 76 64 14 64
Opens at 18:00, closed Sun	28 rue de l'Exposition, tel. 01 47 05 80 39
Closed Sun–Mon	139 rue St. Dominique, tel. 01 47 53 73 34
Closed Sun	135 rue St. Dominique, tel. 01 45 55 15 05
Open daily	21 avenue de la Bourdonnais, tel. 01 47 05 59 81
Closed Sun	27 rue Augereau, tel. 01 47 05 51 22

	Price		
MARAIS AREA—Trendy places amid boisterous nightlife **(see map, pages 204–205)**			
17 Ma Bourgogne	$$$	Vintage eatery with busy waiters serving French specialties	
18 Carette	$$	Modern café serving solid bistro fare with smiles	
19 Royal Turenne	$$	Mostly meat dishes at good prices, live music on weekends	
20 Les Bonnes Soeurs	$$	Blends modern and traditional fare with contemporary ambience and big portions	
21 Brasserie Bofinger	$$	Vintage, sprawling place famous for fish and traditional cuisine with Alsatian flair	
22 Chez Janou	$$	Lively Provençal bistro with Mediterranean cuisine, good tables inside and out	
23 Bistrot de l'Oulette	$$	Tiny, trendy spot serves traditional dishes with a modern twist	
24 Au Temps des Cerises	$	Local wine bar with 1950s atmosphere, tight seating, and character	
25 L'Enoteca	$$	High-spirited and atmospheric, with affordable Italian cuisine (no pizza)	
26 Le Marché and Au Bistrot de la Place	$	Two fun, cheap places on the Marais' most romantic and charming square	
27 Breizh (Brittany) Café	$	Simple Breton place with delicious, organic crêpes, sparkling cider, and more	
28 Chez Marianne	$	Blends delicious Jewish cuisine with Parisian élan in a cluttered wineshop	
29 Le Loir dans la Théière	$	Cozy teahouse ideal for baked goods, hot drinks, and weekend brunch	
30 L'As du Falafel	$	Best falafel in the Jewish Quarter, as well as other tasty dishes	
31 Au Bourguignon du Marais	$$	Handsome wine-bar/bistro with fine cuisine, ideal for Burgundy-lovers	
32 L'Ebouillanté	$	Breezy, romantic crêperie-café, good for an inexpensive meal	

Operating Hours and Days	Address/Phone
Open daily	19 place des Vosges, tel. 01 42 78 44 64
Open daily from 12:00	28 place des Vosges, tel. 01 48 87 94 07
Open daily	24 rue de Turenne, tel. 01 42 72 04 53
Open daily	8 rue du pas de la Mule, tel. 01 42 74 55 80
Open daily	5 rue de la Bastille, tel. 01 42 72 87 82
Open daily from 19:45	2 rue Roger Verlomme, tel. 01 42 72 28 41
Closed Sun	38 rue des Tournelles, tel. 01 42 71 43 33
Mon–Sat until about 22:00, closed Sun	31 rue de la Cerisaie, tel. 01 42 72 08 63
Open daily	25 rue Charles V, tel. 01 42 78 91 44
Both open daily	Place du Marché Ste. Catherine
Serves nonstop from 12:00 to late, closed Mon-Tue	109 rue du Vielle du Temple, tel. 01 42 72 13 77
Open long hours daily	2 rue des Hospitalières-St.-Gervais, tel. 01 42 72 18 86
Mon-Fri 12:00–19:00, Sat-Sun 10:00-19:00	3 rue des Rosiers, tel. 01 42 72 90 61
Day and night until late, closed Sat	34 rue des Rosiers, tel. 01 48 87 63 60
Closed Sun–Mon	52 rue Francois Miron, tel. 01 48 87 15 40
Tue–Sun 12:00–21:30, closed Mon in winter	6 rue des Barres, tel. 01 42 71 09 69

	Price		
ILE ST. LOUIS—Quiet, romantic area perfect for after-dinner strolling (see map on pages 204–205)			
33 Le Tastevin	$$$	Intimate restaurant serving fine meals in a romantic setting under wooden beams	
34 La Taverne du Sergeant Recruteur	$$$	All you can eat and drink for €41 in a rowdy, medieval cellar	
35 La Brasserie de l'Ile St. Louis	$$	Purely Alsatian cuisine served in a vigorous, Teutonic setting	
36 L'Orangerie	$$	Inviting place with soft lighting, comfortable seating, and delicious cuisine	
37 Auberge de la Reine Blanche	$	Tasty cuisine at unbeatable prices in a cozy setting	
38 Café Med	$	Inexpensive salads, crêpes, and plats served in a tight but cheery setting	
LUXEMBOURG GARDEN AREA—Lively near St. Sulpice, quieter near Panthéon (see map, pages 204–205)			
39 La Crêpe Rit du Clown	$	Yummy crêpes on a fun, traffic-free street	
40 Lou Pescadou-Chez Julien	$$	Good bistro fare in an intimate, appealing setting	
41 Santa Lucia	$	Wood-fired pizza, good pasta, and killer tiramisu.	
42 Les Deux Magots and Le Café de Flore	$$	Two famous cafés on a famous boulevard with a famous clientele	
43 La Méditerranée	$$	Gourmet Mediterranean dishes in a lovely setting with a view of the Odéon	
44 Restaurant Polidor	$	Bare-bones bistro with unpretentious cooking and fun old-Paris atmosphere	
45 Le Vin Qui Danse	$$	Warm little place serving tasty dishes and well-matched wines	
46 Le Soufflot Café	$	Library-like interior and great outside seating with brilliant Panthéon views	

	Operating Hours and Days	Address/Phone
	Open daily	46 rue St. Louis-en-l'Ile, tel. 01 43 54 17 31
	Open daily from 19:00	37 rue St. Louis-en-l'Ile, tel. 01 43 54 75 42
	Closed Wed	55 quai de Bourbon, tel. 01 43 54 02 59
	Closed Mon	28 rue St. Louis-en-l'Ile, tel. 01 46 33 93 98
	Open daily from 18:00	30 rue St. Louis-en-l'Ile, tel. 01 46 33 07 87
	Open daily	77 rue St. Louis-en-l'Ile, tel. 01 43 29 73 17
	Mon–Sat 12:00–23:00, closed Sun	6 rue des Canettes, tel. 01 46 34 01 02
	Open daily	16 rue Mabillon, tel. 01 43 54 56 08
	Closed Mon–Tue	22 rue des Canettes, tel. 01 43 26 42 68
	Open daily	Place St. Germain-des-Prés
	Open daily	2 place de l'Odéon, tel. 01 43 26 02 30
	Open daily	41 rue Monsieur-le-Prince, tel. 01 43 26 95 34
	Open daily	4 rue des Fossés Saint-Jacques, tel. 01 43 54 80 81
	Open daily	16 rue Soufflot, tel. 01 43 26 57 56

Rue Cler Area Restaurants

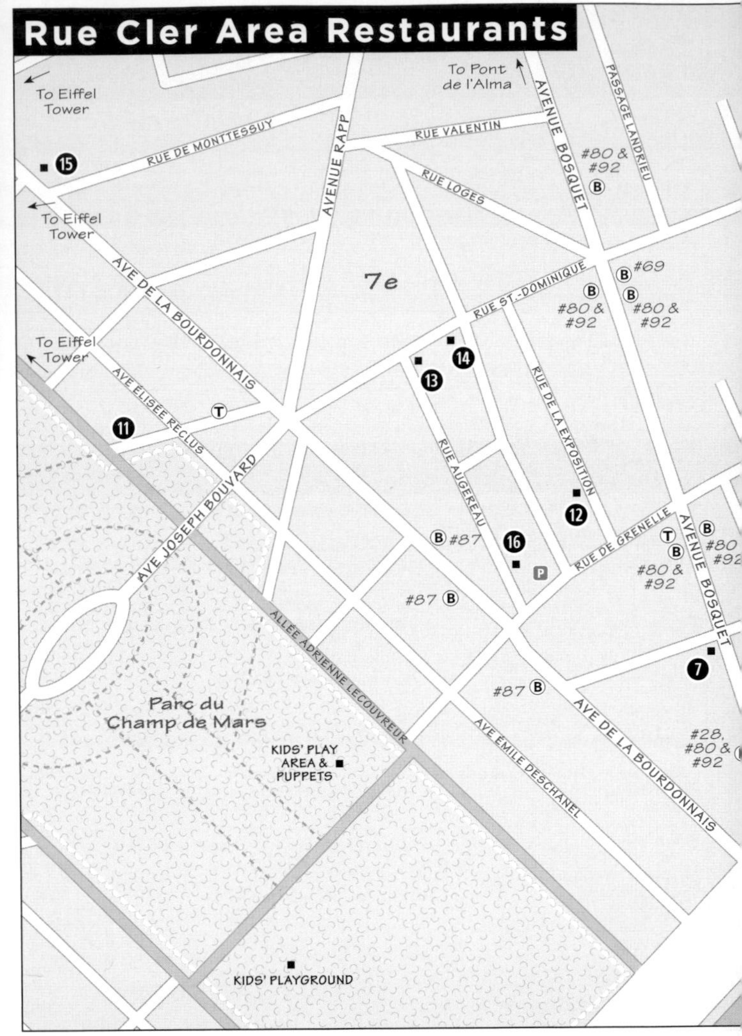

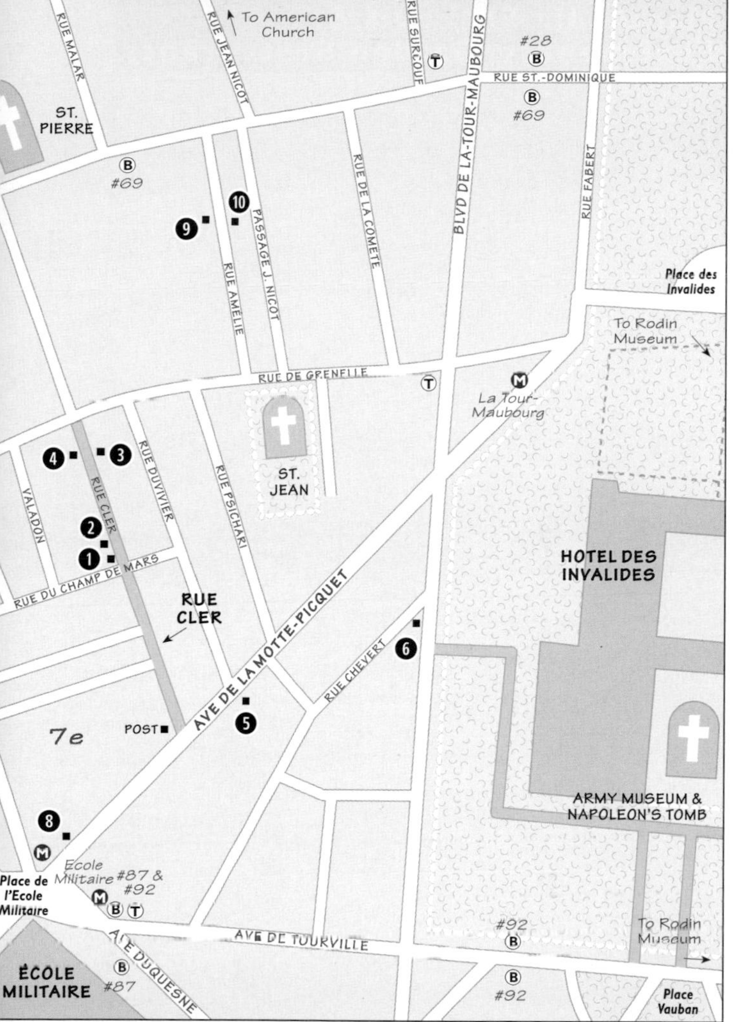

To American Church
RUE MALAR
RUE JEAN NICOT
RUE SURCOUF
BLVD DE LA-TOUR-MAUBOURG
#28
RUE ST.-DOMINIQUE
#69
ST. PIERRE
#69
RUE DE LA COMETE
RUE FABERT
PASSAGE J. NICOT
RUE AMÉLIE
Place des Invalides
To Rodin Museum
RUE DE GRENELLE
La Tour-Maubourg
RUE DUVIVIER
RUE PSICHARI
ST. JEAN
VALADON
RUE CLER
RUE DU CHAMP DE MARS
HOTEL DES INVALIDES
RUE CLER
AVE DE LA MOTTE-PICQUET
RUE CHEVERT
POST
7e
ARMY MUSEUM & NAPOLEON'S TOMB
Ecole Militaire
#87 & #92
Place de l'Ecole Militaire
AVE DE TOURVILLE
AVE DUQUESNE
#92
To Rodin Museum
ÉCOLE MILITAIRE
#87
#92
Place Vauban

Marais, Ile St. Louis & Luxembourg Garden Restaurants

LOUVRE
QUAI FRANÇOIS MITTERAND
PONT CARROUSEL
Seine River
QUAI DU LOUVRE
RUE DU LOUVRE
PONT DES ARTS
QUAI MALAQUAIS
To Orsay Museum
QUAI DE CONTI
RUE DE RIVOLI
R. DES HALLES
BLVD. DE SÉBASTOPOL
1e
Châtelet
RUE PERNELLE
Pont Neuf
QUAI DE LA MÉGISSERIE
Place du Châtelet
TOUR ST. JACQUES
RIVER CRUISES
PONT NEUF
QUAI DE L'HORLOGE
Place Dauphine
CONCIERGERIE
PALAIS DE JUSTICE
SAINTE-CHAPELLE
INSTITUTE DE FRANCE
RUE DES BEAUX-ARTS
RUE VISCONTI
RUE DE SEINE
RUE QUENEGAUD
RUE MAZARINE
RUE DAUPHINE
RUE DES GRANDS AUGUSTINS
QUAI DE LA CORSE
PONT NOTRE DAME
Cité
RUE DE LUTECE
BLVD. DU PALAIS
RUE DE LA CITÉ
Ile de la Cité
RUE ST. BENOIT
RUE JACOB
L'ABBAYE
RUE L'ECHAUDE
RUE BUCI
St. Germain-des-Prés
ST. GERMAIN-DES-PRES
St. Michel
Place St. Michel
RUE ST. ANDRE-DES-ARTS
PASSAGEWAY
Place St. André-des-Arts
RUE DU NOTRE
Place Parvis
NOTRE DAME
POST
RUE DU FOUR
Mabillion
RUELLE COMEDIE
R. JARDINET
R. HUCHETTE
R. SEVERIN
R. HARPE
CANETTES
GUISARDE
Odéon
Place H. Mondor
BLVD.
RUE ST.-SULPICE
Place St. Sulpice
ST. SULPICE
Cluny La Sorbonne
ST. GERMAIN
CLUNY
RUE DANTE
RUE LA GRANGE
Maubert Mutualité
RUE DE TOURNON
RUE DE CONDÉ
Place de l'Odéon
RUE MONSIEUR LE PRINCE
RUE RACINE
MICHEL
THENARD
R. SOMMERARD
RUE MONGE
6e
RUE MADAME
RUE BONAPARTE
RUE FEROU
SERVANDONI
GARANCIERE
POST
THEATRE ODEON
SORBONNE
RUE DES ÉCOLES
RUE DE VAUGIRARD
SANDPIT & WADING POOL (SUMMER ONLY)
LUXEMBOURG PALACE
RUE DE MEDICIS
SAINT-
RUE ST. JACQUES
LATIN QUARTER
WC
Luxembourg Garden
Pond
Place Edmond Rostand
POST
RUE CUJAS
R. VALLETTE
ST. ETIENNE DU MONT
ST.-GENEVIEVE
RUE GUYNEMER
WC
CAFE
BAND-STAND
RUE SOUFFLOT
RUE LE GOFF
Place du Pantheon
MERRY-GO-ROUND
PUPPET THEATER
SWINGS
TENNIS
Luxembourg
BLVD.
RUE GAY-LUSSAC
PANTHÉON
RUE CLOVIS
RUE D'ASSAS
KIDS' PLAY AREA
PATHS
RUE CLOTILDE
RUE DE L'ESTRAPADE
RUE DESCARTES
39 40 41 42 43 44 45 46

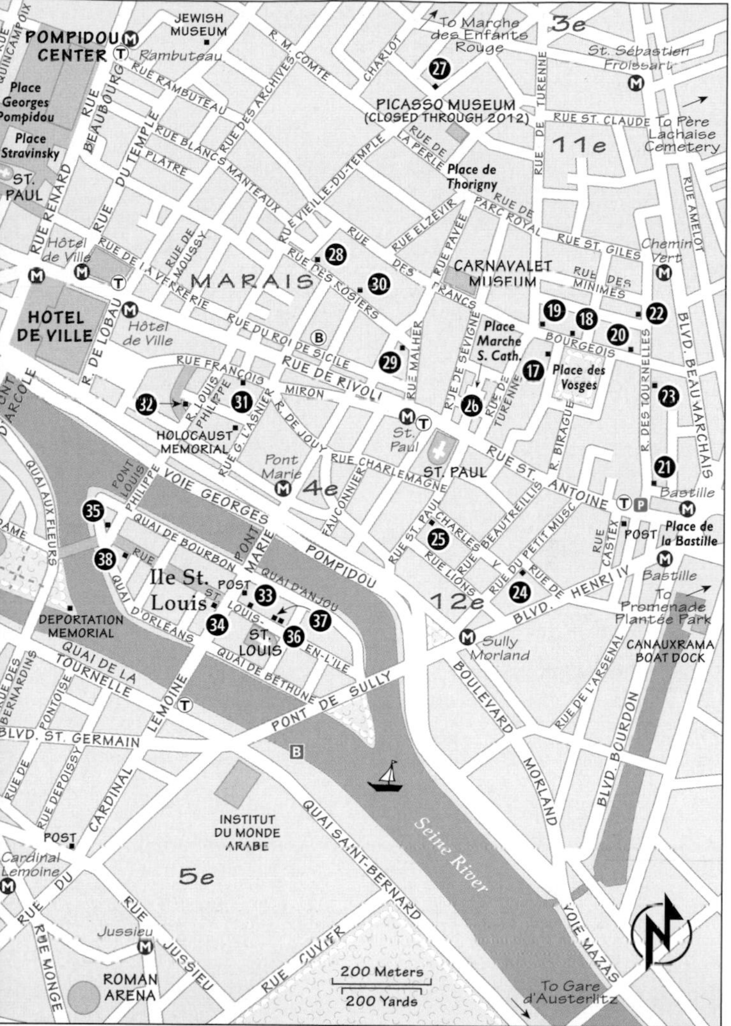
POMPIDOU CENTER
MARAIS
HOTEL DE VILLE
PICASSO MUSEUM (CLOSED THROUGH 2012)
CARNAVALET MUSEUM
Place des Vosges
Place de la Bastille
Ile St. Louis
HOLOCAUST MEMORIAL
DEPORTATION MEMORIAL
INSTITUT DU MONDE ARABE
ROMAN ARENA
Seine River
200 Meters
200 Yards

GARE DU NORD

Practicalities

PLANNING

When to Go

Paris' best travel months—also the busiest and most expensive for flights and hotels—are May, June, September, and October. The summer heat in July and August can be unpleasant (though hotel rates can drop). Paris makes a great winter getaway. Although it's cold and rainy, crowds are less, cafés are cozy, and the city feels lively but not touristy.

Before You Go

You need a passport (see www.travel.state.gov). Call your debit and credit card companies about your plans (see below). Book hotel rooms well in advance during peak season (May, June, Sept, Oct) and consider buying travel insurance. Research railpasses, TGV train reservations, and car rentals. Book an entrance time at the Eiffel Tower, to avoid long lines.

MONEY

France uses the euro currency: 1 euro (€) = about $1.40. To convert prices in euros to dollars, add about 40 percent: €20 = about $28, €50 = about $70. (Check www.oanda.com for the latest exchange rates.)

Withdraw money from a cash machine (known as *distributeur* in France) using a debit card, just like at home. Visa and MasterCard are most commonly used throughout Europe. Before departing, call your bank or credit-card company: Confirm that your cards will work overseas, ask about international transaction fees, and alert them that you'll be making withdrawals in Europe.

Be aware that—while American credit cards are accepted almost everywhere in Europe—they will not work in some European vending machines (e.g., buying Métro tickets from a machine). But don't panic. You can pay with cash, try your PIN code (ask your credit-card company in advance or use a debit card), or find a nearby cashier who should be able to process the transaction.

To keep your valuables safe, wear a money belt. But if you do lose your credit or debit card, report the loss immediately with a phone call: Visa (tel. 08 00 90 11 79), MasterCard (tel. 08 00 90 13 87), and American Express (tel. 01 47 77 70 00).

Helpful Websites

Paris' Tourist Information: www.parisinfo.com
France's Tourist Information: www.franceguide.com.
Passports and Red Tape: www.travel.state.gov
Cheap Flights: www.skyscanner.net
Airplane Carry-on Restrictions: www.tsa.gov/travelers
General Info on Lots of Paris Topics: www.bonjourparis or www.paris-anglo.com
European Train Schedules: http://bahn.hafas.de/bin/query.exe/en
General Travel Tips: For information on train travel, railpasses, car rental, travel insurance, packing lists, and much more—as well as updates for this book—see www.ricksteves.com.

ARRIVAL IN PARIS

Charles de Gaulle Airport

Paris' main airport has three terminals: T-1, T-2, and T-3. All have ATMs, banks, shops, and bars. There are tourist information offices (marked "ADP") in T-1 and T-2. You can travel between terminals on the free CDGVAL automated shuttle train (allow 30 minutes). For airport information, call 3950 or visit www.adp.fr.

To get between the airport and downtown Paris, you have several options:

Taxi: The 50-minute trip costs about €60 for up to three people with bags. For trips from Paris to the airport, have your hotel arrange it a day in advance.

Roissy-Bus: Buses make the 50-minute trip to the Opéra Métro stop in central Paris, arriving on rue Scribe (€9.40, 4/hour, runs 6:30–21:00, buy ticket on bus). From there, it's an easy Métro ride to anywhere in the city.

"Les Cars" Air France Bus: Bus #2 goes to the Arc de Triomphe and Porte Maillot (45 minutes). Bus #4 runs to Gare de Lyon (45 minutes) and the Montparnasse Tower/train station (€16, at least 2/hour, runs 5:45–23:00, toll tel. 08 92 35 08 20, www.cars-airfrance.com). All stops are on Métro lines.

RER-B Trains: This option is cheaper but more complicated. Follow

Paris by Train signs, then *RER* signs. The train serves Gare du Nord, Châtelet–Les Halles, St. Michel, and Luxembourg (€9.50, 4/hour, runs 5:00–24:00, 30 minutes to Gare du Nord).

Airport Vans: These shuttle vans work like those at home, carrying passengers directly to or from their hotels. They cost about €20 for one person, €40 for two, or €55 for three. Ask your hotel to arrange one or try Paris Shuttles Network (tel. 01 45 26 01 58, www.shuttlesnetwork.com), Airport Connection (tel. 01 43 65 55 55, www.airport-connection.com), or the higher-priced but intensive-service Paris Webservices (www.pariswebservices.com).

Orly Airport

Paris' second airport is smaller but its two terminals—Ouest (west) and Sud (south)—have all the conveniences. For flight info call 3950, or visit www.adp.fr. To get into Paris, you can take a taxi (€40); or catch the "Les Cars" Air France bus to Gare Montparnasse, Invalides (near rue Cler), or Etoile (€11.50, buy ticket from driver, 4/hour, 40 minutes); or ask at the airport TI for other options.

Paris' Train Stations

Paris has six major stations, each serving different regions. For example, to go to London on the Eurostar, you leave from Gare du Nord. Trains to Chartres leave from Gare Montparnasse.

The best all-Europe train schedule information is online at http://bahn.hafas.de/bin/query.exe/en. The French national rail website is www.sncf.com. Book TGV trains well in advance at www.tgv-europe.com. To see if a railpass could save you money, check www.ricksteves.com/rail.

HELPFUL HINTS

Tourist Information (TI): Paris' official tourist offices offer little information, and may charge for a basic city map (which you can get free from your hotel). Their website and telephone are more helpful—www.parisinfo.com, tel. 08 92 68 30 00. Both airports have handy "ADP" information offices with long hours and short lines.

English-language bookstores include the venerable Shakespeare and Company (near Notre-Dame, 37 rue de la Bûcherie, tel. 01 43 25 40 93); W.

H. Smith alongside the Tuileries Garden (248 rue de Rivoli, Mo: Concorde, tel. 01 44 77 88 99); and the friendly Red Wheelbarrow in the Marais (22 rue St. Paul, Mo: St. Paul, tel. 01 48 04 75 08).

Hurdling the Language Barrier: Most Parisians speak some English—certainly more English than Americans speak French. Still, learn the pleasantries like *bonjour* (good day), *pardon* (pardon me), *s'il vous plaît* (please), *merci* (thank you), and *au revoir* (goodbye). Begin every encounter with "*Bonjour, madame* or *monsieur,*" or "*s'il vous plaît,*" and ask "*Parlez-vous anglais?*" End every encounter with "*Au revoir, madame* or *monsieur.*" For more French survival phrases, ✪ see page 227.

Time: France uses the 24-hour clock. It's the same through 12:00 noon, then keeps going: 13:00, 14:00, and so on. France's time zone is six/nine hours ahead of the East/West Coasts of the US.

Business Hours: Most businesses are open Monday through Saturday, roughly 10:00-19:00. Smaller shops may close for lunch (12:00–14:00) and on Monday mornings until 14:00. Banks close on Saturday. On Sunday morning, some small markets, *boulangeries* (bakeries), and street markets are open until noon. Handy hole-in-the-wall grocery stores stay open every day until midnight.

Watt's Up? Europe's electrical system is 220 volts, instead of North America's 110 volts. Most newer electronics (such as laptops, hair dryers, and battery chargers) convert automatically, so you won't need a converter plug, but you will need a special adapter plug with two round prongs, sold inexpensively at travel stores in the US.

Laundry: Paris has no shortage of self-serve launderettes, charging about €8 to wash and dry a load—ask your hotelier for the closest one.

Pedestrian Safety: Parisian drivers are notorious for ignoring pedestrians. Look both ways. Don't assume you have the right of way, even in a crosswalk. Be aware that many streets are one-way, and be careful of seemingly quiet bus/taxi lanes. Bicycles are silent but dangerous, lurking in the bus/taxi lane or going the wrong way on a one-way street.

Numbers and Stumblers: What Americans call the second floor of a building is the first floor in Europe. Europeans write dates as day/month/year, so Christmas is 25/12/11. Commas are decimal points and vice versa—a dollar and a half is 1,50, and there are 5.280 feet in a mile.

France uses the metric system: A kilogram is 2.2 pounds; a liter is about a quart; and a kilometer is six-tenths of a mile.

Tipping

Tipping in France isn't as generous as it is in the US.

To tip a taxi driver, round up to the next euro on the fare (for a €4.50 fare, give €5). For longer rides, figure about 10 percent.

At hotels, if you let the porter carry your luggage, tip a euro for each bag. I don't tip the maid, but if you do, you can leave a euro per night at the end of your stay.

For sit-down service in a restaurant, a 12–15 percent service charge is always already included, having been factored into the list price of the food *(service compris)*. Most Parisians never tip. However, if you feel the service was *exceptional,* it's fine to tip up to 5 percent extra. When you hand your payment plus a tip to your waiter, you can say, *"C'est bon"* (say bohn), meaning, "It's good." Never feel guilty if you don't leave a tip.

The French measure temperature in Celsius: 0°C = 32°F. For a rough conversion from Celsius to Fahrenheit, double the number and add 30.

WCs: Paris has some free public toilets (tipping the attendant is appropriate) and some coin-op "toilet-booths" along the sidewalks. Otherwise, use restrooms in museums, or walk into any sidewalk café like you own the place, and find the toilet in the back.

Tabacs: These handy little neighborhood shops sell phone cards, postage stamps, some Métro tickets, parking-meter cards, and...oh yeah, cigarettes. Plus, they're a slice of workaday Paris.

GETTING AROUND PARIS

In Paris, you're never more than a 10-minute walk from a Métro station, and buses are everywhere.

Buying Tickets

The same ticket works on the Métro, RER suburban trains (within the city), and city buses. A single ticket costs €1.70 and is valid for as many transfers as you need to make a single journey within 90 minutes (but not to transfer between Métro/RER and bus).

To save money, buy a *carnet* of 10 tickets for €12.50; the one-day Mobilis pass for €6.30; or the weekly Passe Navigo, a chip-embedded card (€18.85 plus €5 first-time fee, requires postage stamp–size photo).

Which is best? It's hard to beat the *carnet.* Two 10-packs of *carnets*—enough for most travelers staying a week—cost €25, are shareable, and don't expire until they're used. The Passe Navigo only becomes worthwhile for visitors who stay a full week (beginning on a Monday) and use the system a lot.

Buy tickets and passes at most Métro stations or at some *tabac* shops. Some Métro stations have staffed ticket windows (which accept cash and credit cards). All stations have ticket-vending machines (which require coins; some may take bills but none accept American credit cards).

For more information on Paris' public transportation system, visit www.ratp.fr.

By Métro

Europe's best underground train system runs daily 5:30–24:30. Begin by studying a Métro map.

Find the Métro stop closest to you and the stop closest to your destination. Next see which lines connect those two points. The lines are color-coded and numbered, and are known by their end-of-the-line stops.

In the Métro station, signs direct you to the train line going in your direction (e.g., *direction: La Défense*). Insert your ticket in the turnstile, reclaim it, and pass through. Keep your ticket until you exit the system—you may need to show it to a fare inspector (or face a minimum fine of €25), or use it to pass through an exit turnstile.

To make transfers, follow orange *correspondance* (connection) signs. Be prepared to walk significant distances within Métro stations.

Once you reach your final stop, look for the blue-and-white *sortie* (exit) signs. Use the helpful neighborhood maps to choose the *sortie* closest to where you want to go. After you exit the system, toss or tear your used ticket so you don't confuse it with unused tickets.

Be wary of thieves in the Métro—while you're preoccupied buying tickets, passing through turnstiles, and contending wiht the jostle of boarding and leaving crowded trains.

By RER

The RER suburban train line works just like the Métro and uses the same ticket (valid within the city center only; transfers okay between Métro and RER). On your Métro map, the RER routes are the thick lines labeled A, B, C, and so on. Many trains don't stop at every station—check the sign over the platform to see if your destination is listed as a stop.

By City Bus

Paris' excellent bus system works like buses anywhere. Every bus stop has a name, and every bus is headed to one end-of-the-line stop or the other. One bus/Métro/RER ticket gets you anywhere in central Paris within the freeway ring road. It's good for transfers between buses within 90 minutes, but not from bus to Métro/RER, or for multiple trips on the same bus line. You can buy tickets on board for a bit more.

Board your bus through the front door. Validate your ticket or scan your Passe Navigo. Push the red button to signal the driver you want a stop, then exit through the rear door. Rush hour is Monday–Friday 8:00–9:30 & 17:30–19:30.

Bus #69 runs east–west between the Eiffel Tower and Père Lachaise Cemetery by way of the rue Cler, Orsay Museum, Louvre, and the Marais. Scenic bus #73 runs from the Orsay Museum up the Champs-Elysées to the Arc de Triomphe.

By Taxi

Parisian taxis are reasonable, especially for couples and families, who can split the cost. Fares and supplements (described in English on the rear windows) are straightforward and regulated. A taxi can fit three people comfortably, and a fourth for €3 extra.

The meter starts at €2.20, and there's a minimum total of €6.10. A typical 20-minute ride (e.g., place Bastille to Eiffel Tower) costs about €20. Taxis can charge higher rates at rush hour, at night, all day Sunday, to airports, and €1 for each piece of luggage you put in the trunk. To tip, round up to the next euro, or tip up to 10 percent for long rides.

You can try waving down a taxi, or find the nearest taxi stand. To order a taxi, call 3607 (or ask your hotelier); the meter starts running as soon as the call is received, adding about €6 to the bill. Taxis are tough to find during rush hour, when it's raining, and on Friday and Saturday nights.

If you need to catch an early morning train or flight, book your taxi at least the day before; your hotel can help.

By Bike

Paris is great by bicycle. The city is flat, there are more than 370 miles of bike and bus-priority lanes, and Parisian drivers are growing accustomed to sharing the road.

Rental bikes are everywhere, thanks to the city-wide Vélib' program. Locals can just swipe a card at one of 1,450 stations, take a bike off the rack, and return it at any station when they're done. Unfortunately, most Americans cannot use the system, since it requires payment with a chip-and-PIN credit card, which most Americans don't have. Only American Express cards work.

You can rent bikes from Bike About Tours near Hotel de Ville (€15/day, 4 rue de Lobau in Vinci parking garage, www.bikeabouttours.com) or from Fat Tire Bike Tours near the Eiffel Tower (€4/hour, 24 rue Edgar Faure, www.fattirebiketoursparis.com, call 01 56 58 10 54 to check availability). Both places also offer good bike tours.

Sunday cycling is especially peaceful: the city opens up many districts just for bikes (see www.paris.fr and search *"Paris respire"* for details).

COMMUNICATING

Telephones

Making Calls: To call France from the US or Canada: Dial 011-33 and then the local number, without the initial zero. (The 011 is our international access code, and 33 is France's country code.)

To call France from a European country: Dial 00-33 followed by the local number, without the initial zero. (The 00 is Europe's international access code.)

To call within France: Just dial the local number (including the initial zero).

To call from France to another country: Dial 00 followed by the country code (for example, 1 for the US or Canada), then the area code and number. If you're calling European countries whose phone numbers begin with 0, you'll usually have to omit that 0 when you dial.

Phoning Inexpensively: Since coin-op pay phones are virtually obsolete, you'll need a phone card. The best option is a €7.50 international phone card *(carte à code)*, which works with a scratch-to-reveal PIN code. They give you pennies-per-minute rates on international calls, decent rates for calls within France, and can even be used from your hotel phone. Buy them at newsstands and *tabac* shops. Tell the vendor where you'll be making the most calls (*"pour les Etats-Unis"*—to America), and he'll select a good-value brand. Calling from your hotel room can be a rip-off for long-distance calls unless you use an international phone card.

Mobile Phones: A mobile phone—whether an American one that works in France, or a European one you buy when you arrive—is increasingly affordable. You'll find mobile-phone stores selling cheap phones (for as little as $20 plus minutes) and SIM cards at Charles de Gaulle Airport, major train stations, and throughout Paris.

Many smartphones, such as the iPhone or BlackBerry, work in Europe—but beware of sky-high fees, especially for data downloading (checking email, browsing the Internet, and watching videos). Using Wi-Fi can be cheaper.

For more on the fast-changing world of telephones, talk to your service provider or see www.ricksteves.com/phoning.

Internet

Many hotels offer some form of free or cheap Internet access—either a computer in the lobby or Wi-Fi in the room (if you have a laptop). Otherwise, your hotelier can point you to the nearest Internet café. If you're bringing your own laptop, Wi-Fi hotspots (e.g., cafés) are plentiful.

Laptop users can make phone calls to other computers and telephones inexpensively or even free using Skype (www.skype.com) or Google Talk (www.google.com/talk).

Snail Mail

You can arrange for mail delivery to your hotel (allow 10 days for a letter to arrive). Federal Express makes pricey two-day deliveries. Sending a package home via the French Post Office's Colissimo XL mailing box costs about €40 for 12 pounds.

Useful Phone Numbers

Police: tel. 17
Emergency Medical Assistance: tel. 15
Directory Assistance (some English spoken): tel. 12
Collect Calls to the US: Tel. 00 00 11
US Consulate and Embassy: Emergency services Mon–Fri 9:00–11:00, 4 avenue Gabriel, Mo: Concorde, tel. 01 43 12 22 22, http://france.usembassy.gov
Canadian Consulate and Embassy: tel. 01 44 43 29 00, 35 avenue Montaigne, Mo: Franklin D. Roosevelt, www.amb-canada.fr

SIGHTSEEING TIPS

Hours: Hours of sights can change unexpectedly; confirm the latest times from a TI, or at the sight's website, or the general website www.parisinfo.com. Many sights stop admitting people 30–60 minutes before closing time, and guards start shooing people out before the actual closing time, so don't save the best for last.

Typical Rules: Important sights such as the Louvre have metal detectors or conduct bag searches that will slow your entry. Others require you to check (for free) daypacks and coats. To avoid checking a small backpack, carry it under your arm like a purse as you enter.

Photos and videos are normally allowed, but flashes or tripods usually are not. Many sights offer guided tours and rent audioguides (€4–7). Most have an on-site café. Expect changes—artwork can be on tour.

Churches: Many churches have divine art and free entry. They're generally open throughout the day. Churches encourage a modest dress code (no shorts, bare shoulders, or miniskirts), but few enforce it.

Discounts: Many sights offer free or reduced admission for children under 18 and for students (with International Student Identity Cards, www.isic.org). Senior discounts are generally only for EU residents, but it's worth asking—*"Réduction troisième âge?"*

Pace Yourself: In summer, try to schedule a mid-day break at your air-conditioned hotel. Because public restrooms are scarce, use toilets whenever you can at museums, restaurants, and bars.

Free Rick Steves Audio Tours: I've produced free audio tours of many of Paris' best sights. With an iPod (or other MP3 player) or a smartphone, you can tour the Paris Historic Walk, the Louvre, the Orsay, and Versailles. Download them from iTunes (search for "Rick Steves' Audio Tours") or from www.ricksteves.com.

Paris Museum Pass

For many visitors, the Paris Museum Pass is a time- and money-saver. The pass admits you to many of Paris' most popular sights, and lets you skip the (often long) ticket-buying lines. An added benefit is that you can pop into sights you might not otherwise spend the money for.

A pass covering two consecutive days costs €39; four days is €54; and six days is €69. Buy the pass at participating museums, monuments, FNAC department stores, and TIs. Avoid buying the pass at a major museum (such as the Louvre) with long lines.

Most of Paris' major sights are covered by the pass, including the Louvre, Orsay, Sainte-Chapelle, and Versailles. Key sights that are NOT covered are the Eiffel Tower, Montparnasse Tower, Marmottan Museum, Opéra Garnier, and Jacquemart-André Museum. Add up your sightseeing to see if the pass is worth it. The pass can pay for itself with as few as four key admissions in two days. For more info and a full list of sights, visit www.parismuseumpass.com or call 01 44 61 96 60.

To use your pass at sights, boldly walk to the front of the ticket line (after passing security if necessary), hold up your pass, and ask the ticket-taker: *"Entrez, pass?"* (ahn-tray pahs). You'll be ushered directly in.

To make the most of your pass, validate it only when you're ready to tackle the covered sights on consecutive days. Make sure those sights will be open. Sightsee like mad during your "pass" days by visiting sights open late.

Avoiding Lines with Advance Tickets: Even without a Museum Pass, you can still skip ticket lines at many places with long lines. You can buy individual *"coupe-file"* (line-cutting) tickets at TIs and FNAC department stores, or buy online at museum websites or www.parisinfo.com/express-booking.

Affording Paris' Sights

Besides the Paris Museum Pass, here are a few other frugal sightseeing options.

Free Museums and Sights: On the first Sunday of the month, these are free: the Louvre, Orsay, Rodin, Cluny, and Pompidou Center. Always free are the Carnavalet, Petit Palais, Victor Hugo's House, Père Lachaise Cemetery, and the Deportation Memorial. Most churches are free (Notre-Dame, Sacré-Cœur Basilica, St. Sulpice) as are parks (Luxembourg Garden, Champ de Mars, Tuileries, Palais Royal Courtyards). The Rodin Museum's sculpture garden is a mere €1.

Reduced Price: You get a discount if you enter later in the day at the Louvre, Orsay, Army Museum and Napoleon's Tomb, and Versailles.

Free Concerts: Check *Pariscope* magazine's "Musique" section for events marked *entrée libre*.

THEFT AND EMERGENCIES

Theft

While violent crime is rare in the city center, thieves (mainly pickpockets) thrive near famous monuments and on the Métro. Be alert to the possibility of theft, even when you're absorbed in the wonder and newness of Paris. Be on guard when crowds press together, especially at tourist sights, while you're preoccupied at ticket windows, and while boarding and leaving buses and subways. Assume any beggar or friendly petitioner is really a pickpocket, and that any commotion in a crowd is a distraction to pick pockets. Watch out for a common scam where a stranger "finds" a ring and offers to sell it to you. I keep my valuables—passport, credit cards, crucial documents, and large amounts of cash—in a money belt that I tuck under my beltline. Muggings are rare, but if you're out late, avoid dimly lit, empty places, such as the dark riverfront embankments.

Dial 17 for English-speaking police help. Claim lost property at the police station (36 rue des Morillons, Mo: Convention, tel. 01 45 31 14 80).

Medical Help

In France, dial 15 for an ambulance. For minor ailments, first visit a pharmacy (marked by a green cross), where qualified technicians routinely diagnose and prescribe. For more serious problems, ask your hotelier for assistance. Many doctors speak English, but there's the American Hospital at 63 boulevard Victor Hugo in the Neuilly suburb (Mo: Porte Maillot, then bus #82, tel. 01 46 41 25 25). SOS Doctors make house calls to hotels or homes for about €50–70 (tel. 01 47 07 77 77). A good list of English-speaking doctors is available on the website of the U.S. Embassy in Paris (france.usembassy.gov).

ACTIVITIES

Shopping

Chic Paris has a tradition of marketing some of the world's most elegant, trendy, and overpriced clothes, jewels, and foods. The shops with their window displays are works of art themselves. Stroll some of the fashionable neighborhoods and indulge in a little window-shopping, which the French call *faire du lèche-vitrines*—"window-licking."

Most shops are open Monday to Saturday 10:00–19:00.

Shopping Etiquette: Entering a small shop, greet the clerk with *"Bonjour, Madame* (or *Mademoiselle* or *Monsieur*)*,"* and bid them *"Au revoir"* when leaving. Ask before handling clothing—*"Je peux?"* means "Can I?" It's okay if you're "just looking"—*"Je regarde, merci."*

Grand Department Stores: Paris invented the modern department store—different items under a single roof, with fixed prices—and several venerable places are still in business. The Galeries Lafayette flagship store, near the Opéra Garnier, features a sensational belle époque dome, a rooftop viewpoint, and fashion shows every Friday at 15:00 (40 Boulevard Haussman, www.galerieslafayette.com, reserve fashion show at tel. 01 42 82 30 25). A block west is Printemps, with cheaper prices and a better rooftop view.

Place de la Madeleine Neighborhood (Mo: Madeleine): This ritzy area forms a miracle mile of gourmet food shops, four-star hotels, glittering jewelry stores, exclusive clothing boutiques, and people who spend more on clothes in a day than I do all year. Stroll counterclockwise around place de la Madeleine, starting with the bastion of gourmet food stores, Fauchon. Peruse the deli, the bakery, the candy store (there are several different entrances), and stroll downstairs to the wine cellar to consider a €3,500 bottle of Cognac.

Continuing around the square, don't miss Fauchon's rival, Hédiard (founded 1854), whose small red containers are popular souvenirs. At La Maison des Truffe, smell those truffles and ponder how something so ugly can cost €2,500 a pound. Continue through the tea store and the caviar store—fish eggs can sell for up to €8,000 a pound.

Stroll down rue Royale and turn left on rue du Faubourg St. Honoré to end the walk on the *très* elegant square, place Vendôme, home to upper-crust jewelry stores and the Hôtel Ritz.

Sèvres-Babylone to St. Sulpice (Mo: Sèvres-Babylone): For Left Bank swank, start at the Bon Marché department store, Paris' oldest. Walk down rue de Sèvres, and consider a drink at the terribly cool Au Savignon Café (#19). Continue on to the half-man-half-horse statue (ouch)—you're at a pinwheel intersection of several boutique-lined streets worth exploring. When you're ready, turn right on rue du Vieux Colombier and head to St. Sulpice Church. To finish the walk, continue past the church on rue St. Sulpice and turn left on rue de Seine, to find Gérard Mulot's *pâtisserie* (#76) with arguably Paris' best pastries.

Flea Markets: The granddaddy of oversized garage sales is the Puces St. Ouen, on Paris' northern fringe. Vendors in covered alleys sell everything from flamingos to faucets, but mostly antiques. It runs Saturday 9:00–18:00, Sunday 10:00–18:00, and Monday 11:00–17:00. From the Porte de Clignancourt Métro station, walk straight out of the station and pass under the freeway overpass. Veer left on rue des Rosiers—the main "spine" of the sprawling market—and explore from there. Some find the market a delightful melting pot; for others it's a gritty, crowded, overwhelming experience, with thieves on the prowl. For a smaller, less-touristed flea market, try the Puces de Vanves (Sat–Sun only, 7:00-13:00, Mo: Porte de Vanves).

Open-Air Produce Markets: These are museums for people-watchers. Many neighborhoods have one street or square for traffic free shopping, overflowing with flowers, produce, fish vendors, and cafés. Most are open all day Tuesday through Saturday (except at lunch 13:00–15:00), and Sunday morning.

Rue Cler is refined and upscale (Mo: Ecole Militaire, ✪ see the Rue Cler Walk, page 115). Rue Montorgueil, a half-mile northeast of the Louvre, has a more local scene and the elegant covered arcade, passage du grand Cerf, nearby (Mo: Etienne Marcel). Rue Mouffetard, hiding several blocks behind the Panthéon, starts on picturesque place Contrescarpe and gets grittier the farther downhill you go (Mo: Censier Daubenton). In the heart of the Left Bank, try rue de Seine and rue de Buci (Mo: Odéon).

Souvenirs: You won't need a guidebook to find plenty of shops selling "I Heart Paris" T-shirts, Mona Lisa mouse pads, and Eiffel Tower keychains—especially along rue de Rivoli (near the Louvre) and rue d'Arcole (north of Notre-Dame). The riverfront stalls near Notre-Dame are classy and picturesque if higher-priced.

Sizes: European clothing sizes are different from the US. For example, a woman's size 10 dress (US) is a European size 40, and a size 8 shoe (US) is a European size 38½.

Getting a VAT Refund: If you purchase more than €175 worth of goods at a single store, you may be eligible to get a refund of the 20 percent Value-Added Tax (VAT). It's easiest through a VAT-refund service such as Global Refund (www.globalrefund.com) or Premier Tax Free (www.premiertaxfree.com), which have offices at major airports. For more details, see www.ricksteves.com/vat.

Customs for American Shoppers: You are allowed to take home $800 worth of items per person duty free, once every 30 days. You can also bring in duty-free a liter of alcohol.

As for food, you can take home many processed and packaged foods (e.g., vacuum-packed cheeses, chocolate, mustard) but no fresh produce or meats (canned pâtés are an exception). Any liquid-containing foods must be packed in checked luggage, a potential recipe for disaster. To check customs rules and duty rates, visit www.cbp.gov.

Nightlife

Paris is brilliant after dark. Perhaps the best after-dark activity is to enjoy a leisurely meal, then stroll historic streets, past floodlit squares and fountains.

The *Pariscope* magazine (€0.40 at any newsstand) offers a complete weekly listing of events. It's in French, but it's easy to decipher what's going on in the worlds of *Musique, Cinéma, Théâtre, Arts,* etc.

Jazz and Blues Clubs: Paris has been a jazz capital since the Roaring 20s. At most clubs, expect to pay (about) a €20 entry plus €7 per drink. Caveau de la Huchette, in the Latin Quarter near Notre-Dame, is a steamy cellar for hot jazz and frenzied swing dancing (5 rue de la Huchette, tel. 01 43 26 65 05, www.caveaudelahuchette.fr). Rue des Lombards, a street in central Paris (Mo: Châtelet), is a teeming two-block-long hive of nightlife. The plush Au Duc des Lombards club offers high-class jazz in a theater-like setting (42 rue des Lombards, tel. 01 42 33 22 88, www.ducdeslombards.fr). Le Sunside, just a block away, has two different stages (60 rue des Lombards, tel. 01 40 26 21 25, www.sunset-sunside.com).

Classical Concerts: Several historic churches regularly host concerts (mostly Baroque-style chamber music) from March to November: Sainte-Chapelle, St. Sulpice, St. Germain-des-Prés, La Madeleine, St. Eustache, and St. Julien-le-Pauvre. Sainte-Chapelle is especially worthwhile for the pleasure of hearing Mozart, Bach, or Vivaldi, surrounded by the stained glass of the tiny church (it's unheated—bring a sweater). Buy tickets there or make reservations (tel. 01 42 77 65 65 or 06 67 30 65 65, www.archetspf.asso.fr).

The Salle Pleyel (north of the Arc de Triomphe) hosts world-class international concerts at high prices (252 rue du Faubourg St.-Honoré, Mo: Ternes, tel. 01 42 56 13 13, www.sallepleyel.fr).

Opera is performed at the massive modern opera house, the Opéra Bastille (Mo: Bastille). The Opéra Garnier, Paris' first opera house, now hosts mostly ballet in a grand belle époque setting (Mo: Opéra). Get tickets for either opera house at tel. 08 92 89 90 90, www.operadeparis.fr, or at their box offices.

Movies: Many theaters run movies in their original language (look for "v.o."—*version originale*). Cinemas cluster around Mo: Odéon. Enjoy the big movie palaces on the Champs-Elysées.

Rowdy Bars and Clubs: For late-night partying (after 21:00), try the rue de Lappe—take the Metro to Bastille, head north and follow the noise. Other areas are around rue Vieille du Temple in the Marais (Mo: St. Paul), rue des Lombards (Mo: Châtelet), and rue des Canettes and Guisarde (Mo: St. Sulpice).

Museums: To check which museums with later opening hours on some nights, ✪ see the Paris at a Glance sidebar on page 10. For a list of free wine-and-cheese art gallery openings (called *vernissages*), check www.paris.artalog.net.

Tours by Night: Consider a Seine River cruise or bus tour. Paris Authentic takes up to three people on informal, fun, off-beat tours in old Deux Chevaux cars (€80, tel. 06 64 50 44 19, www.parisauthentic.com).

Do-it-yourselfers could snag a taxi and make their own scenic tour—from Notre-Dame to the Eiffel Tower along the Left Bank, then returning along the Right Bank (figure about €50 for a one-hour loop, split by up to four passengers).

Night Scenes: The Eiffel Tower viewed from place du Trocadéro is spectacular, and the Trocadéro itself is a festival of hawkers, gawkers, roller-bladers, and entertainers. The Champs-Elysées and Arc de Triomphe glitter after dark. Ile St. Louis (Mo: Pont Marie) is quiet and romantic; perfect for dinner, for sampling Paris' best ice cream shops, and for a stroll to floodlit Notre-Dame.

Get your Left Bank buzz in the area around place St. Germain-des-Prés and Odéon (Mo: St. Germain-des-Prés and Odéon), full of famous cafés, cinemas, and night owls prowling along rue des Canettes, rue Guisarde, and rue de Buci. Montmartre is touristy but lively, and a bit dicey at night. For old-time cabaret ambience, consider Au Lapin Agile (€24, shows in French only, tel. 01 46 06 85 87, www.au-lapin-agile.com), and end the evening in front of Sacré-Cœur Basilica for the glorious city view.

Connecting with the Culture

Make your trip more personal through one-on-one contact with real live English-speaking Parisians. A group called Meeting the French organizes dinners and workplace tours (www.meetingthefrench.com). Paris Greeter has volunteers guiding you through "their" Paris (www.parisiendunjour.fr). Enjoy Your Paris organizes trips to wine tastings, sporting events, concerts, and more (http://fr.enjoyourparis.com). Ô Château wine school near the Louvre offers fun, informal wine-tasting classes (www.o-chateau.com). Cooking schools have pricey demonstration courses—the most famous is Le Cordon Bleu (www.lcbparis.com). Twenty-somethings should check out the people-to-people events at www.meetup.com.

Tours

Seine Cruises: Several companies run one-hour, €12 boat cruises on the Seine, best by night, and worth checking out for their dinner cruises. Bateaux-Mouches has large, open-topped, often-crowded boats departing from the Pont de l'Alma (www.bateaux-mouches.com). Others are Bateaux Parisiens (from the Eiffel Tower, www.bateauxparisiens.com) and Vedettes du Pont Neuf (from pont Neuf, www.vedettesdupontneuf.com).

Those Parisians

The idea that Parisians are "mean and cold and refuse to speak English" is an out-of-date preconception left over from the days of Charles de Gaulle. Parisians are as friendly as any other people, and no more disagreeable than New Yorkers.

Parisians may appear cold when they're actually being polite and formal, respecting the fine points of culture and tradition. Waiters are paid to be efficient, not chatty. Parisians think that those ever-smiling Americans, while friendly, are somewhat insincere. And let's face it: It's tough to keep on smiling when you've been crushed by a Big Mac, Mickey-Moused by Disney, and drowned in instant coffee.

Like many big cities, Paris is a massive melting pot of people from all over France plus recent immigrants. Your evening hotel receptionist may speak French with an accent.

To appreciate the French—slow down. Hurried, impatient travelers can easily misinterpret French attitudes.

Despite its size and modernity, Paris maintains a genuine village feel. People still hold the door open for you in the Métro. People share family news with their neighborhood grocer. And on warm summer nights, the streets and cafés are full of happy Parisians in love with life.

Batobus allows you to get on and off, making their day passes worthwhile for point-A-to-B travel (www.batobus.com).

Bus Tours: Hop-on, hop-off bus tours let you ride through Paris on an open-air bus. Hop on at any of the stops along their loop routes, pay as you board, ride awhile, hop off to sightsee, then catch the next one to carry on. Two similar companies are in business—L'Open Tour (www.paris-opentour.com) and Les Car Rouges (www.carsrouges.com). Paris Vision offers uninspired bus tours at night, and basic excursions outside the city, e.g., to D-Day beaches or the Loire (www.parisvision.com).

Guided Tours: For walking tours of Paris' history, art, and neighborhoods, try Paris Walks (www.paris-walks.com). Context Paris is serious and intellectual (www.contextparis.com). Classic Walks is the antithesis—low-brow and high-fun (www.classicwalksparis.com).

Bike tours guide a dozen cyclists on breezy excursions through neighborhoods. Try Bike About Tours, near Notre-Dame (www.bikeabouttours.com) or Fat Bike Tours, near the Eiffel Tower (www.fattirebiketoursparis.com). Fat Tire also offers pricey four-hour tours by Segway.

If you'd like a private guide (around €160/half-day and up), try Arnaud Servignat (tel. 06 68 80 29 05, www.frenchguide.com), Thierry Gauduchon (tel. 06 19 07 30 77, tgauduchon@aol.com), or Elizabeth Van Hest (tel. 01 43 41 47 31, elisa.guide@gmail.com).

www.ricksteves.com

This Pocket guide is one of more than 30 titles in my series of guidebooks on European travel. I also produce a public television series, *Rick Steves' Europe,* and a public radio show, *Travel with Rick Steves.*

My website, www.ricksteves.com, offers free travel information, free vodcasts and podcasts of my shows, free audio tours of Europe's great sights, a Graffiti Wall for travelers' comments, guidebook updates, my travel blog, an online travel store, and information on European railpasses and our tours of Europe.

How Was Your Trip? If you'd like to share your tips, concerns, and discoveries after using this book, please fill out the survey at www.ricksteves.com/feedback. It helps us and fellow travelers.

French Survival Phrases

When using the phonetics, try to nasalize the n sound.

Good day.	**Bonjour.**	bohn-zhoor
Mrs. / Mr.	**Madame / Monsieur**	mah-dahm / muhs-yur
Do you speak English?	**Parlez-vous anglais?**	par-lay-voo ahn-glay
Yes. / No.	**Oui. / Non.**	wee / nohn
I understand.	**Je comprends.**	zhuh kohn-prahn
I don't understand.	**Je ne comprends pas.**	zhuh nuh kohn-prahn pah
Please.	**S'il vous plaît.**	see voo play
Thank you.	**Merci.**	mehr-see
I'm sorry.	**Désolé.**	day-zoh-lay
Excuse me.	**Pardon.**	par-dohn
(No) problem.	**(Pas de) problème.**	(pah duh) proh-blehm
It's good.	**C'est bon.**	say bohn
Goodbye.	**Au revoir.**	oh vwahr
one / two	**un / deux**	uhn / duh
three / four	**trois / quatre**	twah / kah-truh
five / six	**cinq / six**	sank / sees
seven / eight	**sept / huit**	seht / weet
nine / ten	**neuf / dix**	nuhf / dees
How much is it?	**Combien?**	kohn-bee-an
Write it?	**Ecrivez?**	ay-kree-vay
Is it free?	**C'est gratuit?**	say grah-twee
Included?	**Inclus?**	an-klew
Where can I buy / find...?	**Où puis-je acheter / trouver...?**	oo pwee-zhuh ah-shuh-tay / troo-vay
I'd like / We'd like...	**Je voudrais / Nous voudrions...**	zhuh voo-dray / noo voo-dree-ohn
...a room.	**...une chambre.**	ewn shahn-bruh
...a ticket to ___.	**...un billet pour ___.**	uhn bee-yay poor
Is it possible?	**C'est possible?**	say poh-see-bluh
Where is...?	**Où est...?**	oo ay
...the train station	**...la gare**	lah gar
...the bus station	**...la gare routière**	lah gar root-yehr
...tourist information	**...l'office du tourisme**	loh-fees dew too-reez-muh
Where are the toilets?	**Où sont les toilettes?**	oo sohn lay twah-leht
men	**hommes**	ohm
women	**dames**	dahm
left / right	**à gauche / à droite**	ah gohsh / ah dwaht
straight	**tout droit**	too dwah
When does this open / close?	**Ça ouvre / ferme à quelle heure?**	sah oo-vruh / fehrm ah kehl ur
At what time?	**À quelle heure?**	ah kehl ur
Just a moment.	**Un moment.**	uhn moh-mahn
now / soon / later	**maintenant / bientôt / plus tard**	man-tuh-nahn / bee-an-toh / plew tar
today / tomorrow	**aujourd'hui / demain**	oh-zhoor-dwee / duh-man

In the Restaurant

I'd like / We'd like...	**Je voudrais / Nous voudrions...**	zhuh voo-dray / noo voo-dree-ohn
...to reserve...	**...réserver...**	ray-zehr-vay
...a table for one / two.	**...une table pour un / deux.**	ewn tah-bluh poor uhn / duh
Non-smoking.	**Non fumeur.**	nohn few-mur
Is this seat free?	**C'est libre?**	say lee-bruh
The menu (in English), please.	**La carte (en anglais), s'il vous plaît.**	lah kart (ahn ahn-glay) see voo play
service (not) included	**service (non) compris**	sehr-vees (nohn) kohn-pree
to go	**à emporter**	ah ahn-por-tay
with / without	**avec / sans**	ah-vehk / sahn
and / or	**et / ou**	ay / oo
special of the day	**plat du jour**	plah dew zhoor
specialty of the house	**spécialité de la maison**	spay-see-ah-lee-tay duh lah may-zohn
appetizers	**hors-d'oeuvre**	or-duh-vruh
first course (soup, salad)	**entrée**	ahn-tray
main course (meat, fish)	**plat principal**	plah pran-see-pahl
bread	**pain**	pan
cheese	**fromage**	froh-mahzh
sandwich	**sandwich**	sahnd-weech
soup	**soupe**	soop
salad	**salade**	sah-lahd
meat	**viande**	vee-ahnd
chicken	**poulet**	poo-lay
fish	**poisson**	pwah-sohn
seafood	**fruits de mer**	frwee duh mehr
mineral water	**eau minérale**	oh mee-nay-rahl
tap water	**l'eau du robinet**	loh dew roh-bee-nay
milk	**lait**	lay
(orange) juice	**jus (d'orange)**	zhew (doh-rahnzh)
coffee	**café**	kah-fay
tea	**thé**	tay
wine	**vin**	van
red / white	**rouge / blanc**	roozh / blahn
glass / bottle	**verre / bouteille**	vehr / boo-teh-ee
beer	**bière**	bee-ehr
Cheers!	**Santé!**	sahn-tay
More. / Another.	**Plus. / Un autre.**	plew / uhn oh-truh
The same.	**La même chose.**	lah mehm shohz
The bill, please.	**L'addition, s'il vous plaît.**	lah-dee-see-ohn see voo play
tip	**pourboire**	poor-bwar
Delicious!	**Délicieux!**	day-lee-see-uh

For more user-friendly French phrases, check out *Rick Steves' French Phrase Book and Dictionary* or *Rick Steves' French, Italian & German Phrase Book.*

INDEX

D

E

S

T

U

V

W

PHOTO CREDITS

Title Page

© Sborisov/Dreamstime.com

Table of Contents

© Ben Cameron

Introduction

© Laura VanDeventer, Carol Ries

Historic Paris Walk

p. 14 © sborisov/123rf.com; p. 18, right © Bryan Busovicki/123rf.com; p. 23, right © Konrad Glogowski/flickr.com; p. 32, right © Luke Daniek/istockphoto.com; p. 37, right © Ionut Dobrescu/123rf.com; p. 42, right, Pont-Neuf-Partiel.jpg, commons.wikimedia.org; other images © Rich Earl, Cameron Hewitt, Gene Openshaw, Rick Steves, David C. Hoerlein, Bruce VanDeventer, Rob Unck

Louvre Tour

p. 50, right © James Shin/flickr.com; p. 56, left, Giotto - estigmatização de são francisco.jpg, The Yorck Project*, commons.wikimedia.org; p. 56, right © Réunion des Musées Nationaux / Art Resources NY; p. 57 © The Art Gallery Collection / Alamy, p. 60, left, Andrea Mantegna 088.jpg, The Yorck Project*, commons.wikimedia.org; p. 61, Leonardo da Vinci 020.jpg, The Yorck Project*, commons.wikimedia.org; p. 62 © The Art Gallery Collection / Alamy; p. 64, left, © Dennis Hallinan / Alamy; p. 64, right, Paolo Veronese 008.jpg, The Yorck Project*, commons.wikimedia.org; p. 66 © Réunion des Musées Nationaux / Art Resources NY; p. 67, left, Jean Auguste Dominique Ingres 005.jpg, The Yorck Project*, commons.wikimedia.org; other images © Laura VanDeventer, Bruce VanDeventer, Cameron Hewitt, Gene Openshaw, Rick Steves

Orsay Museum Tour

p. 71 © Erich Lessing / Art resource, NY; p. 74, right, Jean Auguste Dominique Ingres 006.jpg, The Yorck Project*, commons.wikimedia.org; p. 79, right, The Romans of the Decadence.jpg, http://www.allartpainting.com, commons.wikimedia.org; p. 80, right, Édouard Manet - Le Déjeuner sur l'herbe.jpg, Arpingstone, commons.wikimedia.org; p. 83, left © Peter Barritt / Alamy; p. 83, right, Edgar Germain Hilaire Degas 021.jpg, The Yorck Project*, commons.wikimedia.org; p. 85, Edgar Germain Hilaire Degas 012.jpg, The Yorck Project*, commons.wikimedia.org; p. 86, Pierre-Auguste Renoir, Le Moulin de la Galette.jpg, The Yorck Project*, commons.wikimedia.org; p. 90, left, Paul Cézanne 149.jpg, The Yorck Project*, commons.wikimedia.org; p. 91 © Chris Hellier / Alamy; p. 92, right © Purestock, p. 94 © The Gallery Collection/Corbis; p. 95 © MARKA / Alamy; other images © Laura VanDeventer, Rick Steves, Cameron Hewitt

Photo Credits, continued next page

Eiffel Tower Tour

p. 100 © Ann Triling/123rf.com; p. 101 © Domen Colja/123rf.com; p. 103, right © Jose I. Soto/Dreamstime.com; other images © Laura VanDeventer, Rick Steves, Gene Openshaw, Cameron Hewitt

Rue Cler Walk

p. 114 © Ted Tabor/flickr.com; p. 115 © Ted Tabor/flickr.com; other images © Rick Steves, Laura VanDeventer

Versailles Day Trip

p. 126 © Rubens Alarcon/123rf.com; p. 127 © Adriano Rubino/123rf.com; p. 137, © North Wind Picture Archives / Alamy; p. 145, left © Cosmin - Constantin Sava/ Dreamstime.com; p. 145, right © Isantilli/123rf.com; p. 153, right © Jose I. Soto / Dreamstime.com; other images © Gene Openshaw, Rob Unck, Rick Steves, Cameron Hewitt, Carol Ries

Sights

p. 154 © Elena Elisseeva/123rf.com; other images © Rick Steves

Sleeping

p. 178 © Isantilli/123rf.com; p. 179 © Elena Elisseeva/123rf.com

Eating

p. 190 © Elena Elisseeva/123rf.com; other images © Laura VanDeventer

Practicalities

p. 206 © Ritu Jethani/123rf.com; other image © Rick Steves

* Additional Yorck Project information: The work of art depicted in this image and the reproduction thereof are in the public domain worldwide. The reproduction is part of a collection of reproductions compiled by The Yorck Project. The compilation copyright is held by Zenodot Verlagsgesellschaft mbH and licensed under the GNU Free Documentation License. The Yorck Project: 10.000 Meisterwerke der Malerei. DVD-ROM, 2002. ISBN 3936122202. Distributed by DIRECTMEDIA Publishing GmbH.

Unless otherwise noted, copyrights apply to photographs of artwork.

Start your trip at

Free information and great gear to

▸ Plan Your Trip

Browse thousands of articles and a wealth of money-saving tips for planning your dream trip. You'll find up-to-date information on Europe's best destinations, packing smart, getting around, finding rooms, staying healthy, avoiding scams and more.

▸ Eurail Passes

Find out, step-by-step, if a railpass makes sense for your trip—and how to avoid buying more than you need. Get a bunch of free extras!

▸ Graffiti Wall & Travelers Helpline

Learn, ask, share—our online community of savvy travelers is a great resource for first-time travelers to Europe, as well as seasoned pros.

Rick Steves' Europe Through the Back Door, Inc.

Rick Steves

www.ricksteves.com

EUROPE GUIDES

Best of Europe
Eastern Europe
Europe Through the Back Door

COUNTRY GUIDES

Croatia & Slovenia
England
France
Germany
Great Britain
Ireland
Italy
Portugal
Scandinavia
Spain
Switzerland

CITY & REGIONAL GUIDES

Amsterdam, Bruges & Brussels
Budapest
Florence & Tuscany
Greece: Athens & the Peloponnese
Istanbul
London
Paris
Prague & the Czech Republic
Provence & the French Riviera
Rome
Venice
Vienna, Salzburg & Tirol

SNAPSHOT GUIDES

Barcelona
Berlin
Bruges & Brussels
Copenhagen & the Best of Denmark
Dublin
Dubrovnik
Hill Towns of Central Italy
Italy's Cinque Terre
Krakow, Warsaw & Gdansk
Lisbon
Madrid & Toledo
Munich, Bavaria & Salzburg
Naples & the Amalfi Coast
Northern Ireland
Norway
Scotland
Sevilla, Granada & Southern Spain
Stockholm

POCKET GUIDES

London
Paris
Rome

TRAVEL CULTURE

Europe 101
European Christmas
Postcards from Europe
Travel as a Political Act

NOW AVAILABLE:
eBOOKS, APPS & BLU-RAY

EBOOKS

Most guides available as eBooks from Amazon, Barnes & Noble, Borders, Apple iBook and Sony eReader, beginning January 2011

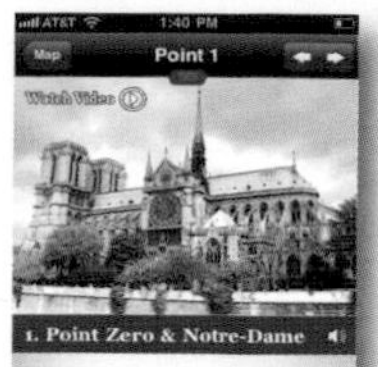

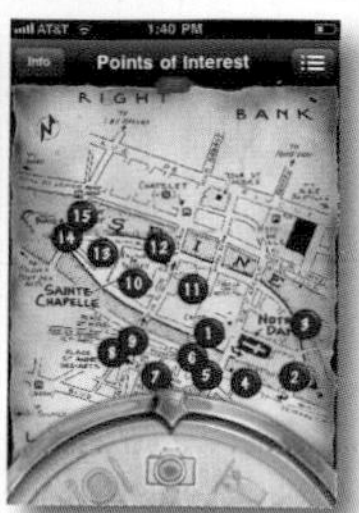

RICK STEVES' EUROPE DVDS

Austria & the Alps
Eastern Europe, Israel & Egypt
England & Wales Europe
European Travel Skills & Specials
France
Germany, Benelux & More
Greece & Turkey
Iran
Ireland & Scotland
Italy's Cities
Italy's Countryside
Rick Steves' European Christmas
Scandinavia
Spain & Portugal

BLU-RAY

Celtic Charms
Eastern Europe Favorites
European Christmas
Italy Through the Back Door
Surprising Cities of Europe

PHRASE BOOKS & DICTIONARIES

French
French, Italian & German
German
Italian
Portuguese
Spanish

APPS

Rick Steves' Ancient Rome Tour
Rick Steves' Historic Paris Walk
Rick Steves' Louvre Tour
Rick Steves' Orsay Museum Tour
Rick Steves' St. Peter's Basilica Tour
Rick Steves' Versailles

PLANNING MAPS

Britain, Ireland & London
Europe
France & Paris
Germany, Austria & Switzerland
Ireland
Italy
Spain & Portugal

JOURNALS

Rick Steves' Pocket Travel Journal
Rick Steves' Travel Journal

Rick Steves guidebooks are published by Avalon Travel, a member of the Perseus Books Group.
Rick Steves books and DVDs are available at bookstores and through online booksellers.

Avalon Travel
a member of the Perseus Books Group
1700 Fourth Street
Berkeley, CA 94710

Printed in China by RR Donnelley
Third printing April 2012

ISBN 978-1-59880-379-2
ISSN 2158-8503

For the latest on Rick's lectures, guidebooks, tours, public radio show, and public television series, contact Europe Through the Back Door, Box 2009, Edmonds, WA 98020, tel. 425/771-8303, fax 425/771-0833, www.ricksteves.com, or rick@ricksteves.com.

Europe Through the Back Door Managing Editor: Risa Laib
ETBD Editors: Gretchen Strauch, Jennifer Madison Davis, Cathy Lu, Tom Griffin, Sarah McCormic
Avalon Travel Senior Editor and Series Manager: Madhu Prasher
Avalon Travel Project Editor: Kevin McLain
Copy Editor: Patrick Collins
Proofreader: Kia Wang Nevarez
Indexer: Stephen Callahan
Production & Typesetting: McGuire Barber Design
Cover Design: Kimberly Glyder Design
Interior Design: Darren Alessi
Graphic Content Director: Laura VanDeventer
Maps & Graphics: David C. Hoerlein, Laura VanDeventer, Lauren Mills, Barb Geisler, Mike Morgenfeld, Brice Ticen
Photography: Rick Steves, Steve Smith, David C. Hoerlein, Gene Openshaw, Laura VanDeventer, Cameron Hewitt, Julie Coen, Barb Geisler, Ben Cameron, Ragen Van Sewell, Robyn Cronin, Rob Unck, Carol Ries, Rich Earl, Rachel Worthman (additional photo credits, page 237)
Front Cover Image: Eiffel Tower © Nicole Hill/Getty; Saint Germain des Pres District © John Kellerman/Alamy

FOLDOUT COLOR MAP

The foldout map on the opposite page includes:

- **A map of Paris on one side**
- **Maps of Greater Paris, France, and Paris Metro on the other side**